Jean C. S.

Distributed by
YEAR BOOK MEDICAL PUBLISHERS • INC.
35 EAST WACKER DRIVE, CHICAGO

Adolescent Pregnancy: Perspectives for the Health Professional

Adolescent

Perspectives for the
Health Professional

Pregnancy:

Edited by

Peggy B. Smith, Ph.D.

Obstetrics & Gynecology

Baylor College of Medicine

Texas Medical Center

Houston, Texas 77030

David M. Mumford, M.D.

Obstetrics & Gynecology

Baylor College of Medicine

Texas Medical Center

Houston, Texas 77030

G. K. Hall & Co. 70 Lincoln St. Boston, MA 02111

G. K. Hall & Co.
Medical Publications Division
70 Lincoln Street
Boston, Massachusetts 02111

80 81 82 83 / 4 3 2 1

Adolescent pregnancy.

Includes index.
1. Pregnancy. 2. Youth—Sexual behavior. 3. Sex instruction for
youth. 4. Pregnancy, Adolescent—United States. 5. Adolescent
mothers—United States.
I. Smith, Peggy B. II. Mumford, David M.
RG556.5.A36   613.9'55   79-13482
ISBN 0-8161-2121-4

The authors and publisher have worked to ensure that all information
is this book concerning drug dosages, schedules, and routes of
administration is accurate at the time of publication. As medical
research and practice advance, however, therapeutic standards may
change. For this reason, and because human and mechanical errors
will sometimes occur, we recommend that our readers consult the
PDR or a manufacturer's product information sheet prior to
prescribing or administering any drug discussed in this volume.

Contributors

PEGGY L. BUNCH, J.D.

> Assistant Health Planning Coordinator
> Department of Obstetrics and Gynecology
> University of Texas Health Science Center
> Dallas, Texas

JOSEPH CALIFANO, J.D.

> Former Secretary
> Department of Health, Education and Welfare
> Washington, D.C.

ALBERT G. CRAWFORD, PH.D.

> Research Associate
> Center for Research on the Acts of Man
> University of Pennsylvania
> Philadelphia, Pennsylvania

CARLA W. DOWBEN, J.D.

> Associate Professor
> Department of Obstetrics and Gynecology
> Southwestern Medical School
> University of Texas Health Science Center
> Dallas, Texas

FRANK F. FURSTENBERG, JR., PH.D.

> Professor of Sociology
> Center for Research on the Acts of Man
> University of Pennsylvania
> Philadelphia, Pennsylvania

CONTRIBUTORS

RALPH W. INGERSOLL, PH.D.

>Associate Dean of Education
>Baylor College of Medicine
>Texas Medical Center
>Houston, Texas

RAYMOND H. KAUFMAN, M.D.

>Ernest W. Bertner Chairman and Professor
>Department of Obstetrics and Gynecology
>Baylor College of Medicine
>Texas Medical Center
>Houston, Texas

KONSTANTIN KOLENDA, PH.D.

>McManis Professor
>Department of Philosophy
>Rice University
>Houston, Texas

JOAN SCHEFF LIPSITZ, PH.D.

>Director
>Center for Early Adolescence
>University of North Carolina
>Chapel Hill, North Carolina

NANCY MCCORMICK, M.S.

>Research Assistant
>Department of Obstetrics and Gynecology
>Baylor College of Medicine
>Houston, Texas

DAVID M. MUMFORD, M.D.

>Professor
>Department of Obstetrics and Gynecology
>Baylor College of Medicine
>Texas Medical Center
>Houston, Texas

ALFRED N. POINDEXTER, M.D.

>Assistant Professor
>Department of Obstetrics and Gynecology
>Baylor College of Medicine
>Texas Medical Center
>Houston, Texas

IVOR L. SAFRO, M.D.

>Assistant Professor
>Department of Obstetrics and Gynecology
>Baylor College of Medicine
>Texas Medical Center
>Houston, Texas

PATRICIA SCHILLER, M.A., J.D.

>Founder and Executive Director
>American Association of Sex Educators, Counselors,
>and Therapists
>Washington, D.C.

PEGGY B. SMITH, PH.D.

>Assistant Professor
>Department of Obstetrics and Gynecology
>Baylor College of Medicine
>Texas Medical Center
>Houston, Texas

DAVID D. YOUNGS, M.D.

>Attending Physician
>Departments of Obstetrics & Gynecology and Psychiatry
>Maine Medical Center
>Portland, Maine
>Consultant on Adolescent Pregnancy
>Joseph P. Kennedy Jr. Foundation
>Washington, D.C.
>Former Andelot Director
>Center for Social Studies and Human Reproduction
>Johns Hopkins Hospital
>Baltimore, Maryland

Contents

Acknowledgments

Appreciation is expressed to the various persons in the professional and support staffs who have implemented clinical and research activities cited in this book. Their suggestions, experience, and compilations have significantly contributed to the observations made. Additional thanks is extended to Pat Armstrong and Melba Mata for their diligent typing of the preliminary drafts and to Ruth Christ, Susan Nenney, and Teresa Johnson for their assistance in copy editing and proofing. Special acknowledgment is given to Dr. Abel J. Leader, Director of the Baylor Population Program and Mrs. Susan Franzheim of the Franzheim Synergy Trust, Houston, Texas, for their interest and support.

Our final thanks go to the many unnamed but real contributors to the book, the countless adolescents who cooperated in diverse programs and research projects involved in the studies presented. Because of the open sharing and honesty of these young people, we are beginning to gain meaningful interpretations and valid insights into adolescent reproductive behavior. We hope that this comprehension will lead to wisdom by those charged with addressing the problems identified.

Peggy B. Smith, Ph.D.   David M. Mumford, M.D.

Foreword
Joseph Califano, J.D.

For most of us, the birth of a child is an occasion of great joy and hope, an investment in the future, a consecration of life. But for hundreds of thousands of teenagers—particularly those who are unmarried—the personal consequences are tragic.

For an adolescent mother, often barely beyond childhood herself, the birth of a child can mean a dismal future of unemployment, emotional trauma, and impaired health. The statistics are startling:

1. Eight out of ten women who become mothers by age 17 never complete high school.
2. Of all the children born out of wedlock almost 60 percent end up on welfare.
3. The baby of a teenage mother is twice as likely to die during the first year of life than the baby of an older mother.
4. The likelihood of a low-birth-weight baby, a condition associated with a number of health problems, including severe mental retardation, is 30 to 50% higher for teenagers.

The personal tragedy is only exceeded by the enormity of the problem. In 1976, there were about 1 million pregnant teenagers. Of these, some 400,000 were under age 17, and another 30,000 were under 14. About 60,000 of these young women gave birth and fully 25% of those were pregnant again within the first year.

The social costs of teenage pregnancy are also substantial. Adolescent pregnancies cost the government between one and three billion dollars each year, and in 1975, there were 250,000 teenagers with at least one child on Aid to Families with Dependent Children (AFDC). Indeed, about half of all mothers in AFDC families were women who had their first child during adolescence.

Adolescent pregnancy is a problem enmeshed in a complex of physical, social, cultural, and economic factors. The population of teenagers has swelled in the postwar period to over 40 million young people. The decreasing age of puberty, largely attributable to better nutrition, is another contributing factor to the growing rate of teenage pregnancy. For girls, the average age of puberty in the United States is 12.8 years with about 13% reaching puberty at age 11 or younger. And clearly, changing sexual mores are a major factor. In 1976, about 11 million teenagers between ages 15 and 19 had experienced sexual intercourse.

Any program dealing with the problem of adolescent pregnancy must have two principal objectives: (1) it should help to prevent unintended pregnancies, and (2) it should assist teenagers who become pregnant. If the objectives are clear, the solution is not.

To this end, the legislative proposal submitted by President Carter is built around four core principles which we believe are the beginnings of an effective teenage pregnancy program:

First, the proposal pursues the twin goals of prevention and care. Prevention is obviously the first line of defense and a significant portion of the budget will go toward family planning and other educational programs.

Second, the program seeks to expand comprehensive services for adolescents who risk becoming pregnant or who need pregnancy-related care. One excellent example of comprehensive care is at the Johns Hopkins Medical School were pre- and postnatal care, vocational counseling, family planning, and many other related services are provided. Their effort has markedly reduced the incidence of low-birth-weight babies, school drop-outs, and repeat pregnancies. The New Futures School in Albuquerque, New Mexico, is another good example. They have reduced the rate of repeat pregnancies to 8%, and more than 70% of the mothers in the program return to school after the birth of their children.

Third, the legislative proposal encourages experimentation with a wide variety of local approaches. There is no single answer to the problem of adolescent pregnancy, and so it is preferable to allow communities considerable latitude in designing and operating programs of prevention and care.

Fourth, it is extremely important that the program eventually developed and funded build upon the existing resources and institutions, from the families and the churches to the schools and the community.

Adolescent pregnancy is one of the most pressing, persistent, and poignant problems facing our society. It is obviously not a problem that can be solved through a government program. Only by experimenting with a broad range of programs and by involving those persons and institutions that most affect teenagers can we even begin to deal with the problem of adolescent pregnancy. Whatever our limitations, however, we must not fail to act when the personal and social costs of a problem are so great and potentially tragic.

Preface

The 1970s will probably be viewed by some as benchmark years in the area of adolescent childbearing and rearing. Federal, medical, educational, and private groups who have been impressed by the growing body of statistics concerning the consequences of teenage sexuality have voiced concern over the number of adolescents who, by either default or design, find themselves pregnant. The origins of this concern are obviously multidimensional and are often phrased in provocative terms. Adolescent pregnancy is frequently seen by health servers as unwanted, unplanned, and epidemic; they claim it is a social problem, the primary source of illegitimacy and an economic millstone. Proposed solutions run the gamut from "strengthening the family," offering widespread sex education in schools, and frequent dispensing of free contraceptives to the liberalization of abortion and family planning policies for low-income teens. Vested interests from diverse cultural, religious, and political backgrounds make national consensus on this issue difficult. Accordingly, the ills of teenage pregnancy receive different kinds of attention in the streets, in health units, from the pulpit and on the steps of the state and national legislatures.

Beneath this crosscurrent of overt activity, however, some issues and knowledge basic to the teen pregnancy problem still lie dormant. The underlying psychology of adolescent sexuality and the decision-making process involved in pregnancy are as yet relatively unexplored. The historical, cultural, and long-term ramifications of early child rearing lack adequate anthropological or social interpretations. Evaluation of ongoing programs, both educational and medical, are conspicuously absent. The fact that pregnancy in the postpubertal teen is often viewed as genital, physiological, and medical completely ignores the motivational aspects of this phenomenon. Finally, the impact of adolescent sexuality in other areas, such as the cost of health care and welfare, and its relation to other medical problems such as venereal diseases, is not commonly considered.

The first objective of the book is to provide information on, and insight into, some of the vital aspects of adolescent pregnancy. Both the audience and the authorship are cross-disciplinary. There are admitted problems with this approach. The Tower of Babel phenomenon may arise through the use of parochial jargon, and occasional "chauvinist" or "straightjacket" thinking may be evident. The recruitment of authors who are not only knowledgeable, but who are also communicators, has alleviated much of this difficulty. Another potential drawback is that the chapters differ in approach, concepts and amount of information and detail. For instance, the material on psychiatric aspects of adolescent pregnancy is less referenced, more tentative and shorter than the biomedical discussions. This does not imply in any way that the psyche of the pregnant teen is not important. Rather it indicates that a well-integrated and expansive body of knowledge on the subject has not yet arisen. On the other hand, the reader will notice that social and educational issues are widely explored.

Another objective of the chapters, perhaps overly ambitious, is to collect a volume that will catalyze new approaches to the many problems surrounding teen pregnancy. There are no "right answers." Indeed, in many instances we do not even know the right questions. From these readings it may be that some fundamental, or new questions may be raised or old questions rephrased which might supply a springboard for innovative efforts to improve the life situation of the adolescent mother. A corollary of this suggests that cross-fertilization among disciplines of thought may produce worthwhile conceptual hybrids. It is the editors' bias that the many professionals now involved in the problems of adolescent pregnancy may have much to contribute to each other if only the opportunity is given for dialogue, discussion and for joint action.

The book also has some remedial aspirations. With the intense and sometimes hurried emphasis now placed on teen pregnancy, some of the evolving perceptions have lost their accuracy—indeed, in some cases, their validity—or have been based on erroneous assumptions. As a result, a growing body of misinformation has developed among some service persons. Some of the ideas reflect old misconceptions and even prejudices. For example, the assumptions that pregnant teenagers commonly make money from welfare, do not love their children, or are usually promiscuous, are misleading at best, and at worst, quite destructive.

The segments of this book are intended to be "reality training"—at least in reality as it exists today. New approaches, when offered, should not rest on old foundations of sand.

As the title of the book implies, the editors hope to bridge some major gaps by presenting views of diverse health and educational groups. In addition to the physician, other professionals such as the nurse, the social worker, the health professional, the psychologist, the sociologist, the anthropologist, the economist, the educator, and the committed lay worker all spend significant time and energy dealing with pregnant adolescents. The readings provide a multifaceted mirror to help each person see his or her effort in its relationship to the service of the common cause. The book also provides reservoirs of information applicable to individual fields.

1 Adolescent Psychosexual Development

Joan Scheff Lipsitz, Ph.D.

Americans view adolescence as a particularly troubled time in life. In the past 10 to 15 years, statistics of distress have become commonplace. Every year more than one million teenagers become pregnant; violence makes schools the least safe place for seventh graders to be; the adolescent suicide rate climbs annually; incidents of running away have doubled since 1965; alcohol abuse is affecting an increasing number of adolescents. Each year there are new television dramas and documentaries on school violence, juvenile prostitution, teenage pregnancy, urban gangs, and other social dilemmas that leave adults feeling helpless and vulnerable.

Omitted in this barrage of statistics and media events is a clear understanding of what it means to be an adolescent in America. All these statistics refer to approximately 20 to 30% of the adolescent population. Does the chronicle of teenage catastrophes indicate that adolescence is a more difficult period of life than adulthood, even a pathological stage? Evidence would suggest not. More than 70% of American teenagers make their way through adolescence without unwanted pregnancies, running away, skirmishing with the law, or suffering undue emotional stress. We can say no more about the adult population.

Although adults feel vulnerable in their dealings with adolescents, they tend to overlook adolescents' extreme vulnerability to adults, who define, regulate, and even create many aspects of adolescence. Given adolescents' vulnerability to adults' perceptions of them, society must beware of labeling their behavior as pathological, of seeking single-cause solutions, and of generalizing the behavior of a minority to all. It is crucial to keep a firm perspective about the normalcy of adolescence.

Very little about teenage pregnancy is self-evident. For instance, while the absolute number of pregnancies has risen, this may be explained by the fact that the young population segment is the largest in our country's history. The overall rate of teenage pregnancy has remained almost stable (Baizerman 1977). Of great concern, however, is the rising rate of *young* adolescents who become pregnant. The only age group in America for

1

whom the birth rate is not declining are girls 15 and under. The earlier incidence of pregnancy, combined with the fact that the largest increase is found among young *whites,* may help explain our new societal concern for teenage pregnancy in general.

In our concern we are in danger of ignoring normal adolescent development and its milestones. This oversight is dangerous for two reasons. First, the vast majority of adolescents who are coping remarkably well during a time of growth and change are dependent upon the expectations of society-at-large for their well-being. We must perceive them appropriately in order to help promote their healthy development. Second, we are too accustomed to a medical model in which we learn about normalcy through pathology. It is instructive to reverse the process and see what explanatory power can be gained by looking at characteristics of normative adolescent development and their implications for patterns of behavior that deviate from our expectations.

Characteristics of Adolescent Development

Adolescent development is marked by biological, socioemotional, and cognitive changes which take place in historical and cultural contexts.

Biologically adolescence is that time of life marked by a characteristic growth spurt and the onset of puberty. Using 1840 as a baseline, records regarding the onset of puberty indicate that it has been occurring four months earlier every decade. The average age of menarche was once 17; it is now 12.9. Even if, as it now appears, this trend has stopped and the mean age of menarche remains approximately 12, adolescents are biologically older than many assume them to be. They are capable of reproduction at what for many is a shockingly early age. Thus, earlier responsibility for their sexual behavior is required of them than was required of their grandparents. We are often asked whether there is a marked increase in all forms of adolescent sexual behavior at an earlier age, or whether there is merely an increased openness. Perhaps the telling question is whether people developmentally capable of earlier reproduction are also developmentally capable of assuming personal responsibility for their fertility.

Ironically, during eras when adolescents were biologically younger, society considered them socially older than it does today. For instance, junior high schools were established in the early part of this century

2

partly to prepare young adolescents more quickly for early entry into the labor force. Now we have mandated a prolonged adolescence through child labor laws and compulsory education requirements. Adolescents are considered socially younger even as they are biologically older. The phenomenon of the "child parent" is partly a function of earlier physiological maturation and partly a function of our perception of all adolescents as children. We do not know the relationship between the earlier onset of puberty and socioemotional development. Although in the aggregate the mean age of menarche is 12.9, the variance is approximately four years. Since girls mature on the average two years earlier than boys do, there can be six years' difference in biological age between a quickly maturing girl and a slowly maturing boy. The internal and external stimuli (the reaction of others) each is exposed to differ considerably (Hill 1973). We can assume that these stimuli will affect socioemotional development, but we do not know much beyond the levels of hypothesis and common sense about the nature of the interrelationships between biological and socioemotional ages.

Individuation

Socially and emotionally adolescence is a time of individuation, of forming a conscious sense of individual uniqueness as well as a sense of solidarity with group ideals (Erikson 1968). What is at stake is the formation of a sense of personal identity, a continuity between one's perception of oneself from one moment to the next and congruity of one's perception of oneself with others' perceptions of oneself. A part of that self to be explored is one's sexual identity, including gender roles, sexuality, and the capacity for intimacy. Individuation requires detachment, a shifting of emphasis from parents to peers. The greatest shift from family to peer orientation occurs in relation to association or companionship (with whom does the adolescent prefer to socialize?), and the least, in relation to identification and norms (whom does the adolescent single out for admiration, for a model, for value setting?). This process of "desatellizing" usually occurs earlier in girls than in boys, and more rapidly in large families with four or more children (Bowerman and Kinch 1969). Individuation also requires risk-taking in role experimentation, and the testing out of personal relationships. We expect of healthy adolescents that they will engage in risk-taking behaviors with a vibrant and spontaneous sense of adventure, tempered by a necessary sense of danger and unfettered by crippling inner constraints.

Adolescence is portrayed in the literature and through our media as being a time of inevitable, tumultuous storm and stress. Researchers have found, to the contrary, that approximately 70% of adolescents go through this time of life with relative serenity (Douvan and Adelson 1966). If rebelliousness is to occur, it is most likely to lead to troubled relationships (especially with parents) during *early* adolescence. After parents and adolescents negotiate the hurdle of early adolescence, there appears to be a higher degree of mutual tolerance and understanding (Offer 1967), particularly when parents adopt a democratic (instead of an authoritarian or permissive) parenting style (Kandel and Lesser 1972).

Commitment

Just as individuation is a task of adolescence, so is commitment. For the first time in their lives adolescents feel themselves to have a future, a personal destiny. They also see themselves as part of society, a member of a generation. The growing capacity for commitment allows an adolescent to plan a future which is informed by a sense of self in a social frame of reference. Just as it is ironic that society sees adolescents as childlike now that they are biologically mature, it is also ironic that society now deprives adolescents of meaningful outlets for their growing sense of commitment while at the same time expecting them to be responsible. As Mathis (1976) points out, one cause for adolescent distress is "the obvious uselessness of the adolescent in our society." Although physically and mentally capable of fulfilling many occupational roles, the adolescent finds little opportunity for achieving ego growth and identity through practical mastery of significant tasks.

Intellectual Growth

Adolescence is a time of remarkable intellectual growth and change. The importance of this cognitive development during adolescence is beginning to gain the recognition it has long been denied. It is during early adolescence, around age eleven, that a shift from what Piaget calls "concrete operations" to "formal operations" becomes a human possibility. Thus, at some point during adolescence the young person may begin to reason on the basis of symbols and propositions, to think about thinking, to examine values in light of principles, to consider contingencies, to anticipate possible consequences.

We do not understand the relationships among biological, socioemotional and cognitive development. We do not understand the relationship between social cognition and social behavior during adolescence. We are unsure about the nature of the relationship between moral development and cognitive development. We are especially confused about whether concept development is culture-dependent, and what the implications of this dependence are for adolescent behavior and social services. What we do know is that adolescent social behavior and cognitive development are issues that have previously been seen as "psychological" in the sense of emotional and social, but are now being examined in light of cognitive stages of development.

The area of self-esteem is a case in point. The onset of formal operations makes it possible for adolescents to step aside from themselves and see themselves as others see them. This can lead to extremely egocentric behavior in which one is overly sensitive or self-conscious about what others actually see—what Elkind (1967) calls "the imaginary audience." At the same time, the ability to see oneself as others do can lead to a sense of social isolation and privateness based on the assumed uniqueness of personal feelings—what Elkind calls "a personal fable." There is, then, a certain fragility of self-esteem during adolescence which is normal and is dependent upon cognitive development both for its onset and resolution.

Adolescent Development and Pregnancy

In the following pages we will attempt to answer the questions, what aspects of normal adolescent development are related to an adolescent's unplanned pregnancy, and how are these characteristics influenced by society, including the family.

SEXUALITY

American culture is ambivalent about sexuality and especially about children's sexuality. The character of the ambivalence is suppression of adolescent sexual expression in the family, school, and church, but public, commercial exposure of sexuality. Because many adults view young adolescents as children in adults' bodies, their sexual behavior appears incongruous, even indecent. What is acceptable in adult behavior is promiscuous for adolescents.

Because of this ambivalence, there is a constant attempt to keep sexual topics hidden. What adolescents need to know about sexuality is kept secret in adults' face-to-face relationships with them. And yet sex is ubiquitous publicly. With spermicidal creams on supermarket shelves, so-called "sophisticated adult" magazines openly displayed on newsstands, and sexual innuendoes on T.V. programs from morning game shows through midday soap operas to evening's "Soap," the silence in private relationships is a mockery.

If adolescents do not remain silent, adults are critical of their tendency to be open about their sexual behavior. As Mathis (1976) says, "Adolescent sexuality makes the adult world uncomfortable. This discomfort goes beyond that which might be realistically produced by the dangers of pregnancy and venereal disease. Perhaps the repressed adolescent fantasies of the present adult are being acted out so that they cannot be ignored." The conspiracy of silence, the all-too-apparent adult discomfort, and the teasing public sexuality may isolate and confuse the young adolescent at a time of changing feelings and bodies. The message is clearly contradictory: sex is omnipresent, fun, harmless, adult, and somehow forbidden. Early physical maturation, risk-taking behavior, a desire for adult symbols, and mixed messages from society are ill-suited to one another.

INDIVIDUAL UNIQUENESS AND EDUCATION

The hallmark of adolescent development is its variability, both interindividuals and intraindividual. Adolescents vary widely among each other in developmental ages. Also, each adolescent's growth is not so orderly that biological, emotional, social, and intellectual development are synchronized. This variability indicates that one's perceptions of personal sexuality and fecundity are changeable and dependent upon emotional, social, and cognitive development. Therefore, concepts and techniques for intervening in an adolescent's life in reference to issues like contraception must differ not only depending on social and cultural backgrounds, but also developmental ages. As the United States Department of Health, Education and Welfare's (HEW) task force on adolescent pregnancy concluded in its "Decision Memorandum," education, contraceptive, health and service programs must be sensitive to differences in ages (1977). "Adolescence" is an aggregated category which has little to do with developmental realities.

SHIFT FROM FAMILY TO PEER ORIENTATION

The nature of the adolescent's shift from family to peer orientation is of critical importance. Parents' reactions to "desatellization" may be extreme. At the first sign of the adolescent's shift from seeking parental to seeking peer companionship, parents may overreact with negligence or extreme parenting styles and thereby inadvertently pressure the adolescent toward a shift in normative and identificative desatellization as well as an associative shift. The adolescent is thereby pushed into a premature and extreme shift in orientation because parents have mistaken normal tension about companionship for rebellion about values. Adult awareness about normal adolescent development can prevent this push-out phenomenon.

At the same time, Cvetkovich and co-workers (1975) point out that women who have more individual control over their lives, with greater scholastic and vocational interests, are more likely to use contraception. They report that, contrary to expectation, the more independent of parental influence, the more likely the adolescent is to use contraceptives. "Seemingly, a necessary component of premeditated sex is that the adolescent is well on the way to developing an identity as a person separate from his parents." They also cite the 1973 work of Kantner and Zelnik who found that in their national sample young women who were living alone, who were in households not headed by a father, or who reported a low degree of confidence-sharing with parents were more likely to use contraceptives than women with the opposite characteristics. The most stable and supportive family environment does not therefore guarantee, and may actually hinder, adequate adolescent contraceptive practice. Adolescents need to be able to consent to their own health care not only because of their families' inadequate support, but also because of their apparently adequate support. As the "Decision Memorandum" recommends, "While family relations and communication should be emphasized, the adolescent should be able to obtain all needed services on his/her own consent" (HEW 1977).

7

MALE CONTRACEPTIVES

It should be noted that unlike most studies which overlook female adolescent development, studies about contraception and pregnancy overlook males. Cvetkovich and co-workers (1975) did not uncover "a single indepth analysis of male adolescents regarding contraception." HEW's "Decision Memorandum" recommends: "Programs and policies must be sensitive to providing support and assistance to the male adolescent" (1977). This will have to be done on an inadequate research base.

EXPLORATION OF SEXUALITY

Adolescents must be free to explore their developing sexuality. They also must be able to take risks in interpersonal relationships. And yet at the same time, they must be helped not to endanger themselves physically and emotionally. Mathis (1976) points out that the analytic literature is replete with warnings about the serious consequences of adolescent sexual activity. For instance it is argued that the young adolescent in our culture is not sufficiently mature to have an intimate heterosexual experience; that a premature sexual involvement impedes one's developing capacity for intimacy; and that acting out sexual desires rather than sublimating them compromises ego growth and the ability to form mature relationships. Mathis takes a middle ground in the debate over adolescent sexual behavior. Many adolescents can be injured by "premature or unrestrained sexual activity," but damage is not the necessary outcome of heterosexual gratification in adolescence. "Perhaps it is not the activity per se which holds the major potential for damage, but rather the combination of the activity, the social clime in which it occurs, and the developmental background of the individuals involved." Since much of overt sexual behavior is not sexually motivated, it is necessary that we look at the motivations which are specific to adolescent psychosocial development in order to resolve in individual cases the health or harm of sexual behavior.

We would have to look at the resolution or lack thereof of such developmental tasks as individuation and commitment, and such processes as "desatellization," developing closeness with peers, integration of body image, the conquering of self-consciousness, reexamination of values, and role definition—and this is certainly not an exhaustive list. As Mathis (1976) says, "There is far more to adolescent behavior than the purely sexual, and much of that behavior may be of greater importance in the total picture.''

The current milieu in which adolescents develop exerts undeniable pressure towards overt sexual behavior which many adolescents may find uncomfortable. This pressure is hard enough for many adults to cope with. For adolescents it may demand as massive a denial of anxiety-provoking reality factors as did the Victorians' repression of sexual impulses (Mathis 1976).

DEVELOPMENT OF SOCIAL COMMITMENT

Adolescents require meaningful outlets for their growing sense of social commitment. A society which puts its young people on ''hold'' in order to reduce strain on a glutted job market denies its youth that obvious definition of the future *qua* job which stabilized previous generations of adolescents. We do not even offer many opportunities for unpaid youth participation.

Adolescents are extremely vulnerable to sociohistorical forces. Those adults who were adolescents during the depression or during the years of World War II or during the expansive postwar years had different expectations of their possible futures which radically influenced their experience of themselves as adolescents. To be an adolescent with a newly developed sense of destiny facing a 35% youth unemployment rate or a constricted job market after college is to be turned inward, away from the future, and intensively toward the present. If the present is too much with this generation of adolescents, it may be because the future holds so little promise. Society can make few arguments about delayed gratification in such a context.

ADOLESCENT COGNITIVE DEVELOPMENT

The nature of adolescent cognitive development has important implications for teenage pregnancy. Planned Parenthood's widely distributed report, *11 Million Teenagers: What Can Be Done About The Epidemic of Adolescent Pregnancies in the United States,* states that about half of sexually active unmarried teenagers say they did not use a contraceptive the last time they had intercourse. Four out of five had had sexual relations without using contraception at some time. The major reasons for not using contraception were that the teenagers assumed they could not become pregnant because of the time of their menstrual cycle, because of age, and because of infrequency of intercourse. Planned Parenthood recommends better education as a remedy, along with more adequate service programs and contraceptive methods more suited to episodic sexual activity (Alan Guttmacher Institute 1976).

On the basis of researchers' recent work on adolescent cognition, we would have to question what that "better education" would be, what services "adequate" programs would actually deliver, and which methods are well-suited to adolescents' needs. Cvetkovich and co-workers (1975) report that ". . . one of the most striking characteristics of teenage illegitimacy is that many adolescents who have the benefit of best sex education and have available contraceptive materials, do not use contraception." Acceptance of one's own sexuality is a more important correlate with contraceptive use than sex education, knowledge of sex and contraception, or religious background is (Goldsmith 1972; Kantner and Zelnik 1973).

Acceptance of sexuality requires cognitive as well as emotional maturity. Most discussions of pregnancy prevention assume the adolescent's capacity to anticipate consequences, to consider what is a probable outcome of personal behavior, or to project oneself in one's "mind's eye" into the future. In other words, prevention is based on an ability to approach problem-solving by engaging in formal operational thought. If studies fail to find differences in amounts of formal sex education between contraceptive seekers and pregnant adolescents, the reason may lie beyond access to informal information, squarely in the ability of the adolescent to premeditate objectively about issues related to sexuality. Or, as Baizerman (1977) asks, can the young adolescent understand the idea of prevention and therefore act so as to keep herself from becoming pregnant? Does she have the cognitive maturity for prevention? The capacity to use operational thought does not guarantee the application of its method to the area of sexuality. Conversely, preventive techniques predicated on operational thought cannot be adopted by preoperational thinkers.

Cvetkovich and co-workers (1975) found that many girls "did not know at the time that there is a probabilistic relationship between intercourse and becoming pregnant. This may be due to the difficulty that young adolescents have in thinking in probabilistic terms." For instance, an adolescent may have been certain that she could not become pregnant because "we only did it a few times." "This seemingly is (an) example of how the laws of probability are applied in a lopsided manner. It is an example of the classical gambler's fallacy—the chances of getting pregnant are considered to be cumulative across incidents of intercourse rather than being independent."

Baizerman (1977) agrees that many adolescents may not have reached the stage of cognitive development that permits probabilistic thinking. There is an important change from "it won't happen to me" to "it *may* happen to me." Thus, risk-taking, which is so important a need of healthy adolescents, is related to teenage pregnancy by the ability or inability of the teenager to predict based on probability. "To understand the idea and experience the feeling that one is not fully in control of events external to oneself is to (begin to) understand as an adolescent and not as a child. . . . It is to understand and experience the notion that the future is problematic and may not happen the way one predicts."

It stands to reason, then, that a developmental perspective of cognition should pervade curriculum development and direct service delivery. Health education is usually based on the unexamined assumption that students can be taught to "prevent" something. Service delivery systems are usually based on the client's ability to transform knowledge into new behaviors. Both ignore the inability of many adolescents to *know*, not in the sense of abstract processes assessable by an I.Q. test, but in the developmental sense of the word.

A further point to be made about cognitive development is that levels of moral reasoning about sex have been found to be lower than those relating to social, political, and economic issues which are nonsexual. Thus, 16- and 17-year-olds may appear to reason based on principle rather than on fear of punishment, hedonism, or approval of others. When studied more closely, their level of reasoning in relation to sexual dilemmas is depressed in comparison with nonsexual dilemmas. These are several possible explanations: sexuality is a charged area which depresses reasoning; adolescents have little opportunity to practice reasoning about sex because of adults' insistence on silence, and therefore, there is a developmental lag; adults applaud a lower level of reasoning (i.e., reasoning based on obedience rather than principled conscience) where sex is concerned (Wilson 1978). Whatever the explanation may be, curricula and service delivery must take this lack of cognitive developmental synchrony into account and also provide opportunities for practicing reasoning in the sexual realm.

Finally, counseling an adolescent girl or boy about particular methods of birth control must be predicated on development beyond figurative toward operative thinking. Cobliner (1974) suggests that one can overcome the barriers of figurative (concrete) thinking by the ubiquity and frequency of information provided in places where adolescents congregate. Availability is not enough; actual delivery of services is necessary. And the method of present contraceptive devices must not be solely predicated on operative thinking.

Conclusion

Adolescence is a time of growth and change, marked by milestones that are highly variable in individuals' development. Each developmental phenomenon has implications for the incidence and prevention of unplanned teenage pregnancy. Adolescence is also a time in life that is dependent upon culture and historical events for its definition. For a girl growing up in New York City in 1956, a pregnancy was a traumatic developmental interruption occurring in the context of 6.7% illegitimacy rate. In the last part of the 1970s, when the rate approaches 50% in many cities (and is over 50% in Washington, D.C.), teenage pregnancy has a different cultural meaning, and therefore a different personal impact on the development of many adolescents.

In considering the medical, psychiatric, social, and ethical implications of adolescent pregnancy, we will continue to ignore the impact of adolescent development and of its sociohistorical context at our common risk.

The questions which should set the tone for any further discussion of unplanned adolescent pregnancy are posed by Mathis (1976):

(1) Why and how are most adolescents surviving the enormous stresses of the present age quite well; and given even a partial answer to that question,

(2) How can we help prevent the remaining minority from becoming social casualties?

References

Alan Guttmacher Institute. *11 million teenagers: what can be done about the epidemic of adolescent pregnancies in the United States*. New York: Alan Guttmacher Institute, The Research and Development Division of Planned Parenthood Federation of America, 1976.

Baizerman, M. Can the first pregnancy of a young adolescent be prevented? A question which must be answered. *J. You. Adole.* 6:343–351, 1977.

Bowerman, C. E., and Kinch, J. W. Changes in family and peer orientation of children between fourth and tenth grades. *In Adolescent development,* ed. M. Gold, and E. Douvan. Boston: Allyn and Bacon, 1969.

Cobliner, W. G. Pregnancy and the single adolescent girl: The role of cognitive functions. *J. You. Adole.* 3:17–29, 1974.

Cvetkovich, G. et al. On the psychology of adolescents' use of contraceptives. *J. Sex Res.* 2:263, 1975.

Douvan, E. and Adelson, J. *The adolescent experience.* New York: John Wiley and Sons, 1966.

Elkind, D. Egocentrism in adolescence. *Child. Dev.* 38:1025–1034, 1967.

Erikson, E. *Identity: youth and crisis.* New York: W. W. Norton, 1968.

Goldsmith, S. et al. Teenagers, sex and contraception. *Fam. Plann. Perspect.* 4:32–38, 1972.

Hill. J. P. Some perspectives on adolescence in American society. Position paper prepared for the Office of Child Development, United States Department of Health, Education, and Welfare, mimeographed, Washington, D.C., May 1973.

Kandel, D. B., and Lesser, G. S. *Youth in two worlds.* London: Jossey-Bass, 1972.

Kantner, J. F., and Zelnik, M. Contraception and pregnancy: experiences of young unmarried women in the United States. *Fam. Plann. Perspect.* 5:21–35, 1973.

Mathis, J. L., Adolescent sexuality and societal change. *Am. J. Psychother.* 30:434, 1976.

Offer, D. *The psychological world of the teenager.* New York: Basic Books, 1967.

United States Department of Health, Education, and Welfare, Decision Memorandum: Initiative to address adolescent pregnancy and related issues, mimeographed. August 4, 1977.

Wilson, W. C. "Adolescent moral development and sexual decision." Sex and Youth: A Symposium. Reprinted from *Top of the News.* Winter 1978.

2 Administrative Concerns Ralph W. Ingersoll, Ph.D.

Concern for the person has to be the central focus of any discussion of teenage pregnancy. How the young girl feels, what she understands, who her friends are and how she makes decisions are factors that contribute to potential solutions to this social condition which affects all of society. The problems are complex, and, while administrators often seek simple solutions, it is reasonable to predict that none are close at hand. Will what is known about learning and behavioral change be effective? Are the existing institutions of society capable of rallying to the needs of teenage girls? Should the government intervene, and at what level? What further research should be conducted? How will the research findings be implemented? Is it possible to bring the emotional issue of teenage pregnancy before the public in the same manner that the more socially acceptable physical condition of hypertension has been given national attention during the past few years?

The Individual

Most parents of a teenage girl will recognize that she is very uncomplicated in her approach to problem solving; typically the answers to most problems are either yes or no; I like it or I do not. She has not yet learned to be clever or evasive as adults sometimes are, yet she seems very complex when one attempts to change her behavior. Lessons learned in the past often cause interference and complicate the change process, so that hit-or-miss behavior-change programs will be found wanting and ineffective.

How then should an administrator approach the teenage pregnancy problem? Probably most importantly with an open and creative mind. A basic understanding of individual responses is also essential. Lack of this understanding has contributed to the ineffectiveness of most large-group educational programs in changing behavior. It is essential, too, that research be conducted in both program design and application.

BASIC DRIVES

Humans, very much like other animals, have certain basic drives that must be met for survival. However, very little of what individuals strive for most of the time would be considered essential. Basic needs such as caring for the body, eating, having sexual intercourse, and caring for the young are much more under conscious control in the human being than in other·animals. Learning experiences stimulate us to meet and sometimes override our basic bodily needs. In relation to sexual needs Beach (1956) states:

> "The principal differences between man and the lower mammals lies in the extent to which the sexual arousal mechanism is affected by symbolic factors. . . . Human sexual arousal is subject to extensive modification as a result of experience. Sexual values may become attached to a wide variety of biologically inappropriate stimulus objects and partners. Conversely, responsiveness in the usual heterosexual situation may be partly or completely blocked."

The effect of experience on mating has been studied extensively in animals. Deutsch (1973) states that when "immature male rats were trained to avoid females in heat, they would show inhibition of mating behavior when they became mature." Deutsch cites other studies indicating that "sexual behavior is similar to other types of behavior in that it is susceptible to interference effects. Particularly relevant are studies which have shown enhancement of sexual activity when, as a result of learning, one would expect the opposite to occur."

MOTIVATION

Many factors contribute to learning to walk or ride a bike; similarly, sexual activity is complex behavior which cannot be described as a simple act. The sequence of events leading up to the activity are directed by a motive. Motivation is a key concept in the explanation of behavior. Berelson and Steiner (1964) describe a motive as "an inner state that energizes, activates, or moves (hence motivation), and that directs or channels behavior toward goals. In short, a motive results in and hence can be inferred from purposeful, means-end behavior." Primary motives are generated by physical needs; however, learning can and does modify these basic needs. Individuals and groups, like some members of the clergy, will renounce certain basic needs in order to reach some nonbiological goal. Behavior in humans is much less dependent upon basic drives than is animal behavior, and humans are far more responsive to teaching. Every individual has the personal need to belong. The learned need to be accepted, to be cared for, and to be loved motivates each of us.

Klausmeier (1971) has suggested that "remote, intermediate and immediate goals are related to the developmental level of the individual . . . present success and expectations of future success have a desirable effect on motivation. . . . failure has a definitely undesirable effect." He further suggests that both changes in motivation and lowered-goals can be predicted when individuals experience failure. Young people can overcome failure; self-confidence can be learned when goals are realistic. Therefore, a value system consistent with desired behaviors can be learned, and a system of individually oriented motivation which will produce behavior change can be outlined. Modeling and reinforcing desired behaviors, giving adolescents individual attention, providing them with feedback, and using peer and family assistance are all factors in providing positive motivation.

SOCIOECONOMIC STATUS

According to the 1975 work of Ryder and Westoff, teenage pregnancy can be more closely related to socioeconomic status than to other factors. The experience of international population programs, reported in 1976 by Freedman and Berelson, reveals that responsive individuals tend to be older and of higher parity. Such programs, however, do have a demographic impact and a potential effect on the birth rate. Many of the international programs reach the less educated, the rural residents, and the poor, all of whom would normally come to modern fertility control later than much of the world. Administrators of these programs report that the complexities of motivation, methods and programs, do not resolve into simple dichotomies in periods of social change, so there appears to be room for the innovative intervention. Results of the studies reported were directly associated with the social setting and the program effort.

Robertson (1973), discussing social factors and family planning, states, "It is clear that the poor and the near-poor have to struggle to support two times as many children on less than half the amount of median earnings." She goes on to state that research and study in family planning by social scientists is greatly needed. The basic question to be answered concerns the necessary and sufficient conditions that make family planning possible. Administrators no longer accept the view that all that is needed is an adequate supply of effective contraceptives and information about them.

Society

In order to understand society's attitudes toward individuals and groups within society, it is helpful to consider the problem from a historical perspective.

THE DILEMMA: HISTORICAL PERSPECTIVE

The problems of the teenage girl in part reflect society's attitudes and mood swings from generation to generation. The attitudes of our recent past concerning women in general are easily forgotten by some. The following brief essay written about one hundred years ago may jog our memories regarding the attitudes of a decade ago. The Rev. William Little (1910) stated:

> God made himself to be born of a woman to sanctify the virtue of endurance; loving submission is an attribute of a woman; men are logical, but women, lacking this quality, have an intricacy of thought. There are those who think women can be taught logic; this is a mistake. They can never by any power of education arrive at the same mental status as that enjoyed by men, but they have a quickness of apprehension, which is usually called leaping at conclusions, that is astonishing. There, then, we have distinctive traits of a woman, namely, endurance, loving submission, and quickness of apprehension. Wifehood is the crowning glory of a woman. In it she is bound for all time. To her husband she owes the duty of unqualified obedience. There is no crime which a man can commit which justifies his wife in leaving him or ap-

plying for that monstrous thing, divorce. It is her duty to subject herself to him always, and no crime that he can commit can justify her lack of obedience. If he be a bad or wicked man, she may gently remonstrate with him, but refuse him never. Let divorce be anathema; curse it; curse this acursed thing, divorce; curse it, curse it! Think of the blessedness of having children. I am the father of many children and there have been those who have ventured to pity me. "Keep your pity for yourself," I have replied, "they never cost me a single pang." In this matter let women exercise that endurance and loving submission which, with intricacy of thought, are their only characteristics.

Consider the difficulties facing a teenager growing up in a society that has recently moved from the former position toward the following contradictory situation described by Nancy Press Hawley (1973) in *Our Bodies, Ourselves:*

We are simultaneously bombarded with two conflicting messages: one from our parents, churches and schools, that sex is dirty and therefore that we must keep ourselves pure for the one love of our lives; and the other from *Playboy, Newsweek,* etc., almost all women's magazines, and especially television commercials—that we should be free groovy chicks.

NATIONAL CONCERN

The testimony of Julius Richmond on July 24, 1978, before the Education Select Subcommittee, House Committee on Education and Labor stated that:

For hundreds of thousands of teenagers, particularly the majority who are unmarried, the birth of a child can usher in a dismal future of unemployment, poverty, dropping out of school, family breakdowns, emotional stress, dependency on public agencies and health problems for mother and child.

It is estimated that about one in ten adolescent girls age 15–19 become pregnant each year. The following statistics are important for developing a perspective on the teenage mother and her child.

Eight of ten women who have become mothers by age 17 never complete high school.

Of all children born out-of-wedlock, almost 60% are supported by welfare.

A baby born to a teenage mother is more than twice as likely to die during the first year of life as a baby born to an older woman.

The likelihood of low-birth-weight babies is 30% to 50% greater for teenagers. Low birth weight is associated with a number of conditions which can cause life-long health and disability problems, such as severe mental retardation.

Of the teenagers who give birth, at least 25% become pregnant again within a year, and a far higher percentage reportedly become pregnant again within two years of their first child's birth.

Behavior Change

To achieve the desired goal of reducing teenage pregnancy, several problems must be recognized and resolved.

First, research demonstrates that health and illness behavior is culturally patterned (Landy 1977; Logan and Hunt 1978; McLain 1977; Colson 1972; and Paul 1975). Croog, as early as 1961 in a study of army inductees reported ethnic differences in health attitudes and behavior that are related to socioeconomic status. Zola (1966) indicated that there are reported differences between Italian and Irish ethnic groups, particularly with respect to patients' decisions to seek care. Scott (1975) reports a study of ethnic populations in inner city Miami of Bahamanians, Cubans, Haitians, Puerto Ricans and American Blacks. One finding that relates to population studies is that ethnicity accounted for variations among the five groups' beliefs about the menstrual cycle and individual choices of methods of fertility regulation. Hessler (1975) indicates large differences in health beliefs of Chinese Americans. He is critical of research that views ethnic populations as uniform. Suchman (1964) found that social class was independently related to social organization and health orientation. Once social class and parochialisms are controlled, ethnic differences decreased greatly. He further found that a social network within the family is at work. These and other studies suggest that socioeconomic status and cultural patterns should be included in the design of an educational program.

19

Second, problems of population control and teenage pregnancy must be recognized as issues of national importance. Many writers have presented the problem; however, probably none more eloquently than Hardin in his 1978 essay "The Tragedy of the Commons." The author states:

> The commons, if justifiable at all, is justifiable only under conditions of low-population density. As the human population has increased, the commons have had to be abandoned in one aspect after another. . . . Every new enclosure of the commons involves the infringement of somebody's personal liberty. It is the newly proposed infringements that we vigorously oppose; cries of rights and freedoms fill the air . . . the most important aspect of necessity that we must now recognize is the necessity of abandoning the commons in breeding. No technical solution can rescue us from the misery of over population. Freedom to breed will bring ruin to us all.

Finally, a number of contemporary researchers who have developed theories in the moral domain have tended to establish a "double standard" for females. Building on the work of Piaget, Kohlberg (1969) cites six stages of moral judgment, leading from dependencies (Stage 1) in childhood to independence (Stage 6) and assertion in judgment in adulthood. Kohlberg believes that the woman's judgment in moral issues will go beyond Stage 3 (law and order) as she begins to rely less on past experiences. Gilligan (1977), in a response to Kolhberg entitled "In a Different Voice," suggests that:

> When birth control and abortion provide women with effective means for controlling their fertility, the dilemma of choice enters the center of women's lives. Then relationships that have traditionally defined women's identities and framed their moral judgements no longer flow inevitably from their reproductive capacity but become matters of decision over which they have control. Released from passivity and reticence of a sexuality that binds them in dependence, it becomes possible for women to question . . . what it is that they want and to assert their own answers to that question.

The researcher's dilemma is the problem of the conflicting responsibilities facing the teenage girl. One can be certain that she will choose the path of least resistance.

References

Beach, F. Characteristics of masculine sex drives. *Nebraska symposium on motivation*. Lincoln, Nebraska: University of Nebraska Press, 1956.

Berelson, B., and Steiner, G. *Human behavior*. New York: Harcourt, Brace and World, 1964.

Colson, A. The differential use of medical resources in developing countries. *J. Health Soc. Behav.* 12:226–237, 1972.

Croog, S. H. Ethnic origins, educational level and response to a health questionnaire. *Human Organization*. 20:65–69, 1961.

Deutsch, J. A., and Deutsch, D. *Physiological psychology*. Homewood, Illinois: The Dorsey Press, 1973.

Freedman, R., and Berelson, B. The record of family planning programs. New York: The Population Council, 1976.

Gilligan, C. In a different voice. *Harvard Educational Review*. 47, November 1977.

Hardin, G. The tragedy of the commons. *Science*. 162, 1978.

Hawley, N. P. and the Boston's Women's Health Book Collective. *Our bodies, ourselves*. Simon and Schuster, 1973.

Hessler, R., and Nolan, M. *New intraethnic diversity, health and human condition*. North Scituate, Mass.: Duxbury Press, 1975.

Klausmeier, H., and Ripple, R. *Learning and human abilities*. New York: Harper and Row, 1971.

Kohlberg, L., and Kramer, R. Continuities and discontinuities in childhood and adult moral development. *Hum. Dev.* 12:93–120, 1969.

Landy, D. *Culture, disease and healing: studies in medical anthropology*. New York: MacMillan, 1977.

Little, W. *Population and evolution and birth control*. San Francisco, California: W. H. Freeman and Company, 1969.

Logan, M., and Hunt, E. *Health and the human condition*. North Scituate, Mass.: Duxbury Press, 1978.

McClain, C. Adaptation in health behavior. *Soc. Sci. Med.* II:341–348, 1977.

Paul, B. *Health, culture and country: case studies of public reactions to health programs*. New York: Russel Sage Foundation, 1975.

Richmond, J. Testimony before house subcommittee on education and labor. July 24, 1978.

Robertson, M., and Uriccho, W. Social factors in family planning. *Natural Fam. Plann.* Washington, D.C.: The Human Life Foundation, 1973.

Ryder, B., and Westoff, C. Wanted and unwanted fertility in the United States, 1965 and 1970. Research Reports, Vol. I, Commission Population Growth and American Future. Washington, D.C.: Government Printing Office, 1975.

Scott, C. The relationship between beliefs about menstrual cycle and choice of fertility regulating methods within five ethnic groups. *Int.*

J. Gynecol. Obstet. 13:105–109, 1975.

Suchman, E. Sociomedical variations among ethnic groups. *A. J. S.* 70:319–331, 1964.

Zola, I. Culture and symptoms: an analysis of patients' presenting complaints. *Am. Sociol. Rev.* 31:615–630, 1966.

3 Psychiatric Aspects of Adolescent Pregnancy

David D. Youngs, M.D.

A prerequisite to understanding psychiatric aspects of adolescent pregnancy is an appreciation of the developmental tasks facing adolescents today in our society. All too frequently, one is confronted with a variety of myths and biases which substitute for a clear and intelligent explanation of adolescent behavior. As Lipsitz has noted in *Growing Up Forgotten: A Review of Research and Programs Concerning Young Adolescents* (1976), common myths about young teenagers today include: (1) most experience this period as one of tumultulous upheaval; (2) in general adolescents can be treated as a homogeneous group; and (3) young adolescents are really children or at least in a transitional stage. Lipsitz goes on to conclude that "these and other misconceptions are important because they are destructive. They reflect a deep mistrust or even dislike of young people in these formative years."

Traditional Views

Pregnant adolescents have traditionally been described as promiscuous, emotionally disturbed, naive, or the products of troubled families. Unfortunately, none of these descriptions has provided a framework for understanding adolescent pregnancy or how best to deal with this problem. Furthermore, by attributing such illegitimacy to loose morality, lower class status, or acceptable minority behavior, serious efforts at understanding this phenomenon have been unnecessarily delayed.

The recent interest among community leaders, government health agencies, and the media with respect to teenage pregnancy is most likely a result of both the dramatic increase in such pregnancies as well as the extension of this problem into the middle class. Prior to the last decade little research effort was devoted to adolescent problems in general or pregnancy in particular. Fortunately, this situation is beginning to change. For example, Congress has recently passed the Adolescent

Health Services and Pregnancy Prevention and Care Act which will provide much needed financial support for research and services for these youngsters.

The purpose of this chapter is to review briefly traditional psychiatric thinking about adolescent pregnancy and to discuss in more detail newer concepts and experiences relevant to pregnant adolescents.

Psychopathology and Illegitimacy

In earlier works illegitimacy was seen as a general index of pathology. Kasinin and Handschin (1941) interpreted illegitimacy as a psychological problem reflecting an unresolved oedipal complex. These pregnancies were thought to represent hysterical dissociations in which the girl acts out her incest fantasies. Explanations of the development of psychopathology in individuals have varied.

Within the illegitimacy framework, personality types were often used as possible explanations of the problem. Rosen and co-workers (1961) found that, while it was difficult to characterize as a group adolescent females who had illegitimate babies, they manifested a certain cluster of personality traits. The most frequently suggested were sociopathic, unsuspecting, unprepared, passive, rejected, isolated, and lonely girls. Psychological tests were often used to collaborate the relationship of psychopathology and illegitimacy. Wagner and Slemboski (1968) administered the Rorschach Test to unmarried women aged 18 to 26 years and found high scores of doubt, uncertainty, and feelings of loneliness manifested by the tested group. Psychopathology became more demonstrable in cases of multiple repeat pregnancies. Malmquist, Kiresuk, and Spano (1967) found young mothers exhibited distortions in object relations and had a narcissistic character structure. Schonholz and co-workers (1969) also found similar traits in a group of indigent, pregnant adolescents studied in New York City. He noted 85% of the patients in the study were chronically depressed.

Giel and Kidd (1965) in reviewing student charts from the University of Edinburgh found that, when compared to matched controls, pregnant students had a higher rate of psychiatric consultation prior to the pregnancy. This increased frequency of consultation was assumed to be an indicator of neuroses.

Psychoses were also identified by some as an antecedent condition to illegitimacy. Balsalm and Lidz (1969) found that the single pregnant adolescent who required psychiatric consultation during pregnancy manifested depression and had borderline or frank psychotic experiences.

Other explanations have also been proposed as the cause of illegitimacy. The possible psychopathology manifested in mother-daughter relationships has been suggested by Friedman (1966) as a factor in illegitimate pregnancy among young women. Barglow and co-workers (1967) suggest that a girl's relationship with her own mother often casts a long shadow over the events prior to a pregnancy. Schaffer and Pine (1972) suggest that pregnancy, especially in an adolescent, reflects a conflict in the mother-daughter process. Specifically, those authors feel that pregnancy brings to the fore conflicts between being mothered and being a mother. Conversely, depression is seen as a precipitating agent in illegitimacy in a white Jewish population studied by Heinman and Levitt (1960). In this group pregnancy is described as a situation which is dynamically linked to depression and is a common reaction subsequent to the experience of an important loss through either death or separation.

Before concluding the discussion on the relationships between psychopathology and illegitimacy, some attention should be focused on the phenomenon of suicide during pregnancy. Young women experiencing out-of-wedlock pregnancies seem to be especially vulnerable. In 1965 Otto reported on suicide attempts made by pregnant women under the age of 21. He found that 43% of the pregnant women in his sample indicated that pregnancy was the provoking factor of their suicide. In addition, significant emotional problems had been encountered in this group with a large proportion of infantile and hysterical personalities manifested in the girls. Babikian and Goldman (1971) also found suicidal preoccupation in the repertoire of behaviors in a subset of their pregnant population.

Oliven (1965) in his text on sexual hygiene for the professional indicates that sexual activity, including indiscriminate "petting," is considered a serious behavioral disturbance and is a symptom of emotional illness. Moreover, the author predicts that certain varieties of adolescent promiscuity offer a very poor prognosis regardless of treatment. As Oliven states, "These girls will most certainly continue their behavior and make the transition to part-time or full-time prostitution." While prostitution is not uniformly proposed as the eventual life style for these girls, similar negative consequences for her psyche have been described. Deutsch

(1967) indicates that, when adolescents act out sexual desires and impulses rather than sublimating them, ego development is compromised, along with disturbed object relations.

In summary, then, we find a review of the earlier conventional works on adolescent pregnancy overwhelmingly negative in tone. We would agree with Hatcher (1973) that many writers on adolescent pregnancy and sexuality bring both theoretical and personal biases to their studies leaving very few writings based on a thorough analysis of objective data. Thus the limited amount of useful literature on adolescent pregnancy may be due to the widespread personal prejudices and feelings aroused by the phenomenon.

Contemporary Views

Numerous changes in contemporary psychiatry have lead to a renewed interest in normal as opposed to abnormal psychological development. For example, Erikson's classical eight stages of man treats personality development as a normal process (1950). Inherent human processes such as cognitive growth (Piaget 1969) and moral development (Kohlberg 1963) seem to proceed in an orderly fashion for the majority of individuals. Human personality unfolds according to steps that are determined by the person's readiness to approach, be aware of and interact with a widening social horizon. Society supports this process and helps in monitoring its speed and sequence. While some risks are associated with each stage, they can be dealt with and overcome in a variety of supportive ways. An appreciation of this developmental approach is an important factor in understanding adolescent pregnancy.

Similarly, traditional thinking about human sexuality has also experienced a psychological renaissance. Sexuality is now defined as a normal aspect of human growth and development, an essential aspect of "humancss." Schiller (1977) emphasizes that sexuality is an integral part of the total personality and a fundamental dimension of human awareness and development. Others such as Calderone (1976) have expanded this concept of human sexuality by suggesting that sexuality per se is not limited to genitalia but encompasses the whole being including all sex-related thoughts, fantasies, information, self-images, feelings, and experiences. Mitchell (1976) suggests that certain sexual feelings and behaviors are normal and necessary components of adolescent growth and development. For the adolescent the need to be intimate is a basic human desire which permeates all adolescent patterns, habits, friendships, and interests. More recently, pregnancy has also been placed in the context of the female developmental life cycle. Bibring and Valenstein (1976) document this phenomenon through their professional experiences with unselected pregnant females. These psychiatrists concluded that pregnancy, like puberty and menopause, is a period of normal life crises involving profound psychological as well as biological changes. Moreover, these crises represent important developmental steps with similar characteristic phenomena. In pregnancy, as in puberty and menopause, new and more complex emotional and adjustive tasks confront the individual. These tasks often lead to the emergence of unsettled conflicts from earlier developmental periods and require a need for new adaptive skills. These authors point out that the crises are necessarily time limited, normal, and primarily precipitated by the psychological and biological stress of pregnancy.

Other authors who have drawn similar conclusions have attempted to build on the strengths associated with the pregnancy crises. LaBarre (1967) explores psychodynamic factors in pregnancies of married adolescents focusing on the actual strengths of teenagers as they deal with pregnancy. Optimism, courage, and adaptability are cited as positive forces which can be used to deal functionally with the crises associated with a pregnancy.

It has been the author's experience that adolescents living in situations where there is marked social disorganization, poverty, fragmentation of families, and few community resources are likely to experience much greater difficulty in their attempts to grow up. Pregnancy among these youngsters represents a different management problem than with the middle class adolescent. Youngs and co-workers (1977) found in providing obstetrical and psychiatric care for over 200 pregnant adolescents, that frank psychopathology, particularly psychosis, is uncommon and appears to be no more prevalent among pregnant teenagers than their non-pregnant counterparts. Delinquent behavior, characterized by the use of drugs and problems with school authorities also appeared to be uncommon. However, Youngs did find that low self-esteem and academic difficulties were more frequently noted in this population. The author, therefore, suggests it is probably the low academic achievement and the yearning for sources of recognition and self-esteem which encourages pregnancy and the discontinuation of schooling.

Whatever the multiple influences which result in pregnancy among poverty-level inner city youngsters, carefully planned and comprehensive medical and social services have shown promise in achieving reasonably adequate adolescent development. Certainly many of these youngsters have major informational deficiencies in the area of human sexuality, reproductive physiology and family planning techniques. To ascribe the significant increase in teenage conception to the wish for pregnancy and a baby overlooks the fact that approximately 30% of teenagers will terminate their pregnancy if provided the opportunity (Alan Guttmacher Institute 1976).

While our understanding of the adolescent's psychological motivation for pregnancy is limited, relevant research data is beginning to become available (Hatcher 1973). Also, studies on the various social and family dynamics commonly found among pregnant teenagers are providing new and useful information. Abernethy (1975), for example, has been able to characterize adolescents "at risk" for pregnancy using criteria which do not depend on sexual or contraceptive practices. While her findings are preliminary, she identifies such dimensions as self-esteem, feelings about one's parents, and various aspects of the parents' marriage as important considerations in predicting vulnerability of young women to pregnancy. In particular, she found that adolescents who become pregnant are more likely to be dissatisfied with their mothers as role models, express a preference for their fathers, even to an exclusive degree, or report significant hostility within the parents' marriage. In contrast, parents who are affectionate and close are more likely to foster their daughters' identities as women and enhance their self-esteem, thus diminishing the probability of precocious sexual behavior and possible conception (Abernethy 1975).

A common mistake in dealing with adolescents of any race, social class or geographic setting is to group them together in a common category. To do this is to overlook the significant social, intellectual, and psychological differences, among others, that exist between a typical 13-year-old and a typical 18-year-old.

In working with pregnant, middle-class adolescents, Hatcher has found that these young women can successfully be divided into *early, middle,* and *late* stages of psychosocial development. Futhermore, while these stages do not always parallel chronological age, such categorization is highly predictive of how the adolescent experiences pregnancy. For example, the early adolescents in her study were less likely to recognize that they were pregnant until later in pregnancy than the middle or late adolescents. Furthermore, the early adolescent's sense of responsibility, knowledge about conception and contraception, motivation for pregnancy, sense of herself as a mother, as well as other factors were highly distinctive.

S. L. Hatcher's (1973) work provides us with a useful framework not only to understand the developmental issues important for young adolescent women in general, but specifically how these issues may express themselves during pregnancy. For a more detailed discussion of these issues, the interested reader is referred to her work.

Earlier community-based attempts to deal with adolescent pregnancy have focused on contraceptive services and sex education-family life programs. While valuable in their own right, these approaches have not provided a primary focus on the adolescent's emotional needs, but rather a symptomatic, and oftentimes, simplistic approach to the problem. Many investigators working in the area of adolescent pregnancy have come to accept the fact that pregnancy among members of this age group is not generally the result of serious social or psychological pathology, but rather that pregnant adolescents have the same emotional needs as other young people, and require an appreciation of this fact if their immediate care is to be successfully provided. And finally, pregnancy precipitates additional psychological and intrafamily conflicts that require careful and caring management, if the experience of pregnancy for these youngsters is to be a constructive and adaptive one.

In conclusion, it is our belief that appropriate care for the pregnant adolescent can be enhanced by a recognition of the psychosocial antecedents of teenage conception as well as an understanding of the personal and emotional needs of a young pregnant woman.

References

Abernethy, V. et al. Identification of women at risk for unwanted pregnancy. *Am. J. Psychiatry* 132:1027–1031, 1975.

Alan Guttmacher Institute. *Eleven million teenagers*. New York: The Research and Development Division of Planned Parenthood Federation of America, 1976.

Babikian, H. M., and Goldman, A. A study in teenage pregnancy.

Am. J. Psychiat. 128:111–116, 1971.

Balsalm, A., and Lidz, R. Psychiatric consultation to a teenage unwed mothers' program. *Conn. Med.*, 33:447–452, 1969.

Barglow, P. et al. Some psychiatric aspects of illegitimate pregnancy during early adolescence. *Am. J. Orthopsychiatry* 37:266–267, 1967.

Bibring, G. L., and Valenstein, A. F. Psychological aspects of pregnancy. *Clin. Obstet. Gynecol.* 19:357–371, 1976.

Calderone, M. It's society that is changing sexuality. *Sexuality today and tomorrow.* ed. S. Gordon and R. W. Libby. North Scituate, Massachusetts.: Duxbury Press, 1976.

Deutsch, H. Selective problems of adolescence, with emphasis on group formation. Psychoanalytic Study of the Child Series, Monograph 3. New York: International University Press, 1967.

Erikson, E. H. *Childhood and society.* New York: W. W. Norton, 1950.

Friedman, H. L. The mother-daughter relationship: its potential in treatment of young unwed mothers. *Social Casework* 47:502–506, 1966.

Giel, R., and Kidd, C. Some psychiatric observations on pregnancy in the unmarried student. *Br. J. Psychiatry* 111:591–594, 1965.

Hatcher, S. L. The adolescent experience of pregnancy and abortion: a developmental analysis. *J. You. Adole.* Vol. II, #1, 1973.

Heiman, M. and Levitt, E. The role of separation and depression in out-of-wedlock pregnancy. *Am. J. Orthopsychiatry* 30:166–174, 1960.

Kasanin, J. and Handschin, S. Psychodynamic factors in illegitimacy. *Am. J. Orthopsychiatry* 11:66–84, 1941.

Kohlberg, L. Moral development and identification in child psychology.

The 62nd Yearbook of National Society for Student Education, Part I. Chicago: University of Chicago Press, 1963.

LaBarre, M. Pregnancy experiences in married adolescents. *Am. J. Orthopsychiatry,* 38:47–55, 1968.

Lipsitz, J. *Growing up forgotten: a review of research and programs concerning young adolescents.* Lexington, Massachusetts: Lexington Books, 1976.

Malmquist, C.; Kiresuk, T.; and Spano, R. Mothers and multiple illegitimacies. *Psychiatric Quarterly* 41:339–354, 1967.

Mitchell, J. J. Adolescent intimacy. *Adolescence* XI:275–280, 1976.

Oliven, J. *Sexual hygiene and pathology.* Philadelphia: J. B. Lippincott Company, 1965.

Otto, U. Suicidal attempts made by pregnant women 21 years. *Acta Paedopsychiatr. (Basel)* 32: 276–288, 1965.

Piaget, J. The intellectual development of the adolescent in adolescence: psychological perspectives. ed. Caplan and Lebovic. New York: Basic Books, Inc., 1969.

Rosen, E. J. et al. A psychiatric, social and psychological study of illegitimate pregnancy in girls under the age of sixteen. *Psychiatr. Neurol. (Basel).* 142:44–60, 1961.

Schaffer, C., and Pine, F. Pregnancy, abortion and the developmental tasks of adolescence. *American Academy of Child Psychiatry J.* 11:511–536, 1972.

Schiller, P. *Creative approach to sex education and counseling.* New York: Association Press, 1977.

Schonholz, D. H. et al. An adolescent guidance program: study in education for marital health. *Obstet. Gynecol.* 34:610–614, 1969.

Wagner, E. E. and Slemboski, J. Psychological reactions of pregnant unwed women as measured by the rorschach. *J. Clin. Psychol.* 24:467–469, 1968.

Youngs, D. D. et al. Experience with an adolescent pregnancy program: a preliminary report. *Obstet. Gynecol.* 50:212–219, 1977.

4 Adolescent Sexuality, Pregnancy, and Childbearing

Ivor L. Safro, M.D.

Close to 13 million of the 60 million women who gave birth in 1975 became parents before they became adults (Alan Guttmacher Institute 1976). Adolescent girls in the U.S. have amongst the highest childbearing rates in the world. Approximately 10% of U.S. teenagers become pregnant and 6% give birth each year. Only Rumania, New Zealand, Bulgaria, and East Germany have higher rates in this age group.

There are about 21 million people between the ages of 15 and 19 in the United States. Of these, about 11 million are estimated to have had sexual intercourse, and of these, about 4 million are young women. In addition, about 20% of the 8 million 13- and 14-year-old boys and girls are believed to have had intercourse. This problem is not only related to the lower socioeconomic groups. Two-thirds of the pregnancies of girls between 15 and 19 years of age are conceived out of wedlock. (See also chapters 8 and 11 for discussions of contraception and abortion.)

Of the 600,000 U.S. teenagers who became pregnant each year, 28% conceive after marriage and give birth; 10% of the young women conceive prior to marriage and give birth; 21% have births out of wedlock; 27% terminate their pregnancies by induced abortion; and 14% have miscarriages.

In addition, about 30,000 girls 15 years or younger get pregnant every year! Almost all of these pregnancies resulted from conception out of wedlock. Approximately one-fifth of all American births are to women still in their teens; 247,000 are to adolescents 17 and younger; 13,000 to girls younger than 15. Two-thirds of the infants are born out of wedlock and one-third are born to married parents. The following statistics highlight the adverse effects of pregnancy on the health of mothers and their babies:

(1) Six percent of all first babies and almost 10% of second babies born to girls under 15 years of age die in the first year

of life. This mortality rate is two to four times higher than that for babies born to women in their early twenties.

(2) Low birth weight is twice as prevalent among teenagers as in older women. This means that adolescent mothers, who bear 19% of all the U.S. infants, have 26% of all the low birth weight infants.

A 7-year United States study shows that white children born to mothers 15 years and younger are 2.4 times more likely to be born with neurologic defects than infants born to mothers in their early twenties.

(3) The death rate from complications of pregnancy, birth, and delivery is 60% higher for women who become pregnant before they are 15; women who are 15 to 19 years old are twice as likely as older women to die from hemorrhage and miscarriage.

(4) Toxemia and anemia are the worst hazards. In the 15-to-19-year age group, mothers are one and one-half times more likely to die from toxemia. Mothers under 15 years are three and one-half times more likely to die from toxemia. Battaglia and co-workers (1963) state that the increase in perinatal toxemia was not due to race or primiparity. Adolescent mothers are 11% more likely to suffer from nonfatal anemia. Women of 20 to 24 years old have rates for anemia of 8.8% and 6.9% respectively.

From 1966 to 1976 there has been an 18.4% reduction in the number of teenagers giving birth. This is greater than the national trend that shows a decline of 12.1% in total births and 9.3% in teenage births over the same period.

Some studies indicate that teenagers with adequate prenatal care do not, as a group, have greater problems than older childbearing women and in general have lower complication rates than women over the age of 40 years (Battaglia and co-workers 1963). A survey by the National Center for Health Statistics showed that more than 50% of adolescents received no health care in the first trimester and 16% had no health care in the second trimester. Apparently the greatest concern for health is for girls under the age of 15 who apparently show an increased risk of anemia, abnormal bleeding, toxemia, difficult labor, and cephalopelvic disproportion. Some obstetricians working with teenagers are of the opinion that even good prenatal care does not overcome the biologic problems of the adolescent mother. In general, teenagers appeared for family planning only after a year or more of sexual activity or after an abortion or when seeking a pregnancy test (Stubblefield 1978).

The prematurity rate was higher in the 15-year-old age group than in the over-15-year olds, and the increased perinatal mortality rate in this age group was proportionately related to the increase in number of premature infants born to these girls. Among the patients seen in this age group, the incidence of contracted pelvis was assessed to be about 35.7%. Probably immaturity of the pelvis causes this condition which is possibly related to age rather than to race. There did not appear to be an increased incidence of congenital anomalies in the under-15-year-old group.

Prenatal Care of the Adolescent

Ideally, pregnant women should be seen by their physicians early in gestation, examined monthly until the seventh month, and then bimonthly until the 36th week, and weekly from the 36th week until delivery. Unfortunately, private doctors are often reluctant to accept these patients, particularly if they are poor and not married. The quality of teenage care should be the very best that is available to the rest of the community. Often the cooperation of the social worker-psychiatrist is necessary.

PATIENT HISTORY

A history of previous pregnancies, particularly of abortions or deliveries is essential for good patient care. Complications of previous pregnancies, and any fetal abnormalities or fetal loss are very important. Family history particularly of diabetes or high blood pressure or twinning should be noted carefully.

The time of the last menstrual period, any recent vaginal bleeding, attempted abortion, fetal movement, and the time of occurrence should be recorded. It is important to record the normal menstrual cycle of the patient in order to establish her eventual time of delivery. History of any current illness or exposure to hormonal preparations or other medications is also of value. A complete medical and surgical history should be taken. Particular attention should be paid to previous exposure to rubella, herpes, and any other venereal diseases.

PHYSICAL EXAMINATION

A complete general physical work-up is mandatory at the first prenatal examination. In adolescents, particularly those from lower socioeconomic groups, a surprising number of general medical and possibly surgical problems may be uncovered. A Papanicolaou smear and a culture for gonoccoccus from the endocervix should be obtained at the time of the first vaginal examination. During the obstetric examination, the utmost sensitivity and tenderness must be exhibited toward the patient. If requested, her mother should be present at the examination and every effort be made to prevent the examination from being perceived as traumatic. In addition to correlating dates to determine the length of gestation, detailed physical examination of the uterus, including auscultation of the fetal heart with a Doptone should be done if the pregnancy is beyond 12 weeks.

Assessment of the pelvic capacity should be delayed until about 36 weeks of the pregnancy. This procedure is rather painful and unnecessary in the early stages of pregnancy when cephalopelvic comparison is of no value. Assessment of pregnancy duration can be made by ultrasonic measurements of the biparietal diameter of the fetal head after 20 weeks.

EDUCATION

If possible, it may be best to have the young woman attend her regular school and classes until the onset of labor. Some public school systems provide special classes. In some cities special schools, evening programs, or home tutoring are available for pregnant teenagers.

Prenatal group classes and discussions are helpful. For both married and unmarried couples, the father of the infant may wish to be directly involved in the antenatal period and with the delivery. If this is the case, it would be advisable for him to attend classes on prenatal care and labor instruction with the mother.

At first and subsequent visits each patient should be instructed to report any vaginal bleeding, vomiting, dysuria, any intercurrent illness, visual defects, abdominal pain, swelling of the face, fingers, or escape of fluid from the vagina.

Douches are contraindicated because of the danger of air embolism. Frequence of intercourse until term should be determined by the patient's libido and comfort and avoided if bleeding or cervical dilatation or rupture of membranes are present.

Since full skeletal maturation is not complete in some girls until the age of 17 or later, the nutritional demands of pregnancy are superimposed on a continuing maternal growth process.

The patient is advised to follow a balanced diet as recommended by the Food and Nutrition Board (1974) including sufficient protein, carbohydrates, fat and roughage. Patients are warned against taking any medication, drinking alcohol, or smoking, against doing any vigorous exercise, and against having any x-ray examination particularly by a dentist unless the gynecologist is told in advance about the examination.

Several studies have shown that about a third of pregnant women do not take mineral supplements, particularly if the purpose of the medication is not explained. In animal studies, it has been shown that maternal dietary deficiencies result in relatively small offspring.

Specific Dietary Allowances

Although the adolescent mother may still be growing, the Recommended Dietary Allowances issued by the Food and Nutrition Board (1974) for the National Research Council serve as an acceptable guide for the pregnant adolescent.

Calories
An increase in maternal weight of 28 pounds or approximately one pound per week in the latter half of pregnancy is acceptable. Teenagers should be urged not to diet during pregnancy. Additional calories may be recommended if the mother is still growing, underweight, or particularly active.

Protein
The most recent recommendation during pregnancy is the intake of 75 grams of protein per day.

Vitamins
An adequate diet should obviate the need for routine vitamin supplements in healthy individuals.

Vitamin A. Recommended daily allowance of 5,000 IU (International Units). Excessive amounts should not be consumed as hypervitaminosis A can be toxic to infants and in animals has proven to be teratogenic.

Vitamin D. Intake of 400 IU a day is sufficient to meet the requirements of pregnant adolescents. Hypervitaminosis D may be a serious condition leading to hypercalcemia in the infant. Neill (1968) has suggested that excessive ingestion of vitamin D by a pregnant woman may possibly be the cause in the offspring of supravalvular pulmonic and aortic stenosis and of physical and mental retardation.

Minerals and Iron

Pritchard (1969) recommends with supplementation with 30 to 60 mg of a simple iron salt (ferrous gluconate or ferrous fumarate) once a day in the latter half of pregnancy.

Calcium. It is generally felt that a normal well-balanced diet will almost certainly provide all the minerals and vitamins needed for pregnancy as well as the average woman's calcium intake even without additional food consumption. If the patient has lactose intolerance or has a dislike for milk, calcium supplementation will be necessary.

Salt

The danger of sodium restriction in normal pregnancy is the provocation of an exaggerated normal renin-angiotensin-aldosterone cycle leading to sodium depletion. The risk of sodium depletion is heightened by the use of diuretics. Sodium should therefore not be restricted during normal pregnancy (American College of Obstetricians and Gynecologists 1972).

Common Medical Problems Associated with Adolescent Pregnancy

Breast tenderness, nausea, and vomiting are common complaints in early pregnancy. The latter usually lasts about 12 to 14 weeks, but may be severe and may even last for the duration of the pregnancy. Instructions regarding diet should include: identification of nonirritating foods; encouragement of patient to eat small amounts of food frequently after awakening in the morning; and provision of information about the blood sugar level, its importance particularly in the early phases of pregnancy and the times of day when blood sugar is likely to be low.

Occasionally vomiting is of such a severe nature that it may endanger the life of both the mother and the infant and may require admission to a hospital, intravenous medication, sedation and, very rarely, termination of the pregnancy. In all cases a detailed history concerning any psychosocial or emotional problems should be taken and dealt with adequately by the physician in charge.

Early pregnancy is also sometimes associated with lassitude and fatigue and with an urge to sleep particularly in the late afternoon prior to the evening meal. The best advice that one can give the patient is to follow her natural urge and to take some extra rest. Food cravings are common, and later in the second trimester the appetite normally becomes quite voracious, usually associated with an increased fetal demand.

HEADACHES

Causes of headaches in pregnancy are hypertension (pregnancy-induced or otherwise), muscle spasm, and osteoarthritis of the cervical spine. The physician should always bear in mind the possibility of an underlying cerebral tumor and should the headaches be persistent and not relieved by ordinary pain medication then a neurologic opinion is well-advised.

LEUKORRHEA AND VAGINAL DISCHARGE

There is a modest increase in vaginal discharge normally in a healthy pregnancy caused by increased secretion of the cervical glands. Vaginal pruritus or perineal itching is usually associated with infection by *Candida albicans* or *Trichomonas vaginalis*.

The treatment of trichomoniasis in pregnancy is rather difficult as metronidazole is contraindicated in early gestation. *Candida* can be effectively and safely controlled with nystatin suppositories.

VARICOSE VEINS

Patients who develop varicose veins usually have a family history of varicosities, and often their mothers have had similar symptoms. Elastic stockings should be worn from the time of awakening; elevation of the foot of the bed and rest during the daytime with elevation of the feet will afford some comfort.

HEMORRHOIDS

Hemorrhoids are best treated by altering the bowel habits and by using a high bulk diet regimen. Topical local anesthetics can be used to alleviate the pain of the hemorrhoids. External hemorrhoidal hematoma is best treated by incision and drainage under local anesthesia.

VIRAL INFECTIONS

Important viral infections during pregnancy are rubella, cytomegalovirus (CMV) and herpesvirus II. Extensive studies have now shown that maternal viral infections may or may not be halted by the placenta. Rubella, CMV, coxsackie virus B and polio virus reach the fetus by a transplacental route but directly ascending infections via the cervix are also possible. Rubella vaccination is absolutely contraindicated during pregnancy as the vaccine contains live virus that may be transmitted to the fetus.

In CMV infections, an infection was demonstrated in 60% of the mothers (all asymptomatic) of infected infants. When fetal infection is clinically apparent, severe congenital anomalies, resembling those caused by rubella contracted in the second month of development, result. At present there is no way to prevent or treat CMV disease, but work is proceeding on a prenatal vaccine for mothers.

Herpesvirus Type II

Infants are exposed to infection in utero particularly during delivery and in the postpartum period by contact with an infected mother. There is apparently an increased risk of fetal wastage and prematurity due to herpesvirus II infection during pregnancy; when the infant is severely affected hepatic involvement occurs along with ocular and neurologic damage.

It is thought that since herpesvirus II is a common venereal disease and is potentially harmful to the fetus, cervical cultures and Papanicolaou smears for cytopathologic changes should become an integral part of prenatal care. If either a previous history of genital herpes or an active lesion is present, a strong case can be made for delivery by cesarean section. Vaginal delivery is most *definitely* contraindicated if there is any evidence of genital herpesvirus even in the absence of an acute infection.

Hepatitis

Infection occurs with both hepatitis A or hepatitis B and the disease may be transmitted to the fetus in utero. Schweitzer and co-workers (1973) found hepatitis B antigen in 48% of infants born to mothers with acute viral hepatitis whose serum contained the antigen. In asymptomatic mothers only 5% of infants had antigenemia. Hepatitis may also be transmitted with HB antigen to the infant following delivery. The antigen can serve as an indicator of transmission, and antibody may mark the absence of transmission of HB virus from carrier mothers to their children.

Maternal Influenza

The effect of maternal influenza on the fetus is controversial. It has been hypothesized that an increased risk of abortion and congenital anomalies exists if the mother acquires the infection during the first trimester. Killed influenza vaccine is not completely effective but does apparently decrease the morbidity and can apparently be used without risk during pregnancy.

Measles and Small Pox

Measles and small pox are not a problem for American women because of immunization programs and a decreased incidence of the latter in America.

TOXOPLASMOSIS

If the mother acquires toxoplasmosis early in pregnancy, passage of the organism across the placenta may result in severe congenital infections manifested at birth by seizures, hydrocephalus, microcephaly, cerebral calcifications, enlargement of the liver and spleen, and jaundice. No treatment is indicated for women who have had toxoplasmosis before pregnancy unless there is severe eye involvement and in such patients, steroids are generally used. No safe or effective therapeutic agent is presently available for use during pregnancy.

Hypertension and Pregnancy-Induced Hypertension in Adolescents

In adolescent girls, hypertension prior to the onset of pregnancy is quite rare, probably of the order of less than 1%. Pregnancy-induced hypertension or preeclampsia is the most consistently noted high-risk complication in teenage patients; the highest rate is among the youngest mothers. When all reports are considered, the overall teenage incidence ranges from between 7.3 to 29%. All patients during first pregnancies have a rate of about 7%.

TREATMENT

In mild preeclampsia, bed rest in the left lateral recumbent position to improve uterine blood flow is the most important initial therapy. If after bed rest the blood pressure falls to below 120/80 and diuresis results, the patient may be followed as an outpatient and advised to restrict activity.

If a patient is mildly hypertensive and has a diastolic pressure of less than 110 mm Hg, hydralazine (Apresoline) 25 to 50 mg orally every 6 hours is effective. Diuretics are theoretically contraindicated in preeclampsia because of the already existing, low plasma volume. If a patient has severe preeclampsia and a diastolic blood pressure of more than 120, parenteral antihypertensive therapy is indicated. Twenty-five to 50 mg hydralazine intravenously in 500 ml of glucose water should be given for immediate blood pressure control together with 500 mg of Aldomet and 40 to 80 mg of Lasix intravenously. The methyldopa requires 6 to 8 hours for its maximum effect. If diastolic blood pressure is greater than 120 mm of mercury, diazoxide intravenously (30 mg) can be given rapidly with 40 to 80 mg of Lasix. Recently, medical practitioners have tended to recommend that when a patient's blood pressure has been brought under control and excessive excitability of the nervous system has been controlled attempts to effect delivery within 6 to 8 hours should be made using an oxytocin infusion. Cesarean section is indicated when immediate delivery is advisable. This method of delivery is preferable when spontaneous or induced labor fails, when cephalopelvic

41

disproportion exists or other obstetric indications demand a cesarean section. Medical supervision should continue for the first seven to ten days postpartum. Long term follow-up of pregnant adolescents with preeclampsia suggests a 3 to 5 times greater incidence of residual hypertension compared to control women of the same age and weight whose pregnancies have been normal.

Chronic Medical Problems and Pregnancy Complications

BODY WEIGHT

Kreutner and Hollingsworth (1978) surprisingly stated that preeclampsia was found as often in thin girls as in those who were overweight. Both groups had twice as great an incidence of preeclampsia as girls with normal body mass. They also suggested that prepregnancy body weight, as influenced by heredity and environmental factors, had a more important bearing on placental size than nutrition and weight gain during the gestational period. Infant birth weights were positively correlated with prepregnancy weight and placental size. Thin girls had smaller placentas and smaller infants than normal or obese girls.

EMOTIONAL SUPPORT DURING PREGNANCY

Fifty percent of teenagers are sexually active or have borne children by the age of 18. Kreutner and Hollingsworth (1978) claim that 41% of the teenagers became pregnant because they wanted to have the baby. A high percentage of them are not making themselves available to have abortions. The emotional reactions and ability of the pregnant adolescent to cope with the pregnancy are strongly influenced by social circumstances.

If the pregnant adolescent is married and has established a home, her situation may be stable. If her life has economic stability, emotional adjustment is probably similar to those of women in their twenties. Many clinics find a team approach most successful. The key person is a social worker who coordinates care and continually keeps in touch with the patient and her family. If anxiety, depression, and/or drug dependence are problems, expert psychiatric help must be readily available. In Hollingsworth's clinic only 1% of blacks and 12% of whites placed their infants for adoption.

Breast feeding, if possible, should be assiduously taught and encouraged. Home visits by a nurse should be provided at least during the first month after discharge from the hospital.

DIABETES MELLITUS

O'Sullivan and Mayhan (1964) have proposed criteria for diagnosing gestational diabetes. A positive diagnosis is made if two or more blood sugar levels exceed normal values for the pregnancy. In diabetic pregnancies, there is a higher risk of maternal preeclampsia, perinatal death, macrosomic infants, infants with high incidence of birth defects, and neonatal hypoglycemia.

Pregnant women who have sugar in their urine in more than one random sample, a strong family history of diabetes, a previous infant weighing more than 10 lb at birth, a history of previous stillbirth, neonatal death, or a congenital abnormality should have a glucose tolerance test.

Recently Felig and co-workers (1975) recommended that total caloric intake should follow the guidelines established for adolescents by the Committee on Maternal Nutrition of the National Research Council (1974). Approximately 25 lbs are an acceptable weight gain during pregnancy.

Almost all adolescent diabetics require insulin. The dose varies with the severity of the diabetes, the degree of exercise, and several other factors. The amount of insulin should be prescribed to prevent ketoacidosis and low blood sugar. It has been suggested that fewer fetal complications will ensue when blood sugar determinations are maintained in a normal range. Some have advocated continuous hospitalization of the patient from the 30th week of pregnancy with blood sugar monitoring three times per day.

Complications

Complications of pregnancy in patients who are diabetic include an increased incidence of preeclampsia and polyhydramnios. These two complications are ameliorated by bed rest and good control of the diabetes.

43

Fetal mortality is generally 3 to 6 times greater than in nondiabetic pregnancy. Mortality varies with prenatal management, the type of delivery, and the availability of highly skilled neonatal staff. The plan for each delivery must be individualized. Daily placental assessment with 24 hour estriol determinations and fetal monitoring are advisable. After delivery, the mother's blood sugar should be checked every 6 hours and regular insulin given. By the second or third postpartum day, ⅔ or ¾ of the usual prepregnancy insulin dose should be started with further adjustments made as time passes.

The infant of the diabetic mother is larger than normal in size, and blood sugar tends to drop in 10% to 25% of cases. In 5% to 10% of these infants congenital anomalies are present. Respiratory distress syndrome occurs in 25% to 30% and hyperbilirubinemia, in from 5% to 10% of infants. Low blood calcium is present in about 25%.

RENAL DISEASE

Adolescents with chronic renal disease hypertension usually have impaired fertility. Renal function may worsen early in the pregnancy and necessitate therapeutic abortion. Early delivery may be necessary because of the threat of increased intrauterine mortality near term and the risk of premature separation of the placenta in hypertensive pregnancies.

Pregnancy in adolescents with renal transplants are increasing, and Ferris recommends waiting one year after a living homograft and two years after a cadaveric transplant. Management of pregnancy in a transplantation patient is complicated and difficult.

TUBERCULOSIS

All pregnant adolescents should be screened for tuberculosis by skin test and a chest x-ray. If the skin test is negative and the patient is asymptomatic, routine prenatal chest x-ray should be delayed.

There is no deleterious effect of either active or chronic tuberculosis on the pregnancy, no increase in spontaneous abortion.

Antituberculous chemotherapy, serial x-rays, and bacteriological studies should be supervised by an internist who is an expert in tuberculosis.

Drugs

The period during which environmental agents can affect the development of the human embryo is very short and is over by the eighth week of pregnancy. The critical period for teratogenic agents is from 34 to 50 days from the last menstrual period.

OVER-THE-COUNTER DRUGS

Teenagers frequently take excessive doses of over-the-counter medications for symptoms such as constipation and cough. Since over-the-counter preparations cross the placenta and are potentially harmful to the pregnant mother and fetus, the doctor should be aware of their contents.

BARBITURATES

Neonatal withdrawal symptoms and depression at birth have been noted in mothers with a barbiturate dependence. Teenagers frequently use these drugs in combination with others, for example, amphetamines.

ALCOHOL

Severe alcohol addiction by the age of 18 is rare. Alcohol crosses the placenta. Recently described congenital malformation syndrome related to excessive alcoholic intake during pregnancy has infants showing microcephaly, low intelligence, and growth retardation.

MARIJUANA

Unlike nicotine and alcohol, the cannabinoids are fat soluble and may be stored in body tissues, including the brain, for weeks or months. Estimated excretion of the drug takes about 8 days; in mothers who smoke only occasionally there is chronic fetal exposure. Marijuana and the active extract $\Delta 9$ tetrahydrocannabinol isomer both cross the placenta. There is concern that marijuana may cause chromosomal abnormalities. Chronic marijuana smoking impairs cellular-mediated immunity. There is a potential effect of marijuana on the fetal hypothalamus. The American Academy of Pediatrics Committee on drugs recommends avoidance of exposure to marijuana by women who are or may become pregnant.

HEROIN AND METHADONE

Most heroin addicts are infertile because they have amenorrhea, but in sporadic users, pregnancy may occur and the risk to both the mother and infant in utero is mainly that of hepatitis. At birth there are higher perinatal mortality and morbidity rates. The infant may develop heroin withdrawal syndrome. Naloxone is effective against the respiratory depression properties of this drug. Infants of mothers on methadone may also show growth retardation.

LSD

Jacobsen and Berlin (1972) in a large prospective study followed 148 pregnancies in females and their consorts who used LSD before or during pregnancy. They found an incidence of major congenital anomalies 10 to 20 times the expected number for the American population. With this in view it has been suggested that LSD may possibly cause mutagenic changes.

Abortion

In a study by Richardson and Dixon (1976) a significantly higher incidence of spontaneous mid-trimester abortion was found, as was premature labor in teenagers who had a previous elective termination of pregnancy. Eleven patients who had cervical lacerations during termination had a fetal loss rate of 45.5%. The authors suggest a cerclage procedure in a subsequent pregnancy for those with known cervical lacerations.

Postpartum Complications

All available data suggest that the adolescent mother and her offspring are at a greater risk for morbidity and mortality in the immediate postpartum period. Good nutrition and adequate prenatal care can help reduce the risk but unfortunately cannot eliminate it completely.

References

Alan Guttmacher Institute. *11 million teenagers: what can be done about the epidemic of adolescent pregnancies in the United States*. New York: Alan Guttmacher Institute, The Research and Development Division of Planned Parenthood Federation of America, 1976.

Battaglia, F. C., et al. Obstetric and pediatric complications of juvenile pregnancy. *Pediatrics*. 32:902, 1963.

Felig, P. Nutrition maintenance and diet therapy in acute and chronic disease. *Textbook of medicine*. ed. P. B. Beeson and W. McDermott. Philadelphia: W. B. Saunders Co., 1975.

Fielding, J. E. Adolescent pregnancy revisited. *N. Engl. J. Med.* pp. 893–895, October 1978.

Food and Nutrition Boards National Research Council. *Recommended dietary allowances,* 8th ed. Washington, District of Columbia: *National Academy of the Sciences,* 1974.

Jacobsen, C. B. and Berlin, E. M. Possible reproductive detriment in LSD users. *JAMA* 222:1376, 1972.

Jaffe, F. S. and Dryfoos, J. C. Fertility control services for adolescents: access and utilization. *Fam. Plann. Perspect.* 8:167, 1976.

Kreutner, A. K. and Hollingsworth, D. R. *Adolescent obstetrics and gynecology.* Chicago: Yearbook Medical Publishers, Inc., 1978.

Neill, C. A. Etiologic and hemodynamic factors in congenital heart disease. *Human growth.* ed. D. B. Check. Philadelphia: Lea and Trebiger, 1968.

O'Sullivan, J. B. and Mahan, C. M. Criteria for the oval glucose tolerance test in pregnancy. *Diabetes* 13:278, 1964.

Pritchard, J. A., et al. Folic acid requirements in pregnancy induced megaloblastic anemia. *JAMA* 208:1163, 1969.

Richardson, J. A. and Dixon, G. Effects of legal termination in subsequent pregnancy. *Br. Med. J.* 1:1303, 1976.

Stubblefield, P. Personal Communication to Dr. J. E. Fielding. July 26, 1978. (Quoted in *N. Engl. J. of Med.,* p. 894, October 19, 1978).

Schweitzer, I. L., et al. Viral hepatitis B in neonates and infants. *Am. J. Med.* 55:762, 1973.

5 Social Implications of Teenage Childbearing

Frank F. Furstenberg, Jr., Ph.D.

Albert G. Crawford, Ph.D.

Contrary to popular impression, the absolute level of teenage childbearing in the United States has not risen during the past decade, but has actually declined. Moreover, the newly discovered "epidemic" of adolescent pregnancy is not recent; elevated levels of teenage childbearing can be traced to the beginning of the baby boom after the Second World War. Nevertheless, the issue does seem more pressing now than ever before. In this chapter we shall touch on some of the reasons for this issue's prominence. We shall look at the evidence in the literature on the social consequences of teenage childbearing for adolescent parents, their offspring, and members of their family of origin. After assessing this evidence, we shall briefly mention some of the policy initiatives open for us for preventing premature childbearing and for ameliorating its deleterious effects when it does occur.

Teenage Childbearing as a Social Issue

Whether we conclude that adolescent fertility is a problem of growing or diminishing social significance largely rests on how we define adolescence and on how we measure fertility. Table 5.1 presents an array of natality statistics for the period 1966 to 1975, subdivided by age. Depending on the indicator, the specific time period, and the age segment we examine, we may form quite different impressions of the current situation. The statistics can provide either some degree of reassurance or considerable cause for alarm.

As indicated above, when absolute numbers are considered, and if we equate teenagers with adolescents, adolescent childbearing has dropped off significantly since the late 1960s. Even among the school-age population (children up to age 18), there has been a decline in the number of births during the past decade. Of course, one explanation for this downward trend is that the pool of adolescents has not been growing as rapidly in recent years as it did up to 1970. As the share of teenagers in the population diminishes, inevitably there will be a lower number of births, unless the likelihood of their becoming pregnant increases to off-set the decline in their numerical significance. In fact, teenagers, espe-cially the 18- and 19-year-olds, are less, not more, likely to become pregnant. The fertility rate, expressed as the number of births per 1,000 teenagers, has dropped off sharply since the end of the baby boom twenty years ago. Both the shrinking pool of teenagers and the decline in their birth rate, are likely to continue in the near future, suggesting that the absolute number of adolescent births may decline still further in the next few years.

If this is true, then what has generated the intense concern about early childbearing in the past few years? Is adolescent parenthood a socially manufactured problem created by the mass media in order to generate public interest or by government officials in order to extend their social programs? We think not. If we look again at table 5.1, we can find some real basis for the recent wave of attention devoted to the subject; the decline, both absolute and relative, in adolescent fertility has been re-stricted to married teenagers. Out-of-wedlock childbearing has jumped during the same period that marital childbearing among the young has decreased (table 5.2). While most teenagers who have babies are still married when the birth occurs, if present trends continue, this will not be the case for long. In 1950 approximately 85% of the births among the teenage population were to unmarried women; by 1974 the figure was only 60%. When these figures are broken down by age, we can see that the increase in nonmarital childbearing has risen for both mature and younger adolescents. Indeed, a majority of births to females who are under age 18 now take place out of wedlock.

Whether it is justified or not, so-called "illegitimate" births invariably generate more concern about the well-being of the mother and child. Later we shall show that we should be just as concerned about marital as nonmarital teenage fertility. In fact we might argue plausibly that much of the alarm surrounding early childbearing has been provoked by moral concern regarding the fact that an increasing number of teenagers are failing to marry when pregnancy occurs. If these teenagers did marry, the problem might well escape public notice, as it did in the 1950s and early 1960s.

There is reason to suspect that part of the concern about early child-bearing can be traced to a more general apprehensiveness about the rise in adolescent sexual activity. Suppose, for example, that the rate of sexual

Table 5.1
Birth Rates for Women 15–17 and 18–19 Years of Age, by Age
of Mother, United States, 1966 to 1975. (Rates are live births per
1000 women.)

Age of Mother	1975	1974	1973	1972
15 to 17 years	36.6	37.7	38.9	39.2
18 to 19 years	85.7	89.3	91.8	97.3

SOURCE: National Center for Health Statistics 1977.

Table 5.2
Estimated Illegitimacy Rates for Unmarried Women 15–17 and 18–
19 Years of Age, United States, 1966 to 1975. (Rates are illegitimate
live births per 1,000 unmarried women. Population estimated as of
July 1.)

Age of Mother	1975	1974	1973	1972
15 to 17 years	19.5	19.0	18.9	18.6
18 to 19 years	32.8	31.4	30.6	31.0

SOURCE: National Center for Health Statistics 1977.

intercourse rose but that it was accompanied by increased use of contraception and abortion? Would change in the sexual patterns of youth attract public concern even if it occasioned no teenage births or at least no births which occurred out of wedlock? We believe that it would. Our view is that the teenage parent has provided an opportunity for adults to discuss publicly the broader issue of the sexual mores and sexual instruction of the young.

Although we lack good evidence on patterns of sexual behavior among the young prior to the past few years, it is a safe assumption that youth has never even approached the ideal of premarital chastity. Historical records testify that premarital pregnancy has always been common in American society, although there were undoubtedly tremendous regional, religious and ethnic variations in adherence to strict sexual standards in times past (Reiss 1967; Smith 1973). Those variations still persist, though some evidence remains that they may break down in the future as increasing numbers of adolescents opt for a more liberal sexual code.

If we can only speculate about sexual behavior in the past and the

1971	1970	1969	1968	1967	1966
38.3	38.8	35.8	35.2	35.5	35.8
105.6	114.7	115.0	114.9	117.4	121.2

1971	1970	1969	1968	1967	1966
17.6	17.1	15.2	14.7	13.9	13.1
31.7	32.9	31.5	30.0	27.8	25.8

future, we have learned a good deal about recent trends through the national surveys conducted by Zelnik and Kantner (1977). As is shown in table 5.3, the Zelnik and Kantner studies reveal a sharp rise in the proportion of females who have had sexual intercourse at each age and among both blacks and whites. Noteworthy is the change in sexual patterns among whites. Although their overall level of coital experience is lower, their rate of increase is faster, suggesting that white adolescents are "catching up" to blacks. As whites, particularly those in the middle class, are exposed to the risk of pregnancy, the problem of adolescent sexuality will attract wider interest and will command more support for intervention. One form of intervention, of course, has been the availability of abortion. Again, it is difficult to determine the changes in the use of abortion among teenagers, because reliable data only exists since its legalization. Nevertheless, it is likely that the existence of abortion has both "permitted" more sexual experimentation and, at the same time, allowed teenagers to escape the consequences of an unwanted birth. The generally increasing availability of abortion may also help to explain in

51

Table 5.3
Percent of Never-Married Women Aged 15 to 19 Who Have Ever Had Intercourse, by Age and Race, 1976 and 1971.

	Study year and race					
	1976					1971
	All	White		Black		All
Age		%	N	%	N	
15 to 19	34.9	30.8	1,232	62.7	654	26.8
15	18.0	13.8	276	38.4	133	13.8
16	25.4	22.6	301	52.6	135	21.2
17	40.9	36.1	277	68.4	139	26.6
18	45.2	43.6	220	74.1	143	36.8
19	55.2	48.7	158	83.6	104	46.8

SOURCE: Zelnick and Kantner 1977.

part why adolescent fertility may have declined in the face of increased sexual activity and also why a smaller proportion of teenagers today marry upon becoming pregnant. While abortion has served to conceal the growing sexual experience of teenagers and to mitigate the potentially adverse effects of a rise in the adolescent birth rate, it has also drawn attention to teenage sexuality. In no small measure, opposition to abortion has forced attention to an issue that previously would have been swept under the rug. The federal government has been goaded into action by the controversy over abortion. Government officials might have preferred to treat adolescent sexuality as a private concern, relegating it to the jurisdiction of local communities, the churches or the family. Later we shall return to discuss in more detail the alternatives open to various parties interested in preventing premature parenthood.

Research on Early Childbearing

In suggesting reasons why interest in adolescent pregnancies has mounted, we should not ignore the role of researchers in supplying in-

				% increase 1971 to 1976		
White		Black		All	White	Black
%	N	%	N			
21.4	2,633	51.2	1,339	30.2	43.9	22.5
10.9	642	30.5	344	30.4	26.6	25.9
16.9	662	46.2	320	19.8	33.7	13.9
21.8	646	58.8	296	53.8	65.6	16.3
32.3	396	62.7	228	22.8	35.0	18.2
39.4	287	76.2	151	17.9	23.6	9.7

formation both to policy makers and to the general public through the mass media. Until 1970 only scattered studies existed on the topic of teenage parenthood. It is noteworthy that until the mid-1970s, no separate category existed in the *Readers' Guide to Periodical Literature* to designate articles on adolescent childbearing, though there was a heading for teenage marriage. In 1973 the category "pregnant schoolgirls" appeared and then in 1977 this rubric was changed to "teenage pregnancy." The entries on the subject have accordingly increased sharply in the past five years. The review of the literature which follows is not intended to provide a comprehensive guide to this burgeoning area of research, but only to highlight some of the consistent findings that have emerged. For a comprehensive summary of the literature, see Chilman 1977.

In reviewing current research results, we shall give heavy emphasis to the results of the senior author's own longitudinal study of early childbearing conducted in Baltimore, Maryland from 1966 to 1972. Throughout this period the careers of some 400 adolescent mothers were traced from the time of pregnancy to a point five years after the birth of their first child. The young women in the Baltimore study were first contacted when they registered for prenatal care at a hospital clinic. At the time all were under the age of 18 and were pregnant for the first time. Nearly all the women in the study were black, most came from working-class or unemployed households and the great majority (81%) were still single when the initial interview was conducted in 1966 or 1967.

Three follow-up studies were conducted at one year, three years and five years after delivery. Cooperation was excellent throughout the study. In the five year follow-up study, 82% of the original sample were reinterviewed. At the conclusion of the study the children of the young mothers were tested as they were entering the school system.

In order to assess the impact of early childbearing on the life chances of the young mothers and their children, a sample of their former classmates (at the time of pregnancy) were interviewed as well in the three- and five-year follow-up studies. The classmates of the adolescent mothers were well matched in age, racial status and economic background. It turned out that slightly more than half of the classmates also had experienced a pregnancy during their late teens. In the discussion that follows, we shall compare the life situations of the young mothers in 1972 to those of their peers who became pregnant in their late teens and to their classmates who were able to delay the onset of childbearing at least until their early twenties.

We have chosen to feature the results of the Baltimore study not only for reasons of familiarity but also because the findings have been widely supported in subsequent investigations. Research on the consequences of early childbearing has produced a remarkable consistency of evidence that premature parenthood disadvantages the young mother and her child (Presser 1974; Baldwin 1976; Chilman 1977). A recent study by Card and Wise (1978) also confirms the supposition that early childbearing disrupts the life chances of the father as well. Not as much data has been accumulated on the effects of early childbearing on other family members, but we shall report on the results of some ongoing investigations of this topic.

The Etiology of Early Childbearing

Theories about the etiology of early childbearing have often failed to take into account that parenthood is the result of a social process. A major tendency has been to search for psychological or characterological factors which motivate adolescents to enter parenthood prematurely, such as the need for affection, the quest for adult status, resolution of the oedipal conflict, the desire to escape parental control or the inability to foresee a more gratifying future. No doubt some of these reasons apply in some instances. However, most studies show that only a small minority of adolescents become parents because they want to have a child (at least at the time conception occurs). Most become pregnant unwillingly and unwittingly, though to be sure many are reluctant to terminate the pregnancy by abortion once conception occurs. Adolescents typically have reasons why they want a child once they have become pregnant, but these reasons do not necessarily explain why the pregnancy initially occurred.

Too little research has been done on how and why teenagers begin to have sexual relations. The few existing studies show the potent peer group influence, the difficulty parents have in communicating and reinforcing their sexual expectations and the competing interests of young males and females in heterosexual interaction. Clearly, many teenagers are unprepared to assume the responsibility for their sexual behavior. This is partly due to the transition to nonvirginity, which seldom occurs as part of a process of conscious planning.

It follows, then, that regular use of contraception will be relatively rare among adolescents. Since most females do not foresee having intercourse when it first happens, most fail to take the necessary steps to prevent pregnancy from occurring. Occasionally, their male partners are equipped with a condom; typically, however, males do not have the same stake in preventing pregnancy from occurring since they are less affected by the consequences of an early conception. Not surprisingly, then, most studies have shown that only a minority of teenagers use contraception when intercourse first occurs; and, of course, as time elapses a number of nonusers become pregnant.

Individuals who do receive family planning information and instruction are, of course, less likely to experience an unplanned pregnancy. Several studies suggest, however, that many teenagers equipped with the means of contraception have difficulty using them faithfully over a sustained period of time (Ricketts, 1973). While psychological factors undoubtedly play an important part in the rate of contraceptive use among teenagers, we should recognize that contraception is not easy to use even for adults over a lengthy period of time. Accordingly, many adults elect to become sterilized rather than encounter the risks of imperfect use or the dangers associated with the pill or IUD. Teenagers do not have that option and are forced to make use of contraception which is at best technically effective, but nonetheless difficult to use. It is quite likely that if teenagers

55

had to take a pill to become pregnant, early childbearing would quickly vanish as a major social problem.

Approximately a third of all teenage pregnancies and a half of all pregnancies occurring to women under age 18 are terminated by abortion. If pregnancies are generally unwanted, why are abortions not more prevalent? Many teenagers, like their parents, disapprove of abortion. In the Baltimore study, which was conducted before the period of abortion liberalization, it was common for the young mothers to remark when asked whether they had contemplated abortion, "It's not fair to make the baby pay for the mother's mistake." Even though abortion has become more accepted, this attitude militates against it. One suspects that many teenagers are not fully aware of the hardships that will be imposed on them as a result of early childbearing or feel that the price of adolescent parenthood will be offset by the advantages of motherhood (Furstenberg 1978).

The Consequences of Teenage Childbearing

SCHOOLING

As one might expect from casual observation, researchers have consistently found that teenage mothers are more likely to drop out of school than women who delay their first childbirth until they are in their twenties (Chilman 1977; Moore, Waite, Caldwell, and Hofferth 1978). Similarly, women who have their first child out of wedlock have considerably less chance of completing high school than those who delay motherhood until after marriage (Cutright 1973; Card 1978). Significantly, these differences are not merely a product of the women's social background—their race, parents' socioeconomic status, or academic aptitude. In fact the detrimental effect on educational attainment of an early and/or out of wedlock first childbirth is even greater than the detrimental effects of minority status or poor socioeconomic background or a low level of academic aptitude. For this reason, it is fair to conclude that early and/or out of wedlock parenthood is a major *cause* of low educational attainment, and not just another element in a vicious cycle of poverty. Further evidence that adolescent parenthood is a causal factor lies in the fact that between one-half and two-thirds of all female high school dropouts cite pregnancy and/or marriage as their principal reason for leaving school (Coombs and Cooley 1968; Moore, Waite, Caldwell, and Hofferth 1978).

To provide an example of the impact of early childbearing on educational attainment, we shall turn to some findings from the Baltimore study. Five years after delivery, the adolescent mothers in the sample were split almost evenly between those who had dropped out of high school and those who had graduated. By contrast, nine out of ten of their classmates who had not had an early first childbirth had completed high school, and one-fifth of the remainder were still in school. In addition more than one-fourth of all of the classmates had obtained some amount of higher education. On the average the adolescent mothers had had approximately two fewer years of schooling than their classmates in the five-year follow-up study.

Undoubtedly, an important reason why teenage mothers fail to complete their education lies in the enormous difficulties of simultaneously meeting the demands of school as well as those of marriage and/or child rearing. In this regard, some recent evidence shows that marriage may actually be the principal complicating factor. Women whose teenage childbearing leads to an early marriage are twice as likely to drop out of high school as adolescent parents who remain unmarried. Women who marry as adolescents have an 80% chance of dropping out of school, whether they have an early childbirth or not (Moore, Waite, Caldwell, and Hofferth 1978).

This finding is quite surprising and demands more of an explanation than that provided by the heavy demands of conflicting roles. Specifically, why should the demands of marriage be so much more burdensome than those of caring for an infant? Apparently, the women's preexisting motivations and aspirations play a part. The more educationally ambitious young mothers are more likely both to delay marriage and to postpone further childbearing (Furstenberg 1976). Some women, including some with little interest in pursuing occupational careers of their own, opt for marriage and reliance on a spouse rather than seeking preparation for their own employment. Unfortunately, however, this choice all too often works out to the women's disadvantage if their marriages fail.

In spite of the fact that many teenage mothers choose a full-time homemaker role rather than preparing themselves for and seeking employment as well, there is strong evidence that a teenage pregnancy is not merely a convenient excuse to drop out of school. A majority of teenage mothers resume school after delivery (Furstenberg 1976; Moore,

Waite, Caldwell, and Hofferth 1978). Moreover, an early birth is not an insurmountable barrier to graduation from high school, as shown by the fact that a majority of young mothers in the Baltimore study managed to complete this level of schooling. Nevertheless, finishing high school is obviously not just a matter of choosing to do so. As one might expect, teenage mothers from advantageous socioeconomic and family backgrounds are more likely to recoup their losses by completing high school. Along with these advantages of background, such factors as ambition, academic performance, and parental expectations (which are often but not necessarily linked to background) predict whether teenage parents return to and/or remain in school until graduation (Furstenberg 1976; Card and Wise 1978). Additionally, if the first pregnancy disrupts the educational career of the young mother, additional childbearing usually brings it to an abrupt halt. With each successive pregnancy, the proportion of drop-outs rises for the adolescents in the Baltimore study. In fact, this may explain why marriage complicates a woman's schooling even more than an early childbirth. Married women are more likely to experience further childbearing than those who remain single.

OCCUPATIONAL AND ECONOMIC ACHIEVEMENT

Not surprisingly, then, adolescent childbearing also seriously injures a woman's occupational and economic prospects. These consequences are both independent of and even more severe than the disadvantages resulting from minority status or poor socioeconomic background or a low level of academic status (Card 1978).

The Baltimore study provides a good illustration of the detrimental impact of adolescent childbearing. Half of the young mothers were employed at the time of the five-year follow-up study. About two-thirds of these women carried the major burden of supporting the family. And in total three out of five young mothers either were self-supporting or were nonworking women married to wage-earning males. Most of these young mothers were, however, clearly in an economically precarious position. By contrast, their classmates who avoided early childbearing were more likely to be working and were more often completely self-supporting when they worked. At the five year follow-up study, only 15% of the classmates were receiving welfare payments, and only 5% depended completely on public assistance. The latter figure was just one-third as great as the proportion of adolescent mothers who obtained all of their income from welfare.

The dissimilarity between the groups became even more visible when we subdivided the classmates according to whether or not they had experienced a premarital pregnancy. While one-third of the young mothers were receiving at least one-fifth of their income from welfare, only 4% of the classmates who had not conceived premaritally relied at all on public assistance. Moreover, a much higher proportion of the classmates who had not had a prenuptial conception contributed substantially to their own support through employment. Finally, the median annual per capita income in the households of the classmates who had not conceived before marriage ($1,000) was two-thirds greater than that of the young mothers ($600).

The material detriment of early parenthood can be traced to a variety of sources. Typically, adolescent mothers have lower levels of education and experience difficulty in obtaining employment. They are less likely to have enduring marriages and hence cannot count on the economic support of a spouse. They have higher levels of fertility and more rapid rates of childbearing and hence are not in a position to find employment without daycare assistance. For all of these reasons, adolescent childbearers are more likely to become dependent on public assistance. This can happen in two ways, one direct, the other indirect. First, an out of wedlock birth may lead immediately to the need for welfare assistance if aid from the father of the child or from kin is not forthcoming. Second, even when the mother marries, early wedlock carries a greater risk of separation and divorce, leaving the mother in need of economic assistance. Even if her family lends a hand, as they often do, they rarely can shoulder the entire burden of support. Significantly, among the women who remain married, early postmarital births are no more likely to result in welfare dependency than later postmarital births (Moore and Hofferth 1978).

Thus, the consequences of early childbearing for economic independence depend primarily on the woman's marital career. It should be noted, however, that the ultimate economic position of women who marry and whose marriages subsequently break up is worse than that of women who never marry (Furstenberg 1976). Apparently, single women frequently adapt to the insecurity of their situation by finding jobs and thus acquiring some work experience, while the women who enter marriages which ultimately fail often find themselves unprepared to earn a living. Furthermore, these formerly married women may have been less ambitious in the first place.

For all teenage parents—single, married, or formerly married—child-care is essential to their efforts to find stable employment. Thus, a supportive kinship network which can provide child-care support is one of the critical conditions determining whether young mothers can work or must rely on welfare (Furstenberg and Crawford 1978).

Another key factor in the socioeconomic career of the young mother is her childbearing pattern following her first childbirth. Those women who avoid further childbearing are much more likely to be steadily employed than multiparous women. In fact, marital status is largely irrelevant to work patterns when childbearing is held constant. Larger family size further complicates the already difficult problem of arranging for child-care. The presence of a young child presents an especially difficult barrier to employment. Therefore, additional childbearing increases the handicap of the adolescent mother. Her family may offer childcare support after the first pregnancy but withdraw assistance when the second child arrives. Given the cost of childcare, many women find it impossible to locate a job that provides significantly more income than public assistance, especially when they lack education and experience (Furstenberg 1976).

Early Childbearing and Marriage

Adolescents are much more likely to express positive sentiments about becoming pregnant if they plan to marry before or shortly after the child's birth. Accordingly, they are less likely to contemplate abortion if they are about to marry the father of the child (Furstenberg 1976). In fact, although marriage is less likely to follow a teenage pregnancy today than was the case a decade or more ago, many teenagers still resolve an early pregnancy by a precipitate marriage, or, at least, by wedding much earlier than they otherwise might have done (McCarthy and Menken 1979).

In the Baltimore study, the marriage patterns of the young mothers were substantially different from those of their classmates. By age 18 only 21% of the classmates were married, as compared to 41% of the young mothers. The difference was sharper still for marriages that occurred among women not yet 18—11% versus 30%. Premarital pregnancy was not, however, a covert tactic to bring about marriage, for most of the women who entered matrimony did so with obvious reluctance. When asked to reflect on the timing of their marriage, approximately two-thirds of those who had wed claimed that they would have preferred to marry later. Evidence from other investigations confirms that early pregnancy speeds up the nuptial timetable for both men and women (Card 1978).

Both early pregnancy and early marriage impair a couple's chances of conjugal stability. Data from both census materials and surveys explicitly designed to examine the effect of nuptial and birth timing on marriage duration (Card 1978; McCarthy and Menken 1979) convincingly demonstrate that women who marry as teenagers are more likely to separate and divorce than those who marry later and conceive after wedlock. The comparison between the adolescent mothers and their classmates in Baltimore is illustrative. Within three years of their wedding date, nearly half (44%) of the young mothers were no longer residing with a spouse. By contrast, at the same point in their conjugal careers, three-fourths of the ever-married classmates were still living in intact units.

Some evidence indicates that the source of marital instability lies more in early marriage than in early childbearing. Regardless of the woman's age at first childbirth or whether that birth occurs after marriage or not, early marriages are less stable than later ones. In fact, holding age at marriage constant, an early first birth may actually promote marital stability. The child may provide the couple with a reason to remain married in spite of the many problems associated with early marriage, such as psychological immaturity, lack of preparation for parental and conjugal roles, and limited socioeconomic achievement (Moore, Waite, Hofferth, and Caldwell 1978).

Early marriages are thus highly susceptible to dissolution, regardless of whether they are accompanied by early and/or illegitimate births. Nevertheless, this finding does not imply that early childbearing is inconsequential. Typically, the early marriage would not have occurred but for the early pregnancy. Thus, the dissolution of that marriage and the young mother's subsequent impoverishment are results, albeit indirect ones, of the teenage pregnancy.

The Baltimore data points to some reasons why a premarital pregnancy, particularly one which occurs early in life, may disrupt a marriage. First, the bonds between the young couple are often only newly formed. Accordingly, women who had known the father for at least several years before the pregnancy are more likely to survive the first few years of marriage than those who were only recently acquainted when the pregnancy occurred. Additionally, a marriage in the early teens pulls the young mother away from her family of origin, often sooner than otherwise might have occurred. Many young mothers were both psychologically and economically unprepared to depart from the parental household. Indeed, a substantial minority of those who married soon after delivery remained in the parental household, at least for a time. These arrangements, which were partly an adaptation to the economic problems of establishing a separate household as well as to the emotional uncertainties of a newly formed marriage, frequently limited the young parents' commitment to the marriage, particularly when the prospects of that marriage appeared limited.

On the other hand some early marriages do endure in spite of the difficulties that the couples face. It is more likely that an early marriage persists when the mother marries the father of the child (Sauber and Corrigan 1970; Furstenberg 1976). The bond between the parents is strengthened by their common bond to the child. On the other hand, additional childbearing is a major barrier to conjugal stability. The chances of ultimate marital success are smaller for women who have more children after their first, particularly if they are born out of wedlock.

Almost all existing studies show that economic resources are strongly linked to marital stability (Bernard 1966; Carter and Glick 1976; Udry 1966, 1967). Accordingly, in the Baltimore study a crude index of the husband's earning potential turned out to be the best single predictor of marital stability.

Additionally, comparing the economic status of the men who married the classmates with the spouses of the young mothers reveals a noticeable difference between the two groups of men, especially after we separate out the couples who married following a premarital pregnancy. Typically, the early childbearers marry less well, economically speaking. These findings strongly suggest that the most important link in the chain between an unplanned pregnancy and later marital failure is the weak economic position of the male who fathers a child out of wedlock and/or marries a single mother. Most of these men have a low earning potential before they wed. An ill-timed marriage may further limit their prospects for economic advancement by compelling them to terminate school and enter the labor force under less than favorable circumstances.

Given the high rate of marital dissolution among the ever-married adolescent parents (60% five years after their first childbirth), it is surprising that few of them get divorced, even when one takes into account the cost of a divorce. The major reason for the low incidence of divorce among the sample, apparently, is that few of the young women had current plans to marry again. However, women like those in the Baltimore study also face certain objective barriers to remarrying. Most of the adolescent mothers had at least two children by the time their marriages broke up, a situation which presents a formidable challenge to the earning power of potential mates. To add to their difficulties, the young mothers usually have limited economic assets of their own to contribute to a new marriage.

Ironically, the majority (60%) of the young mothers who managed to avoid single parenthood by marrying either before or shortly after delivery ended up as single parents several years later. And many of these women no doubt will never remarry. Therefore, it might be said that once an unplanned pregnancy occurs in adolescence, it seldom matters whether the young mother marries. In time, she may be almost as likely as the unwed mother to bear the major, if not the sole, responsibility for supporting her child.

Teenage Childbearing and Subsequent Fertility

Research has shown that the earlier a woman's age at marriage, the greater her level and pace of subsequent childbearing (Westoff and Ryder 1977). Moreover, regardless of a woman's age at marriage, a premarital first childbirth leads to a higher level of fertility (Coombs and Freedman 1970). Nevertheless, evidence shows that it is not a *premarital* birth but an *early* birth which is correlated with a higher level of childbearing. The earlier a woman's age at first childbirth, the greater the level and pace of her fertility (up to fifteen years later) and the greater the proportion of illegitimate and unwanted births which she experiences (Trussel and Menken 1977). And, significantly, women with an illegitimate first birth do not subsequently bear more children than women whose first birth was within wedlock. Additionally, the consequences of early childbearing vary little by race or level of educational attainment. In fact age at first birth accounts for around half of the racial and educational differences in completed fertility. These results suggest a need for family planning services among all groups of adolescents, younger and older, single and married.

In the Baltimore study, nearly all of the mothers' first pregnancies were unplanned, and most were unwanted at the time conception occurred. One year after delivery, the entire sample was asked when they planned to have their next child. Only 6% said they hoped to become pregnant again "soon." Three years after delivery, only 7% said they were hoping to have another child at the time.

63

Similarly, although some teenagers welcome a second child soon after the first, even when the initial pregnancy was unplanned, the second child more often represents a major setback to the future plans of the young mother, proving especially damaging to her prospects of economic self-sufficiency. Existing evidence seems to support the prevailing belief that a pregnancy in early adolescence signals the beginning of a rapid succession of unwanted births. Although estimates vary, depending on the experiences of the women following the first birth, most published studies show that at least one-half of all teenage mothers experience a second pregnancy within 36 months of delivery (Ricketts 1973).

Many women experienced timing failures in the birth of their second child. Also, within five years after delivery some women had already reached or exceeded the total number of children they wanted to have ever, although they were still in their early twenties. The cumulative probability of becoming pregnant a second and third time shows that nearly all of the ever-married women were running well ahead of their schedules of desired family size. Very few of the single women expressed a desire to have another child before marrying, yet most became pregnant again out of wedlock.

Five years after the young mothers' first child was born, two-thirds of them had had at least two pregnancies, and nearly one-third had had three or more. By contrast, only one-fourth of the classmates had become pregnant more than once, and only 6% had conceived three or more times. The young mothers who never married had, on the average, 1.09 more pregnancies than the single classmates; the difference among the married women was 0.66. This shows that the young mothers' fertility pattern subsequent to their first birth was roughly identical to that of their classmates who deferred their first birth. Nevertheless, we should not underestimate the problems which result from that untimely first childbirth.

Some social characteristics help to account for whether the teenage mothers have another child soon after their first childbirth. The women in the Baltimore study most highly committed to education and those who returned to school immediately following the delivery of their first child were much less likely to experience a second conception in the 12-month period after the birth. Even after four years the women who returned to school had lower rates of second pregnancy than those who did not. This was especially true for the unmarried women. Women may defer childbearing in order to attain their educational goals, but they may also discontinue their educations when they fail to prevent an unwanted pregnancy. Accordingly, we found (even holding educational ambition constant) that women remain in school at least until graduation if they are able to defer further childbearing.

It is often said that public assistance encourages childbearing out of wedlock because it provides a means of supporting additional children for unmarried women. The "broodsow myth," as Placek and Hendershot (1974) so aptly labeled it, received no confirmation from the Baltimore data. The welfare mother was not significantly more likely to become pregnant again after she went on relief than the young mother who was not receiving public assistance. This data suggests that there is no reason to single out the welfare mother as incapable of regulating her childbearing.

Long-Term Consequences for the Children of Early Childbearers

Among the few studies addressing this topic is Card's (1978) reanalysis of the Project TALENT data. She finds that the children of teenage mothers, while in high school, have lower cognitive test scores, lower grades, and lower educational expectations than their classmates, whose parents were at least in their twenties when they were born. Moreover, children of early childbearers have different personality characteristics and interests. Finally, as they grow older (toward age 30), they have lower levels of education, earlier first marriages, and higher rates of marital dissolution. Nevertheless, most of the observed cognitive differences are the result of background disadvantages, particularly higher rates of family instability. Similarly, all of their personality and interest differences can be accounted for by their disadvantages in socioeconomic and family background (other than their "early" birth). The educational disadvantages of these children of teenage mothers are basically a function of their cognitive detriment. Thus, Card proposes a recurrent pattern of disadvantage: early childbearing results in marital dissolution, which in turn leads to cognitive impairment to the child and subsequent educational deficits. This educational disadvantage helps to perpetuate the same cycle of early marriage and childbearing and high fertility among the offspring of early childbearers which their parents first experienced.

Several ongoing studies support Card's finding that early childbearing may be linked to developmental disadvantages for the child. Research by Dryfoos and Belmont (1978) reveals a similar pattern of lower cognitive achievement among the children of early versus later childbearers.

Though the differences observed are slight (on the average approximately three points in I.Q.), they are consistent and recurrent in a variety of samples and do not disappear even after appropriate controls are introduced. Significantly, the research by Dryfoos and Belmont shows no parallel pattern of personality or interpersonal differences between the offspring of early and later childbearers.

Several explanations might account for these differences in cognitive achievement. The differences could be traced to physiological conditions such as prematurity, low birth weight, and complications at delivery. An alternative explanation might be that early childbearers are themselves less intellectually endowed, and the differences observed might be linked to genetic factors or possibly to the parent's capacity to provide early infant stimulation. Finally, it is possible that the young age of the mother makes her a less capable childrearer, which may in turn be reflected in the child's slower rate of development of cognitive skills.

In one sense, then, early childbearing contributes to intergenerational poverty and disadvantage. On the other hand, it should be noted that no vicious cycle, this one included, can persist without society's continued indifference to the problem of economic inequality.

Teenage Childbearing and Family Support

In her extensive review of the literature on the social aspects of adolescent childbearing, Chilman (1977) discusses the need for research on its consequences for other family members.

> No studies have looked at the consequences of early marriage and early childbearing on the parents of the young people involved. To what extent are parents called upon to give financial, child-care and social-psychological support to the young family? What effects may the provision of such supports have on relationships between the older and younger generations? What effects may the provision have on the life styles and plans of older couples?

Two recent analyses conducted by the authors bear on these questions: first a reanalysis of the Baltimore study data (Furstenberg and Crawford 1978); and second an analysis of data collected on two samples of lower income women in Camden, New Jersey (Crawford and Furstenberg 1979).

66

THE BALTIMORE DATA ON FAMILY SUPPORT

The Baltimore study data contain a record of the composition of the adolescent mother's household at each of the four points in the study— during pregnancy and one year, three years, and five years after delivery. When inspected longitudinally, these data on residential situations provide a useful way of mapping one feature of family support over time. From this information, it appears that mothers were much more likely to receive substantial amounts of financial assistance and familial childcare support when they remained with relatives (cf. Cantor and co-workers 1975). Moving out of the parental household, whether to marry or to establish an independent residence, not only reduced the subsidies provided by the family in the form of room and board, but also lessened the chances that a relative would be available to provide daycare. (See also Presser 1978.)

Not surprisingly then most mothers stayed close to home, especially during the early years of the study. At pregnancy, when most of the women were in their early or middle teens, nearly 90% lived with a parent or a close relative. One year after delivery most young mothers (77%) were still living with parents or close relatives. Separation from the family of origin became more common in the ensuing years, but even five years after the birth of their child, nearly half (46%) remained with their parents or other kin. One popular stereotype of the adolescent mother often portrays her as a social isolate, removed from parental or conjugal support, but our data belie this image. Only 26% of the young mothers were living alone at the five-year follow-up; the remainder were residing with parents or other relatives and/or were living in marital units.

In searching for conditions that shape a young mother's residential career, we identified two very general types of determinants. The first is related to the young mother's need for assistance and is accordingly called the ''demand'' factor. The second, relating to the family's capacity to respond, is labelled the ''supply'' factor. In the discussion which follows, we shall make reference to each set of conditions in turn.

Following from what has been said so far, we might anticipate that an adolescent's family shouldered much more responsibility when she remained single than when she married. Detailed inspection of the data certainly bears out this prediction. Especially in the early years of the study, most of the women moved away from their families only after they married. From responses to unstructured questions, we learned that a major deterrent to marriage was that it might require forfeiting family support. The decision to remain in the home after marriage may, of course, be dictated by economic considerations, but we suspect that it also reflects ambivalence about substituting a tenuous conjugal bond for a functioning family network. Not surprisingly, then, those teenage mothers who married but remained in their parents' households were less likely to have stable unions than the other teenage mothers. Few couples who stayed married remained in the women's parents' households for very long. Living with parents as well as a spouse is at best a temporary convenience which permits early marriage but does little to promote its stability.

Surprisingly, age was not an important determinant of the woman's residential careers. Apart from its influence on their marital prospects, age did not account for whether or not the young mothers remained with their parents throughout the study. By contrast, their educational status clearly predicted their residential arrangements. Young mothers who continued their education after becoming pregnant were significantly more likely to remain with their parents than those who dropped out of school. Furthermore, parents often had an explicit understanding with their offspring that they would supply childcare only so long as the young mothers were attending school.

The quality of the relationship between the adolescent mothers and their parents during pregnancy also foreshadowed their subsequent residential choices. In households where the bonds between parents and daughters were close, marriage was less likely to occur. In the event that the young mothers elected to remain single, they usually stayed with their parents. Correspondingly, women who expressed a low level of reliance on their parents were almost twice as likely to move out after delivery, either because of marriage or to establish households of their own.

By the second trimester of the pregnancy, most prospective grandmothers had already signaled their intention to help out after the child was born. The few who stated that they hoped the baby would be given up for adoption were, in fact, less likely to provide childcare assistance following the birth or to provide room and board for the young mother and her child. Thus, the parents' willingness to supply assistance may explain at least a small part of their daughter's residential choices.

Given the inclination of all but a few parents to lend assistance, the family's ability to aid their daughter became a major factor shaping the young mother's residential careers. Adolescents were much more likely to remain in couple-headed households than in female-headed households. Young mothers in couple-headed households were also more likely to return to and remain in school. Evidently, either the greater economic resources of the couple-headed families were used to purchase childcare services, or the grandmother remained at home while the young mother resumed her education.

Moreover, space was more abundant in two-parent households, providing less pressure on the young mother to leave the parental home. Although the data we collected are not fine-grained enough to examine the connection between crowding and separation from parents, it is clear that young mothers were more likely to move out of their parents' household when a second pregnancy occurred. Repeat pregnancy occurred more frequently in female-headed families, which were already pressed for space and strained for resources.

Up to this point, we have touched on some of the circumstances which led to departure from the parental household. However, most adolescents and their offspring stayed in the household for at least several years after the birth of the child. By this time most had completed or had dropped out of school, had married the father of the child or had abandoned plans to do so, were working or had gained stable support from public assistance. Their children were in school or were old enough to be cared for outside the home. In short, the family had often tided the young mother over during the difficult period of the transition to parenthood.

As we have seen, some young mothers benefited from greater amounts of family assistance than others. Does the provision of such support, particularly when it is abundant and long-lasting, improve the life chances of the young mother and her child? The weaknesses of our data preclude a definitive answer, but there are strong hints that young mothers who received significant amounts of aid were more likely to be in an economically favorable position at the conclusion of the study than those who did not. Adolescents who remained with their parents were more likely to advance educationally and economically compared to their peers who left home before or immediately after their child was born. Most participants in the Baltimore study stayed home, at least in part, because they were being provided with childcare assistance by a parent, sibling, or other relative. The last two interviews revealed that the young mothers who lived at home received more help from family members than those who were not residing with relatives. Losing these advantages often forced the adolescent to terminate her education, or, in the event she was working, to quit her job.

How did these collaborative childcare arrangements affect the well-being of the mother and her offspring? Based on the mothers' own reports and on observations by interviewers in the home, there were no sizable differences between the full-time mothers and those who collaborated with a relative. However, the information obtained directly from the children themselves provides a somewhat stronger indication of the benefits of collaborative care. On a test of cognitive performance, the Pre-School Inventory, children of unmarried mothers achieved significantly higher scores when their parents were not their full-time caretakers. As we have already mentioned, the provision of childcare assistance was more likely to occur when the young mother remained with her parents. Thus, unless relatives provided childcare after the young mother's departure as well, moving out often resulted in some cognitive detriment for the child. Perhaps children receive more stimulation when they have multiple caretakers. Also, the quality of care may be higher when the mother receives supervision from an experienced relative or when she simply is relieved of full-time responsibility for childcare.

Even though we do not have the means at hand to explore the differing interpretations of our findings, we can say with some confidence that on the basis of our data family assistance confers certain benefits for the mother and probably for the child as well. How long lasting they are, we cannot say for certain from the Baltimore data.

LONG-TERM CONSEQUENCES FOR KIN

A reanalysis of data on two samples of women from Camden, New Jersey, one with mates and the other without, provides some information on the long-term picture (Crawford and Furstenberg 1979). Comparing the early childbearers (women who had their first child before age 18) with those who entered parenthood later, we discovered some indications that the pattern of reliance on family members for support is not merely short-lived. While the kinship networks of the early and later childbearers were not very different in size, women who had children during adolescence were less likely to have mates and more likely to share a household with relatives. The differences that appear in the probability of living with relatives are slight and might escape notice were it not for the fact that they represent continuities with the picture which emerges from the Baltimore data. It would be erroneous, however, to conclude that early childbearers inevitably develop stronger bonds with kin, for the later childbearers list just as many relatives on whom they can depend as the early childbearers. However, a larger share of these relatives reside outside their home.

The Camden data permit us to examine another issue raised but left unanswered by the Baltimore study. What are the costs to family members of providing assistance to the adolescent mother and her child? Although we have no precise way of reckoning these liabilities, we can see whether the parents and siblings of adolescent childbearers tend to encounter more economic or marital difficulties than the relatives of later childbearers. Given the crudities of the data, it is not possible to provide a refined estimate. All that can be said is that the analysis turned up no evidence supporting the notion that a woman's early childbearing injures the life chances of her close relatives. However, the answer to this question is too important to rest on the results of our inadequate data set.

Consequences of Teenage Childbearing: Implications for Social Programs

In this chapter, we have summarized only a portion of the growing body of research on the consequences of teenage childbearing. Despite the diversity of research designs, populations studied, and measures employed, we have observed a remarkable degree of consistency in the results obtained by researchers. Early childbearing creates a distinctly higher risk of social and economic disadvantages, in great part because it complicates the transition to adulthood by disrupting schooling and creating pressures for early marriage and further fertility. We are disposed to conclude that premature parenthood is one of the principal social mechanisms that perpetuate the cycle of poverty.

This leads us to ask what social measures can be taken to ameliorate the effects of early and unplanned parenthood. As public awareness of the costs of adolescent childbearing has grown in the past decade, services have developed to equip the young parent to handle the economic and psychological demands of childcare. Prenatal services providing medical care to the mother and child, special educational programs permitting the young mother to remain in school during the transition to parenthood, vocational training and job placement, childcare services, and contraceptive instruction are but a few measures in an arsenal of social interventions that has been devised by public and private agencies to reduce the ill effects of early childbearing.

In 1978 Congress approved legislation to support a comprehensive network of programs for the teenage parent. The bill, the "Adolescent

Health, Services and Pregnancy Prevention and Care Act,'' was designed to coordinate and integrate the disparate services as well as to channel some additional moneys to agencies starved for resources. Assuming that appropriations are allocated, what can we expect the effect of this legislation to be on the well-being of young parents and their children?

While we believe that the bill passed by Congress represents a positive initiative on the part of the federal government, we do not hold out much hope that it will substantially alter the life chances of adolescent parents and their children. Our research and the findings of others persuade us that the single most important obstacle facing the teenage parent is economic insecurity.

Lack of skills, minimal daycare support, and the uncertainties of the labor market conspire to create an uncertain economic future for adolescent parents and their children. Unless jobs become more readily available, it is certain that many adolescent mothers will be compelled to turn to public assistance for support. Few are in a position to be fully supported by the child's father, who frequently cannot find work. Families are often willing to extend resources to the young mother, but their assistance is unpredictable. Economic disadvantage erodes the possibility of a stable conjugal partnership, and marital breakup in turn jeopardizes the child's life chances.

In pointing to the need for stable and remunerative employment for teenage parents, we are well aware of the potential costs involved. Childcare services, vocational training, and public service jobs are suffering cutbacks for lack of taxpayer support. Given the political climate, it is unlikely that this trend will be reversed in the near future. Indeed, we do not look forward to much change until a labor market shortage develops in this country, an event that may not occur until in the latter part of this century, when the fertility declines of recent decades begin to shrink the size of the labor force.

In the meantime. we must look to other strategies for coping with the undesirable sequelae of early childbearing. We believe the most promising approach is a much more vigorous campaign to prevent early childbearing. Some encouraging signs can be seen already. Schools are gradually introducing sex education into the curriculum, a step which is bound to provoke a host of political, ethical, and social conflicts in these communities. Nonetheless, it appears unavoidable that parents will thus be encouraged, if not pushed, to share the task of providing sexual socialization to the young. It also seems clear that churches, voluntary organizations such as the scouts, and special interest groups will also take a more active part in equipping youth with sexual knowledge and family planning techniques.

Presently, researchers have little to say about the likely success of such public education campaigns in controlling teenage pregnancies, though only the most optimistic planners believe that sex education and contraceptive services alone will reduce adolescent births to an insignificant number. Obviously, we are assuming that the prevalence of sexual activity is not likely to decline in the immediate future, a proposition with which few experts disagree. Given the many reservations that teenagers have about birth control, the ambivalent feelings which often accompany nonmarital sexuality, and the psychological propensity of adolescents toward risk-taking, we expect a substantial, though perhaps diminished, rate of premarital pregnancy to occur in the years to come.

This prospect raises the sensitive question of whether abortion services are not a necessary backup to contraceptive programs. Although the question of abortion is a private matter, the provision of abortion facilities is a public concern. Reasoned debate is not likely to prevail in the discussion of whether abortion should be made more accessible to adolescents. It is clear to us, however, that the recent legislation passed by Congress, even if accompanied by a similar initiative by state and local government, is not likely to offset the severe economic and social costs of early childbearing. Therefore, our best strategy is to avoid unwanted pregnancies in the first place, and we suspect that contraceptive programs can be sufficiently effective without supplementary pregnancy counseling and abortion services.

In this brief overview of service needs, we have not given adequate space to the immense complexities of providing programs for adolescents. Generally speaking, most health and social service programs have been tailored to suit the convenience of professionals, not the clients they serve. Teenagers looking for contraceptive information and services have had to seek them out, often against considerable obstacles. At relatively low cost, family planning programs have begun to lower these barriers by making service programs more accommodating to the adolescent life style. More flexible clinic hours, more attractive and congenial settings for service programs, outreach by community workers, subsidized transportation, and peer-based counseling are but a few of the innovations that have been made to reach the teenage population.

When we remember that a decade ago relatively few programs existed for the teen population and two decades ago it would have been unthinkable to equip unmarried adolescents with contraceptives, it should be clear that enormous strides have been made in the prevention of unwanted pregnancy. Though these gains have not come easily, they auger well for a more enlightened approach to teenage sexuality in the future.

References

Baldwin, W. S. Adolescent pregnancy and childbearing-growing concerns for Americans. *Population Bulletin*. 21(2). Washington, D.C.: Population Reference Bureau, Inc., 1976.

Bernard, J. Marital stability and patterns of status variables. *J. Marriage and Fam*. 28:421–439, 1966.

Cantor, M. H.; Rosenthal, K.; and Wilke, L. Social and family relationships of black teenaged women in New York City. Paper presented at 28th Annual Scientific Meeting of the Gerontological Society. Louisville, Kentucky, 1975.

Card, J. Long term consequences for children born to adolescent parents. Final Report prepared for the National Institute of Child Health and Human Development. Contract HD-72820. Palo Alto, California: American Institutes for Research, 1978.

Card, J., and Wise, L. Teenage mothers and teenage fathers: the impact of early childbearing on the parents' personal and professional lives. *Fam. Plann. Perspect*. 10:199–205, 1978.

Carter, H., and Glick, P. C. *Marriage and divorce: a social and economic study*. Cambridge: Harvard University Press, 1976.

Chilman, C. S. *Social and psychological aspects of adolescent sexuality: an analytic overview of research and theory*. Report prepared for the National Institute of Child Health and Human Development. Contract N01-HD52821. Institute for Family Development, Center for Advanced Studies in Human Services, School of Social Welfare. Milwaukee: University of Wisconsin, 1977.

Coombs, J., and Cooley, W.W., Dropouts: in high school and after school. *American Educational Research Journal*. 5:343, 1968.

Coombs, L., and Freedman, R. Premarital pregnancy, childspacing, and later economic achievement. *Population Studies*. 24:389–412. 1970.

Crawford, G., and Furstenberg, F., Jr. The long term consequences of early childbearing for women's social networks. Paper presented at the 1979 Meeting of the Eastern Sociological Society, 1979.

Cutright, P. Timing the first birth: does it matter? *J. Marriage Fam*. 35:585–595, 1973.

Dryfoos, J., and Belmont, L. The intellectual and behavioral status of children born to adolescent mothers. Third Progress Report, National Institute of Child Health and Human Development, Contract 7-2805. Columbia University: Alan Guttmacher Institute and the School of Public Health, 1978.

Furstenberg, F. F., Jr. *Unplanned parenthood: the social consequences of teenage childbearing.* New York: The Free Press, 1976.

Furstenberg, F. F., Jr. Burdens and benefits: the impact of early childbearing on the family. Paper presented at the Conference on Perspectives on Policy Toward Teenage Pregnancy, Family Impact Seminar, Washington, D.C., 1978.

Furstenberg, F.F., Jr., and Crawford, A. G. Family support: helping teenage mothers to cope, *Fam. Plann. Perspect.* 10:322–333, 1978.

McCarthy, J., and Menken, J. Marriage, remarriage, marital disruption and age at first birth. *Fam. Plann. Perspect.* 11:21–30. 1979.

Moore, K. A., and Hofferth, S. L. The consequences of age at first childbirth: female headed families and welfare dependency. Working Paper 1146-05. The Urban Institute: Washington, D.C. 1978.

Moore, K. A. et al. The consequences of age at first childbirth: educational attainment. Working Paper 1146-01. Washington, D.C.: The Urban Institute, 1978.

Moore, K. A. et al. The consequences of age at first childbirth:

marriage, separation, and divorce. Working Paper 1146-03. Washington, D.C.: The Urban Institute, 1978.

National Center for Health Statistics, Health Resources Administration, Public Health Service, U.S. Department of Health, Education, and Welfare. Teenage childbearing: United States, 1966 to 1975. *Monthly Vital Statistics Report. Natality Statistics.* 26:77–1120, 1977.

Placek, P. J., and Hendershot, G. E. Public welfare and family planning: an empirical study of the ''broodsow'' myth. *Social Problems.* 21:658, 1974.

Presser, H. B. Early motherhood: ignorance or bliss? *Fam. Plann. Perspect.* 7:8–14, 1974.

Presser, H. B. Sally's corner: coping with unmarried motherhood. Paper presented at the meeting of the American Sociological Association San Francisco, 1978.

Reiss, I. *The social context of premarital sexual permissiveness.* New York: Holt, Rinehart and Winston, 1967.

Ricketts, S. A. Contraceptive use among teenage mothers: evaluation of a family planning program. Ph.D. Dissertation. University of Pennsylvania, Philadelphia, 1973.

Sauber, M., and Corrigan, E. *The six year experience of unwed mothers as parents.* New York: Community Council of Greater New York, 1970.

Smith, D. S. The dating of the American sexual revolution: evidence and interpretation. In *The American family in social-historical perspective*. M. Gordon, ed. New York: St. Martin's Press, 1973.

Trussel, J., and Menken, J. Early childbearing and subsequent fertility. *Fam. Plann. Perspect.* 10:673–674, 1967.

Udry, J. R. Marital instability by race, sex education, and occupation using 1960 census data. *Am. J. Sociol.* 72:203–209, 1966.

Udry, J. R. Marital instability by race and income based on 1960 census data, *Am. J. Sociol.* 52:673–674, 1967.

Westoff, F., and Ryder, N.B. *The contraceptive revolution*. Princeton: Princeton University Press, 1977.

Zelnik, M. and Kantner, J. F. Sexual and contraceptive experience of young unmarried women in the United States, 1976 and 1971. *Fam. Plann. Perspect.* 9:55–71, 1977.

6 Programs for Sexually Active Teens

Peggy B. Smith, Ph.D.

The majority of programs for sexually active adolescents proliferating in the 1960s focused on methods in response to the consequences of teenage sexuality. In some programs the focus was on the prevention of adolescent pregnancy. With an initial nation-wide start in the 1960s of approximately 30 projects, the attempts have continued to grow so that, at last count (1978), over 900 programs have been established that address the needs and problems of sexually active and/or pregnant adolescents. Several converging factors have catalyzed the movement to provide planning programs for the adolescent family. Cultural and sociological trends in the area of human sexuality have changed dramatically during the past decade. Although hesitant to specify a "sexual revolution," Goldsmith (1969) indicated that complex social factors created the dire need for adolescent family planning programs. Moreover, the issues of adolescent sexuality and pregnancy have been exacerbated by another simple factor. The postwar baby boom of the fifties has resulted in more teenagers in the seventies.

Interestingly, Cutright (1972) suggests that the level of sexual activity among teens may not have risen significantly. However, teenage conceptions have increased as a result of good health care, nutrition, and medical technology. These factors have enhanced the capacity of sexually active girls to conceive and carry their fetus to term. Such an explanation is compatible with the documented decline of the onset of menarche in Western European and American populations, as compared to the estimated menarchial age of 17 years in 1840. Zacharias and co-workers (1970) found that the average age of menarche in the United States is now 12.5 years. Although the downward trend has apparently stabilized, this decrease is significant. Very young adolescents and even pre-teens are now physiologically capable of becoming pregnant (Litt, Edberg, and Finberg 1974). For whatever reason, the establishment of family planning services for teens to meet the changing adolescent sexual and fertility trends, has received emphasis recently from both public and private sectors.

Service Delivery Systems

A variety of formats have been devised to meet the needs of the sexually active teenager. Programs for teenage parents in hospitals, schools, and communities provide information and referral and often more comprehensive services. Many family planning programs also offer much broader services to this age group.

The easiest teen group to identify for service in a delivery system is the already pregnant adolescent. The adolescent mother, figuratively speaking, has "acquired" the right to attain postnatal contraception without (or in spite of) parental or social censure. In contrast to a non-pregnant teenager, the adolescent mother legally has in some states more options or facilities that can meet her contraceptive needs. There appear to be several reasons for this anachronistic approach. First, the repeat pregnancy risk for adolescent mothers is very high. Some studies (United States Commission on Population Growth 1973) indicate that such adolescents have a 60% chance of experiencing another pregnancy before the age of 20. Economically, educationally, and vocationally, additional children effectively diminish the adolescent's chances for maximum economic opportunities.

Providing adolescent mothers a priority status for contraceptive services is quite cost-effective. As teenage mothers and their children are easily identifiable, public agency groups can incorporate them more smoothly into various service networks. Vocational re-training, special educational services, and even sex education can be given priority.

A final consideration in favor of aiding "sexually active pregnant girls" is community acceptance. There is usually minimal community opposition to providing contraceptive services to adolescents who have already been pregnant. Their sexual activity has been confirmed by conception and birth. Without such tangible proof, public opposition to the delivery of contraceptive services to teenage girls who have never been pregnant can be quite strong.

Services to already pregnant girls can have a variety of sponsorship. The priority commitment of a service program is often determined by the kind of group which initiates the service. Traditionally, teen services are sponsored by the educational, medical, or lay community.

HOSPITAL-BASED PROGRAMS

Hospital-based programs usually provide only short-term interventions by medical professionals. The initiation of such programs usually meets little community resistance. The high status of medical practitioners and the role of physicians as traditional authority figures facilitate project support.

The sponsorship of teen programs by medical centers provides reinforcement for the maintenance of primary health care. With some coordination, a full spectrum of health and medical staff can be organized to assist program implementation and continuation. In addition, any counseling provided in such programs appears to be well received (Grady 1975). Interestingly, the public assumes that medical personnel, as a result of scientific study, is more capable of assessing behavior nonjudgmentally than counselors in more traditionally conservative settings, such as schools.

The need for programs in a hospital or medical school is documented by medical literature. Pregnant adolescents (Marinoff and Schonholz 1972) and specifically the teenager under 16 years of age (Dott and Fort 1976), run a greater medical and, in some cases, psychological risk (Jekel and Klerman 1973) than all other age groups. Several important prototype programs responsive to these risks have been developed. One special teen program evolved from the general obstetric clinic of Yale-New Haven Hospital (Sarrel and Klerman 1969). In Syracuse, New York, another teen maturity service, the Young Mothers Program, also focused on the medical needs of teen mothers (Osofosky and co-workers 1968). More recent hospital-based programs include mini-nurseries, follow-up care (Grady 1975) and day care instruction (Badger and co-workers 1976).

The general format of most programs now includes a multidisciplinary approach provided by professionals from the medical and allied health professions. The objectives of such programs usually include health maintenance of the mother and baby, encouragement toward continuing educational and vocational activities, and enhanced motivation toward the mother's accepting and using effective contraception. Information and counseling on nutrition, contraception, and medical aspects of childbearing and rearing help achieve such objectives. Many programs also develop psychosocial skills such as making effective decisions and constructing alternative family life styles. Encouragement and referral for educational and vocational entry or re-entry are important keys to the future success of the teen mother. A few hospital-based programs have

79

very strong academic components. In San Francisco, Grady (1975) described five special service centers located within the hospital setting: formal academic education, health education, family planning, home economics laboratory, remedial reading, and group and individual counseling.

Although the majority of hospital/medical based programs concentrate on prenatal service and delivery, some projects attend to the postpartum phase of childbearing as well. At Cincinnati General Hospital (Badger and co-workers 1976) techniques of child care and infant stimulation are presented to postpartum classes of teenagers over a four to five month period. Medical sponsorship not only provides special health and educational opportunities for the teen mother but stimulates wider community involvement to meet the multiple needs of the adolescent mother and her child. The teenage project at Baylor College of Medicine, the Goldfarb Adult Development Clinic, provides a model of an adolescent program with antepartum and postpartum components (Smith and co-workers 1975). In the postpartum phase of this program an entire hospital floor, where all teenagers who have had routine deliveries convalesce during their three-day stay, is used. During obstetrical confinement, individual and group counseling on pediatric care, contraceptives, personal problems, and medical concerns is available to teenage patients. In this way all teenage patients have an opportunity to participate in some organized program before hospital discharge. The Interconceptional Care Program at Grady Memorial Hospital, Atlanta, Georgia (Klein 1974) focuses on the adolescent mother 15 years of age and under and her unique postpartum medical and contraceptive needs. By means of a Special Teen Clinic, the younger adolescent mother participates in a birth control program that maintains a more permissive attitude and uses different health education techniques.

Evaluation of hospital-based programs is important for several reasons. Space in most medical facilities is cramped at best, with little flexibility or tolerance for projects which do not improve the patient's obstetric outcome. Moreover, medical staff time, even when voluntary, is expensive. If other personnel or project sites can provide the same results, with lower direct and indirect costs, a shift from hospital-based programs to other community-based sites would be more efficient.

One of the positively evaluated hospital-based projects is the Young Mother's Clinic of the Yale-New Haven Hospital (Klerman and Jekel 1975). This program incorporates regular prenatal care with weekly group sessions. The results of the program indicate a lowering of medical risks of pregnancy and labor complications. Similar results are also reported in other programs (Osofsky and co-workers 1968). A recent program evaluation (Smith and co-workers 1978) revealed that teen participation in the program significantly enhanced positive benefits for the younger teenager (16 years of age) when compared statistically with older teens.

Some unresolved issues and limitations of hospital-based services for pregnant adolescents are dependent on the lack of assessment. Although evaluation has been initiated in some programs, it is not a widely implemented component of hospital-based programs. Moreover, when evaluation is undertaken, the lack of stated and quantifiable measures of success makes the interpretation of results subjective. This method may reflect an orientation which, by definition, is organized towards the saving of lives, not towards management by objectives. The absence of generally accepted standards makes comparisons among clinical sites and the development of program implementation strategies difficult. Even when comparisons of different formats are attempted, the available assessments may not provide adequate internal information for change. For example, in hospital-based programs for pregnant adolescents, a variety of intervention techniques are utilized in the delivery of services to the patient. As a result, there are many variables which promote positive change; their individual effects are not readily discernible. Designs that have the capacity to differentiate among the complex independent variables are usually not used to evaluate program results. Variables such as personality type and behavior of the implementing staff (for example, the ''friend in the system phenomenon'') might be better documented with more specific assessment techniques.

In medical programs, territorial issues arise among clinical specialties. Pregnancy as a health need requiring clinical intervention has been primarily the responsibility of the speciality of obstetrics and gynecology. However, the declining age of pregnancy of approximately one month per decade (Zackler and Brandstandt 1975) has helped to result in more conceptions among pediatric patients. In 1974, the birth rates among teenagers under 14 years of age had increased as compared to 1961 (Allen Guttmacher Institute 1976). There is a growing need therefore to coordinate the expertise of the pediatrician with the delivery services of the obstetrician. This union could provide counseling on human sexuality and prompt contraception motivation for the very young teenager. To date, a consortium of expertise has not been widely practiced. Cooperative pediatric and obstetrical ventures could easily be expanded to include other medical specialties. The private family practitioner is also in a unique position to work with teenagers on such issues as adolescent sexuality.

In conclusion, several limitations in hospital-based projects have become apparent. Whereas some programs have successfully reduced medical complications, such programs may not be able to successfully accommodate teenagers who become pregnant again (Gordis 1968). The incidence of medical complications for such repeat pregnancies is always significantly high.

SCHOOL-BASED PROGRAMS

Since pregnancy is the most frequently stated reason for the termination of formal schooling (Stine and co-workers 1964; Holmes and co-workers 1973; Foltz and co-workers 1972), educational systems have begun to address the problems of teen pregnancy by implementing school-based programs. Whereas some state legal barriers, such as prohibition of sex education in the schools, still prevent this type of service to nonpregnant students (Paul and co-workers 1976), the educational programs for the pregnant adolescent in the last ten years have expanded greatly. Their attempts include a variety of school, homebound education, special school placement, night school instruction, and T.V. closed circuit teaching formats. For many teens, continuing in their regular school program is the most convenient option. If the choice is available, reasons for continuing in school often depend upon a variety of factors. Priority issues include transportation, extracurricular activities, and maintaining interaction with the teenager's peer and other significant groups (Klein 1974). Ideally, any program in her own school should encompass curricular material and information that especially fits the pregnant girl's needs. Training in child growth and development, budget and financial management, parenting skills, and nutrition are examples of needed elements. Parental and peer pressure and the inability of schools to provide all educational components enhances the need for special school options. One such example was found in the Webster School Model in Washington, D.C. (Howard 1968). Established in the 1960s, this project combined comprehensive services with the regular curriculum. Although a medical component was not initially incorporated in the school program, outside care was mandatory. School staff members did assist in providing linkages to medical care. The Poe School in Baltimore was also a variation of the special school for pregnant girls setting (Washington 1975). One of the issues in this delivery form is that school attendance was not optional but mandatory for any adolescent who found herself pregnant and wished to continue her education.

Whether the service is special school-based or integrated into the regular community education, some important issues still need to be considered. The leadership of school programs must be attuned to the client and to her situation. Many of the coordination responsibilities of an administrator touch sensitive personal areas. Thus, a unique management philosophy must be tailored to the unique problems of adolescence and adolescent pregnancy.

The funding vehicles for programs for pregnant adolescents sometimes create an atmosphere that does not foster progressive programs. One of the primary vehicles for program funding has been through the Title I Elementary and Secondary Education Act and through special education mechanisms, such as handicap resources. The later example indirectly implies that pregnancy is a handicapping condition or perhaps that the pregnant adolescent is less than adequate. Such funding mechanisms often suggest that adolescent pregnancy is a problem exclusively of minority groups and the poor. Although the pregnant teenager may have some additional educational difficulties, she is hardly a handicapped student but one who has to cope with a variety of new and unusual problems.

School-based programs for pregnant adolescents serve a valuable function in fostering and facilitating continued education. Yet, certain project components are often missing in school projects. Special counseling and in-depth guidance for the new problems and personal experiences of these girls is often, especially in regular school settings, difficult to obtain. Specialists are usually not available in many regular schools attended by pregnant adolescents. Moreover, some special counseling situations, such as problem pregnancy counseling and pregnancy termination, are such controversial political and ethical issues that school administrators hesitate to become involved.

Other activities that could be easily implemented by school nurses contain written or unwritten prohibitions. The availability of pregnancy-testing in the school setting could potentially widen the variety of counseling options, opportunities, and/or service entry points. Such a service could be easily performed by a school nurse, but for obvious reasons it is rarely actively encouraged or covertly allowed. Counseling options could also be made available for the father of the baby. However, in most school situations the father's presence or participation is

83

not openly acknowledged. This factor may be changing. Some state adoption statutes now mandate that the father of the baby be involved before parental rights can be terminated.

Several types of learning experiences, such as on-site nurseries in a school setting, are also appropriate curricular components for pregnant adolescent programs. Nurseries not only provide day care for infants (thereby allowing the teenager to return to school) but also generate a valuable firsthand experience and introduction to the process of parenting and childrearing. The opportunity to interact with babies in a nursery setting may also be important for teenagers in their third trimester of pregnancy. Indeed, an on-site nursery may be valuable for teenagers of both sexes. However, school-based nursery programs to date have been difficult to implement. Community resistance and licensing regulations necessitating extensive renovation are significant barriers to the installation of school nurseries.

Two other current facets of school-based programs should be considered. Firstly, there is a significant lack of services for pregnant adolescents. Goldstein and Wallace in a study conducted in 1976 found that a significant number of cities had nothing to offer pregnant adolescents in terms of program development and/or support services. Adolescent pregnancy is certainly not confined to those school systems in which programs exist. Secondly, as with medical-based programs, school programs are not being adequately assessed. Goals and important objectives need to be identified and evaluated. Many programs resort to a simplistic form of headcounting. There are usually citations of figures of average daily attendance or of repeat pregnancies. The literature shows that such techniques may not be an adequate reflection of programmatic success.

Despite all the limitations, school-based programs do have a fairly successful track record. Adolescents who have participated in both regular and special school programs while pregnant have tended, for the most part, to continue their formal education and to control future pregnancies. The majority of these girls have graduated from school and have been able to stay off welfare. Moreover, some researchers indicate that the probability of such successful outcomes is enhanced if teenagers are at the correct age level for their grade level (Goldfarb and co-workers 1977).

COMMUNITY-BASED PROJECTS

Although the majority of programs for pregnant adolescents are either school-based or medical, another type should also be described. This might be called community-based programs. The forms are diverse. Churches, mobile classrooms, health centers, or shopping centers are location options (Howard 1968). Community-based programs have special advantages over the school-based models. For instance, they may allow discussion of human sexuality issues and/or birth control without the traditional prohibitions placed on such information in a school setting. Moreover, as these programs are separate from the medical model, they usually regard pregnancy in a developmental framework rather than a pathologic one. Some projects of this kind were set up by community councils and, because of the wide variety of needs presented by pregnant teenagers, relied heavily on the cooperation of various other agencies. Because of their community location and "draw," community-based projects for pregnant teenagers may be in a better position to provide follow-up for the mother after she delivers and to help mobilize community arrangements for daycare of the infant (Howard 1968).

Maternity homes have often taken a lead in promoting community-based organizations (Lyons 1968). Agencies such as Florence Crittenton have been actively involved in community efforts. These activities usually include a home for pregnant teenagers in which good prenatal care, educational classes, and adoption services are provided. Since currently 9 out of 10 teenagers do not relinquish custody of their baby, the need for such agencies in the traditional role has declined. Future roles for maternity homes may be more involved in the networking and the linking of non-pregnancy services for adolescents, such as programs for children in need of supervision and family counseling.

Some community-based projects, while involved with the issues of adolescent pregnancy, do not offer services directly. Several organizations plan, coordinate, and publicize programs that will meet the needs of adolescent pregnancy. For example, the Austin, Texas Teenage Parent Council, established in 1970, informs the community of many needs of teenage parents and their infants and helps to strengthen and develop new health education and social services. The Austin Teenage Parent Council provides a community forum for information exchange and also provides a vehicle for educating state legislators as well as state and private agency planning staff members. This organization further facilitates service coordination by publishing a list of resources available to pregnant teenagers in the state of Texas.

On the national level the National Alliance Concerned with School-Age Parenthood (NACSAP) served in a similar manner. Operational in the late 1960s, and early 1970s the NACSAP was a multidisciplinary membership organization that provided technical assistance to those who

85

work with school age parents, young families at risk, and the sexually active youth. The goals of this organization were to respond to the immediate crises resulting from adolescent pregnancy and early parenthood and to work with community groups, parents, and agency representatives to develop programs and strategies that can help to prevent high-risk adolescent pregnancy. Another type of network system has evolved in San Antonio. The Teenage Parent Network assists the adolescent parent by referring teen parents to appropriate community agencies which address a wide range of needs. Although this network does not directly provide prenatal or alternative educational programs, it directs young parents to the local organization which can best meet their specific needs. This community-based organization has several unique components. Three way telephone hook-up, home visits, and a liaison agent to service delivery appear to successfully show young parents how to ask for and receive assistance. The planning strategy of the agency staff is also demonstrated to the teenager. By example, she is encouraged to develop her own master plan for reaching community services which meet her basic needs.

Although community-based organizations often provide an important conduit to facilitate teenage services, some limitations are present. By definition, community advocacy agencies usually do not provide direct clinical services. Leadership of such agencies must therefore be very sensitive to changing patient service needs. Some groups have attempted to intensify teenage input through the establishment of adolescent advisory groups and forums. While such techniques, at first blush, may provide valid feedback from consumer groups, further investigation indicates that teenagers who constitute the membership are often chosen in a non-random manner. The representation, therefore, may consist of homogenous populations which lack the entire range of life-experience perspectives.

CLINICAL PROGRAMS FOR NONPREGNANT TEENAGERS

In response to adolescent pregnancy, several programs have attempted to provide family planning services to the nonpregnant girl. The need for such programs is documented not only by the presence of the pregnant adolescent but also by the estimate that 50% of the four million women aged 15 to 19 years of age are in need of family planning services (Tyrer and Josimovich, 1977). The pregnancy prevention approach, once completely blocked by community resistance (Gordon 1968), now appears to have gained momentum. Paul and co-workers (1976) have indicated that legislatures and courts continue to affirm the right of young people to consent for their own health care, including contraceptive services. Such an attitude is part of the larger movement advocating lowering the age of majority. In keeping with the effect of such change, community attitudes concerning adolescent sexuality have also appeared to mellow. Despite the formal disapproval of the United States Presidential Office in 1973 of making contraceptive services available to teenagers, national approval has increased gradually (Blake 1973; Gallup 1978). Although some resistance still exists in the medical profession concerning the provision of family planning services to minors (Minkler 1971), the official position of both the Academy of Pediatrics and the College of Obstetrics and Gynecology wholeheartedly endorses this preventive approach.

In response to the challenge to provide adolescent family planning services, several types of models have evolved. The category or prototype used in various models often plays a role in stimulating community acceptance. The community health care model is holistically oriented and utilizes a multidisciplinary professional staff (Finkelstein 1972). Such family planning units often camouflage contraception under the guise of total health care for teens. The other type of model is more monofocal and contraception oriented. Some agencies (e.g. Planned Parenthood affiliates) provide family planning counseling and contraception to adolescents in a fairly straightforward manner; their approach is enhanced by the heavy community volunteer involvement. Teen clinics of this nature combine family planning services with sex education, contraceptive dissemination, pregnancy and venereal disease testing, and counseling for abortion or prenatal care (Goldsmith 1969; 1972).

While some controversy exists between components of certain service delivery models (Goldsmith 1970), several service criteria are agreed upon. An increasing number of family planning professionals have indicated that parental consent should not be a prerequisite of teen service. The necessity for requiring adult approval (or perhaps simply acquiescence) often becomes an effective block for adolescents seeking family planning provider agencies (URSA 1976).

Parents often have problems coping with the sexuality of their children. Although the general population has acknowledged the need for preventive contraceptive measures for adolescents (Gallup 1978), individual parents, possibly either because of ignorance or denial will often not accept their own child's sexual activity (Furstenburg 1976). In the absence of such an acknowledgement, parents do not assist their children in obtaining contraception. In order to live up to parental expectations, teens will not involve their parents in the procurement of effective methods of contraception.

Some teens face an exacerbated problem concerning the question of parental consent. For some parents, awareness of their progeny's coital behavior may stimulate more than general emotional discomfort. Sexual activity for teens may be a transgression of parental established mores. If such prohibited teenage behavior is exposed, dire parental admonishments and/or consequences are foreseen. These fears are often revealed in the furtive behavior of pregnant girls who are too frightened to reveal their predicament to their parents in spite of the inevitable (without intervention) discovery.

The difficulties parents experience with teen sexuality may reflect their inability to master the concepts of adolescent developmental stages. Some professionals indicate that during teenage psychological development, the need to establish independence may preclude substantive communications with parents, especially concerning human sexual behavior (Erikson 1964).

Another related criterion for teen services is the issue of confidentiality. When teens can only attend clinics organized for the general population, the possibility exists that the teen patient could have an embarrassing or unplanned encounter with a family friend or relative attending the same clinic. The obvious way to avoid such a situation is to set up separate teen clinics for the adolescent clientele. If separate facilities were made available, the staff could focus on the needs and sensitivities of the lifestyle of the teen group rather than on the broad needs of the sexually active adult female population.

Confidentiality then is needed to safeguard the teen not only from parents and family members but also from nonsexually active peers. Adolescents do not want their level of sexual activity to be common knowledge. In response to this attitude, specialists generally agree that family planning centers should not be placed in close visual proximity to schools and educational facilities. The facilities, however, should be accessible by foot or public transportation.

In addition to preserving confidentiality, staff should adopt an open-minded attitude toward teenagers. Careful listening and non-judgmental responses are essential (Goldsmith 1972). Teenagers relax with this approach and openly discuss their problems and need for contraception.

The URSA (1976) study lists a third important service delivery criterion as a prerequisite for effective adolescent family planning services. In order to attract the teenage population, the offered services must be af- fordable to the consumer group. The adolescent population usually depends upon parental stipends as a primary source of income. This income often has an accountability for large expenditures. In light of the strong possibility of parental disapproval, family planning service costs should be minimal at worst and nonexistent at best.

The implementation of these approaches to teenage programs has not been widespread. This containment of services may reflect fiscal rather than attitudinal constraints. While some professionals may feel that sexually active teenagers, because of their behavior choice, should be considered and treated as adults, most agencies surveyed in a recent family planning study (unpublished, Smith 1978) feel that separate teen clinics would be an effective way to provide contraceptive services to adolescents. In a survey conducted among Planned Parenthood affiliates (House and Goldsmith 1972) three out of four clients questioned the scheduling of teen clients with adult women during regular clinic hours. Funding limitations and restrictive overtime policies are usually mentioned as the basic barriers to establishing separate teen services. It is apparent that teenagers are reluctant to visit adult-oriented clinics. Although not documented, this inhibition may be a key cause of the high number of teenagers with unplanned pregnancies (80%) who did not use any birth control when they conceived (Zelnick and Kantner 1978).

CONTRACEPTIVE SERVICES FOR ADOLESCENT MALES

Research and service descriptions focusing on the contraceptive needs, attitudes, and behaviors of adolescent boys do not widely appear in the professional literature. This lack reflects the general state of the art of family planning services for the male population as a whole. Moreover, professionals know less about how to provide services to the male adolescent than to any other male age group (Jekel 1975). There are several reasons for the minimal emphasis on the "male component." Until recently, family planning was primarily a female issue. Culturally, contraception was the responsibility of the woman and consequently any resultant method failure was her fault. This unilateral placement of responsibility was reinforced by the limited variety of effective male methods of birth control. As a result, the family planning service delivery systems developed a strong female orientation and made no deliberate effort to involve the male partner in the decision to use contraception or in the implementation of the method. This bias is often reflected in the lack of male staff members and restrooms for men in family planning facilities.

The one-sided non-male orientation, however, seems to be changing gradually. The increased interest in vasectomy by men appears to indicate their heightened sense of responsibility for decisions in the area of family planning. The literature indicates that such permanent forms of sterilization are now ranked as the most popular methods. Moreover, legally, the rights and responsibilities of alleged fathers have been recently substantiated. In the *Stanley vs. Illinois* decision of the United States Supreme Court, the rights of the single father in the area of child custody were given equal protection under the law. This decision was strengthened by the *Rothstein vs. Lutheran Social Service* decision and by the *Slavek vs. Covanent Children's Home* decision which again guaranteed the rights of the alleged father before the adoption procedures of an illegitimate child could be finalized.

Since the male is no longer anonymous concerning his contraceptive responsibilities nor his legal right to his progeny (albeit illegitimate), new attention has been focused on various aspects of male behavior as it relates to sexual activity and contraception. The onset of early sexual activity for many adolescent males has been well documented. Finkel and Finkel (1975) found that the average age of first male sexual activity was 12.8 years. Furstenburg (1976) noted in his review of research on adolescent parenthood that by age 14, two-thirds of the males were sexually active.

Age also plays a role in partner selection. Researchers (Goldfarb and co-workers 1977; Zelnick and Kantner 1977) observed that the male partner was on the average two years older than the female at first intercourse. This age difference was applicable to all ethnic groups. Selection of contraceptive methods also appears to exhibit some relationship to the male role and teenage sexuality. In spite of the effectiveness of the IUD and hormonal methods of contraception, research indicates that the condom is the primary form of contraception for sexually active adolescent males (Settlage, Baroff, and Cooper 1973). Although adolescents complain about the interference with spontaneity and naturalness of coitus, in 44% of the cases in which some form of contraception was used, the condom remains the method of choice (Minkowski and co-workers 1974). It should be pointed out, however, that the utilization of this contraceptive method is sometimes inconsistent.

Aggressive sexual behavior by the adolescent male may play a role in the female initiation to coitus. Although the significance of this factor is not universally agreed upon (Goldsmith and co-workers 1972), peer pressure and the need for conformity (Garris, Steckler, and McIntire 1976) and intimacy (Cobliner 1974) all encourage coitus. Thus, in the development of human sexuality the impulse for emotional intimacy becomes inevitably interwoven with the impulse for sexual expression and fulfillment. In addition, the man's sexual prowess not only proves his manhood (Eddinger and Forbush 1977) but gives him status within his male peer group (Staples 1971).

The behavioral and psychological literature documents the need for services for adolescent males. However, only two types of service providers are readily apparent in the literature. Of the three types of contraception used by teenagers—withdrawal, douching, and the condom—the condom is the most significant method choice. Thus, attempts have been made to distribute free condoms to adolescent boys through barber shops, pool halls, grocery stores, and restaurants. Arnold and Cogswell's (1971) results of this approach indicate that if boys are given a chance, they will become increasingly more willing to share in the family planning responsibilities (Gobble and co-workers 1969). Nevertheless, there is much to be accomplished. The other service system designed to reach the adolescent male is the rap session. Such sessions not only provide contraceptive information but information on decision making, human sexuality, and moral issues on sexual behavior. This format, however, has not received widespread acceptance.

The major example in the literature of a service provided for the adolescent father (and perhaps the only one) is at Vista Del Mar, a child care service agency in Los Angeles (Pannor, Evans, and Massarik 1971). This program focuses on the problems of the single parent with special emphasis on the single father. The project aggressively involves the father of the baby in the total experience of the pregnancy. The single father's responsibility, reinforced by the ultimate threat of legal action, is viewed as a positive step with beneficial results for the father, the mother, and the future well being of the child (Pannor and Evans 1975).

Although the courts have determined that the rights of the natural father cannot be ignored, few other program description or services for the adolescent father are found in a review of professional literature. Evaluation of the father's role in the pregnancy has been occasionally developed. Some research indicates that the involvement of the father may provide a mixed blessing. Klerman (1975) found that when fathers were involved during the pregnancy a marriage resulted which in turn led to another early pregnancy. Such a result may be counter-productive to the ultimate goal of programs for pregnant adolescents.

Although the degree of paternal involvement in the pregnancy enhanced the chance of establishing permanent relationships (Sauber 1966), the ultimate benefits of the continuation of such a relationship is possibly in question. Furstenburg found that at the one year follow-up, 20% of the mothers had lost touch with the father of the child. At the five year follow-up this figure increased to 37%. Involvement, therefore, of the father may capitulate the couple into a marital contract that is short-lived and that has a documented "high probability of failure."

Recent public interest in the male's role in family planning may indicate that professionals in family planning are recognizing the great potential for male involvement. In January 1978 the National Institute for Community Development performed an extensive review of the literature on this subject. This report (Oresky and Ewing 1978) indicated that male use of contraception was affected by a variety of factors—most notably age, attitude, and education. While encouraging the development of innovative family planning techniques for males, this report underscored the positive potential of a condom designed specifically for adolescents and encouraged "Yankee ingenuity" in the marketing and distribution of this prophylactic. This study also pointed out that programs which promote male-oriented contraception should publicize their efforts by initiating broad-based evaluations of their methods.

Two additional studies on the male's role in family planning were conducted by the National Institute for Community Development. The second (Oresky and Ewing 1978) reviewed the sociological literature on non-family planning activities of males (such as football) to find information relevant to male involvement in family planning and birth control. It was hoped that the existing recruitment methods, motivational strategies, and program design for these other activities could be broadly applied to family planning. The focus therefore shifted from family planning programs *per se* to training programs for disadvantaged youth. This study demonstrated that the peer communication system was probably the most important variable in broad-based behavior change. This finding can be positively applied to family planning methods. A third and final report, (Ewing and Visco 1978) published by this group in July 1978 surveyed model programs with male involvement in family planning. This report found a variety of model programs that actually or potentially served males. These programs varied from the clinical model that used more traditional family planning methods to the information and education model that provided minimal medical services but maximum education.

In conclusion, in the area of contraceptive services to adolescent males, little has been developed or provided. Lacking innovative approaches and technologically advanced methods, the adolescent male who is sexually active and who ultimately finds himself a father has few responsible reproductive options. New approaches are sorely needed.

Summary

Documentation of the need for family planning services for teens comes directly through the empirical study of adolescent sexual behavior (Sorenson 1973; Allan Guttmacher Institute 1977; Zelnick and Kantner 1978), the pregnant teen (Furstenburg 1976; Zackler and Brandstadt 1975) and indirectly through programmatic recommendations (Gordon 1973; Goldsmith 1969; Jekel 1976). Depending upon the catalyzing force, these services are usually presented after the fact, focusing on the pregnant or once-pregnant girl. Scattered attempts have been made to move to pregnancy prevention as a service delivery goal but primary prevention of teen pregnancies through counseling and/or contraception has not been widely tried. Moreover, the role of the male partner is rarely acknowledged, his sexual behaviors are inadequately studied, and the probability of his involvement in responsible reproduction behavior is ignored.

References

Alan Guttmacher Institute. *11 million teenagers: what can be done about the epidemic of adolescent pregnancies in the United States*. New York: Alan Guttmacher Institute. The Research and Development Division of Planned Parenthood Federation of America, 1976.

American Academy of Pediatrics, Committee on Youth. Teenage pregnancy and the problem of abortion. *Pediatrics* 49:306, 1972.

Arnold, C. B. and Cogswell, B. E. A condom distribution program for adolescents. The findings of a feasibility study. *Am. J. Public Health* 61:739–750, 1971.

Badger, F.; Burns, D.; and Rhoads, B. Education for adolescent mothers in a hospital setting. *Am. J. Public Health* 66:469–472, 1976.

Blake, J. The teenage birth control

dilemma and public opinion. *Science* 180:708–712, 1973.

Cobliner, G. Pregnancy and the single adolescent girl: The role of cognitive functions. *J. Youth Adolescence* 3:17–29, 1974.

Cutright, P. Illegitimacy: myths, causes and curses. *Fam. Plann. Perspect.* 3:26–48, 1972.

Dott, A. B. and Fort, A. T. Medical and social factors affecting early teenage pregnancy. *Am. J. Obstet. Gynecol.* 125:532–536, 1976.

Eddinger, L. and Forbush, J. *School-age pregnancy and parenthood in the United States*. Washington, D.C.: National Alliance Concerned with School Age Parents, 1977.

Erikson, E. H. *Children and society*. New York: W. W. Norton, 1964.

Ewing, E., and Visco, E. P. Model programs for involving men in family planning. Prepared for Office of Family Planning, Bureau of Community Health Services, Health Services Administration Contract #240–77–0077. National Institute for Community Development, Inc. Arlington, Virginia: June, 1978.

Finkel, M. L., and Finkel, D. J. Sexual and contraceptive knowledge, attitudes and behavior of male adolescents. *Fam. Plann. Perspect.* 7:256–260, 1975.

Finkelstein, R. Programs for the sexually active teenager. *Pediat. Clin. North Am.* 19:791–794, 1972.

Foltz, A. M.; Klerman, L. V.; and Jekel, J. F. Pregnancy and special education: who stays in school? *Am. J. Public Health* 62: 1612–1619, 1972.

Furstenberg, F. F., Jr. The social consequences of teenage parenthood. *Fam. Plann. Perspect.* 8:148–164, 1976.

Gallup, G. Reflects epidemic of teen pregnancies: growing number of Americans favor discussion of sex in the classroom. The Gallup Poll, news release, Princeton, New Jersey, January 23, 1978.

Garris L.; Steckler, A.; and McIntire, J. R. The relationship between oral contraceptives and adolescent sexual behavior. *J. Sex. Res.* 12:135–146, 1976.

Gobble, F. et al. A non medical approach to fertility reduction. *Obstet. Gynecol.* 34:888–891, 1969.

Goldfarb, A. F. Puberty and menarche. *Clin. Obstet. Gynecol.* 20:625–631, 1977.

Goldfarb, J. L.; Mumford, D. M.; Schum, D. A.; Smith, P. B.; Flowers, C.; and Schum, C. An attempt to detect "pregnancy susceptibility" in indigent adolescent girls. *J. You. Adole.* 6:127–143, 1977.

Gordon, S. *The Sexual Adolescent*. North Scituate, Mass.: Duxbury Press, 1973.

Goldsmith, S. San Francisco teen clinic meeting the sex education and birth control needs of sexually active school girls. *Fam. Plann. Perspect.* 1:2, 1969.

Goldsmith, S.; Gabrielson, M. O.; Gabrielson, I.; Matthews, V.; and Potts, L. Teenagers, sex and contraception. *Fam. Plann. Perspect.* 4:32–38, 1972.

Goldstein, H., and Wallace, H. M. Service for the needs of pregnant teenagers in large cities of the United States. *Public Health Rep.* 93:46, 1976.

Grady, E. W. Models of comprehensive service—hospital based. *J. Sch. Health* XLV:268–270, 1975.

Holmes, M., and Howard, M. How communities finance programs for pregnant school-age girls. Information Series #2, Consortium on Early Childbearing and Childrearing, Washington, D.C., 1972.

House, E. A., and Goldsmith, S. Planned parenthood services for the young teenager. *Fam. Plann. Perspect.* 4:27–31, 1972.

Howard, M. Comprehensive service programs for school-age parents. *Children* 15:193–197, 1968.

Jekel, J. F. Appraising programs for school-age parents. *J. Sch. Health* XLV:296–300, 1975.

Jekel, J. F., and Forbush, J. B. Service needs of adolescent parents. Read at the annual meeting of the American Public Health Association, Maternal and Child Health Section, 21 October 1972, Miami Beach, Florida.

Jekel, J. F.; Klerman, L. V.; and Bancroft, D. R. E. Factors associated with rapid subsequent pregnancies among school-age mothers. *Am. J. Public Health* 63: 769–773, 1973.

Klein, L. Early teenage pregnancy, contraception, and repeat pregnancy. *Am. J. Obstet. Gynecol.* 120:249–255, 1974.

Klerman, L. V. Adolescent pregnancy, the need to new policies and new programs. *J. Sch. Health* XLV:263–267, 1975.

Lipsitz, J. S. *Growing up forgotten: a review of research and programs concerning young adolescents.* Lexington, Mass.: Lexington Books, 1976.

Litt, I. F.; Edberg, S. C.; and Finberg, L. Gonorrhea in children and adolescents: A current review. *J. Pediatr.* 85:595–606, 1974.

Lyons, D. J. Developing a program for pregnant teenagers through the cooperation of schools, health departments and federal agencies. *Am. J. Public Health* 58: 2225–2230, 1968.

Marinoff, S. C., and Schonholz, D. H. Adolescent pregnancy. *Pediatr. Clin. North Am.* 19:795–802, 1972.

McMurray, G. L. Project teen aid: A community action approach to services for pregnant unmarried teenagers. *Am. J. Public Health* 58:1848–1853, 1968.

Minkler, D. H. Fertility regulation for teenagers. *Clin. Obstet. Gynecol.* 14:420–431, 1971.

Minkowski, W. L.; Weiss, R. C.; Lawther, L.; Schonick, H.; and Heidbreder, G. A. Family planning services for adolescents and young adults. *West J. Med.* 120:116–123, 1974.

Mitchell, J. J. Adolescent intimacy. *Adolescence* 42:275–280, 1976.

New American Library. *Population and the american future.* The report of the commission on population growth and the american future. New York, New York: New American Library, 1972.

Oresky, D., and Ewing, E. A review of non-family planning program literature relevant to male oriented family planning programs. Prepared for Office of Family Planning, Bureau of Community Health Services, Health Services Administration Contract #240–77–0077. National Institute for Community Development, Inc. Arlington, Virginia: April, 1978.

Oresky, D., and Ewing, E. Review and annotated bibliography of literature on male involvement in family planning. Prepared for Office of Family Planning, Bureau of Community Health Services, Health Services Administration Contract #240–77–0077. National Institute for Community Development, Inc. Arlington, Virginia: January, 1978.

Osofosky, H. J.; Hagen, J. H.; and Wood, P. W. Program for pregnant school girls. *Am. J. Obstet. Gynecol.* 100:1020–1027, 1968.

Osofosky, H. J.; Osofosky, J. D.; Kendall, N.; and Ragan, R. Adolescents as mothers: an interdisciplinary approach to a complex problem. *J. You. Adole.* 2: 233–249, 1973.

Pannor, R.; Evans, B.; and Massarik, F. The unmarried fathers. New York: Springer Publishing Co., Inc., 1971.

Pannor, R., and Evans, B. W. The unmarried father revisited. *J. Sch. Health* XLV:286–291, 1975.

Paul, E. W.; Pilpel, H. F.; and Wechsler, N. F. Pregnancy, teenagers and the law. *Fam. Plann. Perspect.* 8:16–21, Jan./Feb. 1976.

Rauh, J. L.; Johnson, L. B.; and Burkett, R. L. The reproductive adolescent. *Pediatr. Clin. North Am.* 20:1005–1019, 1973.

Sarrel, P. M., and Klerman, L. V. The young unwed mother. *Am. J. Obstet. Gynecol.* 105:575–578, 1969.

Sauber, J. The role of the unmarried father. *Welfare in Review* 4:15–18, 1966.

Settlage, D. S.; Baroff, S.; and Cooper, D. Sexual experience of younger teenage girls seeking contraceptive assistance for the first time. *Fam. Plann. Perspect.* 5:223–226, 1973.

Smith, E. W. The role of the grandmother in adolescent pregnancy and parenting. *J. Sch. Health* XLV:278–283, 1975.

Smith, P. B.; Mumford, D. M.; Goldfarb, J. L.; and Kaufman, R. H. Selected aspects of adolescent postpartum behavior. *J. Rep. Med.* 14:159–165, 1975.

Smith, P. B.; Wait, R.; Mumford, D. M.; Nenney, S. W.; and Hollins, B. T. The medical impact of an antepartum program for pregnant adolescents: a statistical analysis. *Am. J. Public Health* 68:169–172, 1978.

Sorenson, R. C. *Adolescent sexuality in contemporary America.* New York: World Publishing Co., 1973.

Staples, R. *The black family: Essays and studies.* Belmont, California: Wadsworth Publishing Co., 1971.

Stine, O. C.; Rider, R. V.; and Sweeney, E. School leaving due to pregnancy in an urban adolescent population. *Am. J. Public Health* 54:1–6, 1964.

Tyrer, L. B. and Josimovich, J. Contraception in teenagers. *Clin. Obstet. Gynecol.* 20:651–663, 1977.

Urban and Rural Systems Associates. *Improving family planning services for teenagers.* Final Report submitted to Office of the Assistant Secretary for Planning and Evaluation/Health, DHEW, Contract # HEW-OS 74 304, June, 1976.

Washington, V. E. Models of comprehensive service—special school based. *J. Sch. Health* XLV:274–277, 1975.

Zacharias, L.; Wurtman, R. J.; and Schatzoff, M. Sexual maturation in contemporary American girls. *Am. J. Obstet. Gynecol.* 108: 833–846, 1970.

Zackler, J. and Brandstandt, W. *The teenage pregnant girl.* Springfield, Illinois: Charles C. Thomas, 1975.

Zelnick, M. and Kantner, J. F. Contraceptive patterns and premarital pregnancy among women aged 15–19 in 1976. *Fam. Plann. Perspect.* 10:135–142, 1978.

Zelnick, M. and Kantner, J. F. Sexuality, contraception and pregnancy among young unwed females in the United States. *In Demographic and social aspects of population growth,* eds. C. F. Westoff and R. Parke, Jr. vol. I, Commission Research Reports. U.S. Commission on population growth Washington, D.C., Government Printing Office, 355–374, 1972.

7 Venereal Disease and the Adolescent

David M. Mumford, M.D.

Nancy McCormick, M.S.

The term venereal disease (VD) seems to be losing favor in the contemporary lexicon. Sexually transmitted diseases (STD) will be the designation of the 80s. Over 20 diseases are now listed in this category and the number is climbing (table 7.1). The literary transition may reflect not only our expanded knowledge, but also the changing sexual mores. For simplicity, we will frequently use the term venereal in its specific as well as its general sense, in addition to STD.

Reports limited to sexually transmitted diseases of adolescent women are not copious in the literature, so much of the review which follows depends on studies of adults as well. However, in most instances the application to teenage problems seems clear. Several articles and chapters have served as key references (Handsfield 1977; Hart 1977; Kreutner 1978; Stern 1975).

Classically, the venereal diseases have included syphilis and gonorrhea as major entities, and chancroid, granuloma inguinale, and lymphogranuloma venereum as the so-called "minor" venereal diseases. Since many diseases are now known to be capable of passage by intimate congress, and since the range of acceptable sexual activity by individuals has apparently broadened, the host of diseases now listed as sexually transmitted has lengthened (table 7.1). Most of these infections involve the genital area, but inclusion of rectal, pharyngeal and other areas is increasingly common. With the general augmentation in sexual activity, especially by the young, it is not surprising to find that the venereal disease statistics have shown a continual rise. One of the most common diseases, gonorrhea, has had an extremely rapid elevation. The increase in the teenage group has been much faster than in the general population. Syphilis by contrast is less prevalent, has not shown striking changes and probably only accounts for about 0.5% of adolescent venereal cases (Stern and McKenzie 1975). Gathering valid statistics in the United States on such a sensitive subject is fraught with difficulty and is usually based only on reported cases. Where complete surveys are done, the estimates are much more precise. For example, in a culture and serology study of

Table 7.1 Sexually Transmitted Diseases

Disease	Organism
	Bacteria
Gonorrhea	*Neisseria gonorrheae*
Vulvovaginitis, urethritis	*Haemophilus vaginalis*
Chancroid	*Haemophilus ducreyi*
Granuloma	*Calmmatobacterium granulomatis*
Syphilis	*Treponema pallidum*
Dysentery	*Shigella*
Gastroenteritis, enteric fever	*Salmonella*
Neonatal and infant infections	Group B *Streptococcus*
Lymphogranuloma venereum	Chlamydia
Inclusion cervicitis, vaginitis, and urethritis	Trachoma inclusion conjunctivitis agent
	Fungus
Vulvovaginal Candidiasis	*Candida albicans*
Tinea cruris	*Epidermophyton inguinale*
	Metazoa
Pediculosis pubis	*Phthirus pubis*
Scabies	*Acarus*
	Mycoplasma
Cervicitis, vaginitis, urethritis	*Mycoplasma hominis* or *T. mycoplasma*
	Protozoa
Trichomoniasis (vulvovaginitis)	*Trichomonas vaginalis*
	Viruses
Herpes vulvovaginitis	*Herpesvirus* type 2 (type 1?)
Condyloma acuminatum	*Papilloma virus*
Genital dermatitis	*Molluscum contagiosum virus*
Cervicitis, urethritis	*Cytomegalovirus*
Hepatitis	*Hepatitis B*

740 pregnant teenagers of low socioeconomic rank, we found a 2.4% prevalence for gonorrhea and a 0.7% positive serology prevalence for syphilis (Mumford, Smith and Goldfarb 1977).

After the 1940s, there was great hope that the new antibiotics, penicillin in particular, would wipe out venereal diseases. Indeed there was a significant decline for a while, but then an upswing began. The reasons for the upswing are undoubtedly multiple. The changing sexual mores of teenagers may account for much of the increase. An earlier age of the onset of sexual activity, perhaps coupled with a greater range of partners than was common in past decades, may be partly responsible for the elevated rates. However, enhanced case findings may also be a contributing factor, especially where legislation has allowed adolescents to be treated for venereal diseases without parental consent (Altchek 1972). Another obvious contributing factor is the adolescent's superficial knowledge of venereal diseases. Nonetheless, even when the adolescent is aware of venereal disease he or she may not use contraceptive devices or take protective measures (i.e., the use of condoms, postcoital washings, diaphragms, and the use of certain vaginal compounds which may have antibacterial side effects) which might diminish the chances of venereal infection. Moreover, statistics can sometimes be misleading. For instance, if a new venereal disease program is inaugurated in a community, patients will be actively identified and the subsequent statistics may suggest a tenfold or more rise. The actual incidence of the disease, however, may be decreasing due to the same community action (Hart 1977).

Hart makes another interesting observation which emphasizes the danger in following only incidence figures. He points out that incidence figures are often a poor indication of the total morbidity from a disease (1977). He states, "In the Spanish-Portuguese war (1519), over 5,000 penile amputations were performed for VD. It was estimated that 500,000 cases of syphilis in the French Army in World War I eventually produced 2,000,000 deaths, 157,000 cases of neurosyphilis and 61,000 cases of cardiovascular syphilis." Hart also stresses another thought. With modern drug therapy, the physical complications are less common, but the psychological sequelae, seen so commonly in modern clinics, may be as distressing as the physical consequences of the past. By reducing such psychic sequelae, the total morbidity of venereal disease may be reduced although the incidence may remain unaltered.

Another observation should be made which amplifies an earlier point, the danger of evaluating the extent of a disease by only using reported cases. Nationwide surveys suggest that in the United States only 10.9% of the gonorrhea cases, and only 12% of the infectious syphilis cases were reported (Fleming and co-workers 1970). Moreover, when comparing one region with another, great variables may exist. The type of medical care and services available in a given region (for instance follow-up case work, sex-education programs, contraceptive dissemination services, etc.), may skew the statistical portrait. Thus remedial measures based on statistics which are misleading may be destined to failure unless an appreciation of the range of possible differences is kept fully in mind.

Several final cautions are germane. In estimating the true incidence or prevalence of a disease, the degree of symptoms involved with the illness often determines its recognition. Venereal diseases which are asymptomatic will not be detected as readily as those which give symptoms. Furthermore, the word "incidence" has to be distinguished from the word "prevalence." National and governmental statistics usually reflect *new* cases which constitute the incidence of venereal disease, that is, a measure of the rate at which a disease develops during a specified period of time such as a year. Prevalence, on the other hand, is the number of people in a given population who have a disease at a given point in time. When the infective length of time is short relative to the dynamics of the disease in question, it is possible for prevalence figures to approximate incidence figures. At other times they may be quite different.

Gonorrhea

Gonorrhea and nonspecific urethritis (briefly mentioned later) are today's most common sexually transmitted diseases. If all age groups are considered, next to the common cold, gonorrhea is believed to be one of the most frequent afflictions of humankind. Hart (1977) estimates that the worldwide annual incidence is about 150,000,000 persons; if all sexually transmitted diseases are considered, the annual world total is probably over 400,000,000. In the United States there are probably over 3,000,000 persons with gonorrhea (Handsfield 1977). In 1978 there were, according to the Journal of the American Medical Association's "Medical News" (1979), 1,013,559 reported cases (fig. 7.1). Sixty % of those afflicted with gonorrhea are said to be males, but some authorities dispute this figure and place the estimate closer to 50%. Thirty-five % of those women reported to have gonorrhea are adolescent girls (15 to 19 years old) (Brown 1971). Indeed, the gonorrhea case rate for teenagers may be as high as 510/10,000 (Jerome 1974). An appreciably increased number of acute gonococcal infections are now being found in children between the ages of 12 and 14 (Israel and Deutschberger 1964). Girls, 14 and under, had a gonorrhea rate of 25/100,000 in 1972. An important fact should be born in mind which helps explain a part—but only a part—of the awesome statistics which some label as pandemic. Infec-

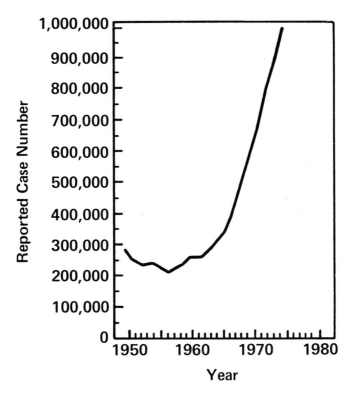

Fig. 7.1 *Gonorrhea in the United States from 1950 to 1978*

tion with gonorrhea does not confer permanent immunity. Even teen-agers may be reinfected. All health service professionals should be aware that, almost everywhere, enlightened legislation has allowed teen-agers to be treated for venereal disease without parental approval.

CHARACTERISTICS

Neisseria gonorrhoeae (N. gonorrhoeae) is a strictly anaerobic oxidase-positive, Gram-negative, diplococcus bacteria whose growth is enhanced by the presence of atmospheric carbon dioxide. The organism is usually identified by a smear, culture, or by fluorescent antibody identification of antigenic presence. The organism attaches to the surface epithelium of the host for 36 to 48 hours (the incubation period) before penetrating to induce a inflammatory reaction.

CLINICAL PICTURE

Asymptomatic endocervical infection is the most common form of gonorrhea in women. When symptoms do occur, they are characteristically mild and consist of signs and symptoms such as vaginal discharge, dysuria, pelvic discomfort, and uterine bleeding. In infants, gonorrhea may occur in the postnatal period in the form of gonococcal ophthalmia neonatorum, oropharyngeal infection, neonatal sepsis and rarely, the arthritis-dermatitis syndrome (Kohen 1974; Pierog and co-workers 1975; Wiesner and co-workers 1973). In the first year of life vulvovaginitis is the most common expression. It may be acquired nonsexually through poor hygiene when the infant shares a bed with an infected parent. However, most investigators state that after the first year of life, pediatric infections are apt to result from sexual molestation (Branch and Payton 1965; Israel, Rissing and Brooks 1975). The clinical picture may be similar to that of adults, but vulvovaginitis is the primary syndrome in girls (Branch and Paxton 1965; Handsfield 1974).

In the postpubertal female, uncomplicated gonorrhea is usually limited to the cervix, but other forms occur (Table 7.2). In complicated forms of gonorrhea, the arthritis-dermatitis syndrome, septic shock, meningitis, tonsillitis, pharyngitis, endocarditis, perihepatitis, and peritonitis, as well as disseminated gonorrhea infections (DGI) may occur. Complicated gonorrhea in the female may provide the picture of acute gonococcal salpingitis with fever, chills, and abdominal pain which often occurs in the perimenstrual intervals. Pelvic inflammatory disease, with residual effects which include infertility, may be a genuine concern for the adolescent female. In the male, gonorrhea may lead to a discharge, urinary symptoms, pain in the perineal, suprapubic or inguinal areas. This may reflect prostatic or seminal vesicle involvement with contiguous spread in the male. Fever may also be present. Epididymitis may be manifested by pain and swelling of the scrotum.

UNCOMPLICATED GONORRHEA

As mentioned above, the endocervix is the primary site of gonorrhea infections in the female. It is frequently asymptomatic. Cultures should be taken from the endocervix or other sites if the clinical history suggests the likelihood of infection in the rectum, pharynx, or urethra. The vagina and introital glands may be infrequent sites of primary infections.

Primary anorectal gonorrhea can occur from anal intercourse in ho-

Table 7.2 Expression of Gonococcal Infection in Women

Asymptomatic Infection	endocervix
	rectum
	pharynx
Symptomatic Infection	cervicitis
	cystitis
	proctitis
	pharyngitis
Local Complications	endometritis
	salpingitis
	bartholinitis
	peritonitis
	perihepatitis
Disseminated Gonococcal Infection	arthritis
	dermatitis
	endocarditis
	meningitis

mosexual or heterosexual relations. One report indicates that 36% of a group of women with endocervical gonorrhea had positive rectal cultures (Dans 1975). Anorectal gonorrhea is usually asymptomatic but may present with rectal burning, tenesmus, discharge, or bleeding. Kreutner cites a case from the literature in which an adolescent female developed anorectal gonorrhea from intercourse only between her thighs (Kreutner and Hollingsworth 1978).

Presumably with the increase in fellatio as a common form of sexual activity, the oropharynx has become a more common source of infection for girls. Oropharyngeal gonorrhea is said to be acquired primarily by fellatio and infrequently by cunnilingus (Handsfield 1978). Weisner reports that up to 20% of women and homosexual men who have gonorrhea at some site have an oral infection as well (1973 and 1975). Kissing and autoinnoculation from genital or anal sites may be a less common form of transmission. Handsfield reports that oral gonorrhea is usually asymptomatic but acute tonsillitis or pharyngitis may occur (1978). When culturing the oral area, proper microbiological fermentation studies must be done to distinguish the gonococcal *Neisseria* from other normal oropharyngeal *Neisseria*.

COMPLICATED GONORRHEA

Complicated gonorrhea may take various forms (table 7.2). The most significant is an ascending endocervical infection of the female which results in pelvic inflammatory disease (PID) with endometritis, salpingitis, or peritonitis. It is said to occur in 20% of female gonorrhea cases (Eschenbach and Holmes 1975). The spread may have repercussions in the form of infertility, ectopic pregnancy, or chronic pelvic pain. Such complications may require surgery.

The gonococcal spread is thought to usually occur with the onset of menses. Presumably the alkaline menstrual blood acts as a good culture medium and paves the way for the endometritis. On the other hand, Eschenbach, Harnisch and Holmes (1977) believe that pelvic inflammatory disease of nongonococcal origin may develop throughout the menstrual cycle. If a woman has asymptomatic gonorrhea and has an abortion or IUD insertion, spread to the upper tubes may be facilitated.

The major symptom of pelvic inflammatory disease is lower abdominal pain. Other common complaints are vaginal discharge, intermenstrual bleeding, menorrhagia, dysuria, or other urinary symptoms. Eschenbach and Holmes report that fever is present in only a third of the cases and chills may occur. Leukocytosis and an elevated erythrocyte sedimentation rate may occur in approximately half of the cases (1975). Physical examination usually reveals cervical discharge and tenderness. Bimanual examination may elicit uterine and bilateral adnexal tenderness, often with adnexal masses. Cultures during the acute phase of the endocervical disease are usually positive.

If the disease progresses to a subacute state, the symptoms may be less acute with dull pain or pressure predominating. The findings may be unilateral and the leukocytosis may be absent. Moreover, cultures at this stage may be negative if the disease is past four weeks (Litt and co-workers 1974). Other complications are acute perihepatitis (Fitz-Hugh-Curtis syndrome) and peritonitis. Litt and co-workers have found the former to be more common in adolescents. Pleuritic and right upper quadrant pain may accompany the perihepatitis. Chronic salpingitis is apt to follow inadequate treatment. Physical examination may reveal unilateral tubal masses. The consequences for pregnancy may be serious. Eschenbach and co-workers (1975) report that *N. gonorrhoeae* causes from 50 to 80% of the cases of pelvic inflammatory disease— more of the initial episodes, and less of the recurrent ones. Nongonococcal pelvic inflammatory disease may be caused by a variety of individual organisms which under normal conditions are thought to be nonpathogenic—i.e., normal cervicovaginal flora such as aerobic and anaerobic streptococci, *Bacterioides fragilis,* and coliforms. Presumably these organisms are not transmitted sexually, yet the pelvic inflammatory disease in which they are found is associated with the same social and personal factors that are predictive of sexually transmitted diseases (Handsfield 1978). It is unknown whether these organisms enhance the development of other sexually transmitted microflora which might be the culprits. McCormick and co-workers (1979) have suggested that *Chlamydia trachomatis,* an intracellular parasite (to be discussed later) is a cause of certain genital diseases such as nongonococcal urethritis, pelvic inflammatory disease, and epididymitis, in addition to its previously known role in trachoma, lymphogranuloma venereum and inclusion conjunctivitis. The roles of *T. mycoplasma, Mycoplasma hominis,* and cytomegalovirus (CMV) in pelvic inflammatory disease are less certain but under study (Eschenbach and Holmes 1975).

DISSEMINATED GONOCOCCAL INFECTION (DGI)

The most common expression of disseminated gonococcal infection is the arthritis-dermatitis syndrome. Patients with this entity present with arthropathy, dermatitis, or both. In one large DGI study by Handsfield, Weisner and Holmes (1973) a majority of the patients had the combined presentation; 22% had arthropathy alone; and 7% had dermatitis alone. One patient had endocarditis.

Probably the most common cause of acute infectious arthritis in adolescents and young adults is from disseminated gonococcal infections. Although some estimates are lower, it is often said that 1 to 3% of infected gonococcal patients may develop arthritic complications (Handsfield, Weisner and Holmes 1973). Females appear unusually susceptible to DGI and 75 to 90% of the cases are found in this sex. Kreutner and Hollingsworth (1978) report that pregnancy may predispose to arthritic complications.

A variety of host factors including menstruation, pregnancy, complement deficiencies, liver disease and pharyngeal gonococcal infections may predispose to the dissemination of the bacteria (Handsfield 1975, 1977). Dermatitis is usually found on the extremities, and lesions may be erythematous, papular, petechial, pustular or even necrotic or hemorrhagic. Polyarticular arthritis is usually asymmetric and may include tenosynovitis as well. The wrists, knees, ankles, and small joints of the hands and feet are primarily involved. Handsfield describes the typical rash described as scant with no more than 5 to 30 eruptions and usually located on the extremities (1978). Both the arthritis and dermatitis are thought to be due to the hematogenous spread of the bacteria to the skin and synovium. The multiplicity of findings reinforces the notion that DGI is a systemic disease. Fever, chills, myalgia, and leukocytosis may be prominent. The primary site of infection in both women and men with DGI is usually asymptomatic. Handsfield notes that pelvic inflammatory disease and disseminated gonococcal infections rarely occur simultaneously (1978). Gonococcal endocarditis and meningitis are rare manifestations of gonococcal infections.

TRANSMISSION AND OTHER ASPECTS

Several authors state that the risk of a female's acquiring gonorrhea from an infected male is 80 to 90%, whereas the male has an estimated 22% risk of being infected by a female with gonorrhea (Felton 1973; Holmes, Johnson and Trostle 1970; Rigg 1975). In suspected cases, gonococcal pharyngitis should be considered in adolescent girls who admit to fellatio and in adolescent boys, even those without symptoms.

Although asymptomatic gonorrhea may be present in 80 to 90% of females, Handsfield states that the actual percentage may be lower (1978). He feels that if proper investigations are done, a truer figure for the asymptomatic state of endocervical gonorrhea in women would be 50 to 60%. He also points out that milder signs and symptoms such as vaginal discharge or dysuria may not be attributed to the gonorrheal infection.

There is increasing evidence to suggest that the male may frequently be asymptomatic also. Hart mentions that as recently as 1972 Lucas, an expert venereologist, wrote, "Tests of cure are ordinarily not necessary in males, since the cessation of symptoms is usually tied to cure of gonorrhea." More recently, Gilstrap (1977) suggests an absolute prevalence of asymptomatic gonorrhea in men of 1 to 1.5% in sexually active groups such as overseas military personnel. Yet other literature reports indicate that male contacts of women with documented gonococcal pelvic inflammatory disease or DGI may have a 40% asymptomatic rate (Handsfield 1974; Portnoy 1974; Gilstrap and co-workers 1977). Crawford and co-workers (1977) estimate 2 to 10% of gonorrhea-infected men may never become symptomatic. Some of the differences in symptom expression may be due to the geographical distribution of certain gonococcal strains, which are less likely to cause symptoms. Yet, as implied above, other men may go through a symptomatic stage to a quiescent asymptomatic phase without cure. Documentation of these events in male adolescents is not available, but it is likely that in the younger age group, the same disease dynamics occur. The implications for the sexually active female partner are obvious. Indeed, as a general precept, it can be said that a gonococcal infection is usually acquired from individuals who are insufficiently symptomatic to have sought medical attention (Handsfield 1977). Understanding the importance of the occult, asymptomatic or noncomplaining pool of gonococcal patients cannot be overemphasized. All contacts of persons found to have gonorrhea should be examined and cultured regardless of the presence or absence of symptoms.

DIAGNOSIS

Gonorrhea is commonly diagnosed by the utilization of microbiological techniques such as Gram-stained smears, bacteriological culture, or by the direct fluorescent antibody test. Accuracy of test results for some of these methods varies according to such factors as whether the tested material is from male or female patients and how carefully and promptly the specimens are processed. The more recently developed serologic assays still have limitations for individual diagnosis, but may have some utility in epidemiologic screening.

Gram-stained smears, when positive, can be highly sensitive and specific under one condition—if tested on symptomatic men with urethral exudate. Test accuracy depends upon technical expertise in detecting the typical Gram-negative "kidney bean" shapes within the polymorphonuclear leukocytes. If a smear is unequivocal (either positive or negative) and the examiner is a highly experienced technician, culture confirmation may not be necessary although it is always desirable (Handsfield 1978). In almost every other clinical case (male or female), culture is mandatory. Gram-stained smears for gonococci are usually very insensitive diagnostic indicators, giving 50% false negatives in most infection circumstances according to Handsfield (1978). In females, positive smears may result from other forms of *Neisseria* found in the vagina. Suspected gonorrhea in rectal, cutaneous, or pharyngeal sites also require culture in addition to smears.

The commonly used Thayer-Martin selective culture medium tends to inhibit overgrowth of gonococcus from contaminating bacteria or fungi (Kellogg 1977). However, some reports indicate that the antibiotics used in this medium may occasionally inhibit *N. gonorrhoeae* as well. Therefore, many authorities suggest that nonselective media (e.g., "chocolate" agar) should always be used when culturing difficult-to-grow gonorrhea. Such gonococcal infections include those in blood, cerebrospinal fluid, and skin lesions. All gonococcal cultures are grown in a 5 to 10% CO_2 atmosphere which facilitates the growth of the diplococci. An alkaline pH and a temperature of 35 to 36° are vital. Transport media such as Transgrow may be satisfactory but usually give lesser yields than standard selective media (Kellogg 1977; Martin and Lester 1971). Their use should be restricted to situations in which there may be a delay of 12 hours or more before specimen processing. Because of its fragile nature, special care in culturing *Neisseria* is mandatory.

For men, it is best to culture from a small calcium alginate-tipped swab which has been inserted 2 to 4 cm into the urethra. Handsfield (1978) states that culturing the residual of the first 10 to 15 mm of a voided urine specimen after centrifugation may also be done.

All pregnant, adolescent girls should be cultured initially at the time of the first prenatal examination, again, if exposed to gonorrhea, and in the last month of gestation. For women, a single endocervical culture is usually 80–90% accurate (Kellogg 1977). Repeated endocervical cultures or a simultaneous rectal culture may improve the chances of recovering the organisms somewhat—probably by 5 to 10% (Bhattacharyya, Jephcott and Morton 1973). Thus, the cost/benefit ratio is not unusually high when culturing repeatedly or from other sites in the female. However, depending on the patient's sexual behavior or clinical picture, repeated cultures, or cultures from nonendocervical locations may be important. If bacteremia is considered, multiple blood cultures must be done because the bacteremia may be intermittent (Holmes, Weisner and Pedersen 1971). Posttreatment culturing is discussed in the treatment section.

Specific, direct, fluorescent antibody testing from material from an infected site is sometimes utilized. For skin lesions, culture or smears may be positive in less than 10% of the cases; whereas the fluorescent antibody test has been reported to be positive in as high as 59 to 88% of the cases (Barr and Danielson 1971; Tronca and co-workers 1974).

TREATMENT

In 1974 the United States Public Health Service made specific recommendations for the treatment of gonorrhea. Penicillin was the drug of choice for uncomplicated gonorrhea. Now the Public Health Service has expanded their recommendations to four drug regimens which can be used for the treatment of uncomplicated gonorrhea: aqueous procaine penicillin G; tetracycline hydrochloride; ampicillin; or amoxicillin (Center for Disease Control 1979).

Aqueous procaine penicillin G, 4,800,000 units, injected intramuscularly (IM) at two sites with 1 gm of probenecid by mouth is preferred in patients requiring a single-dose treatment. Probenecid prolongs the blood level of penicillin. With this regimen the cure rate should be 95% or more (Jacobs and Kraus 1975). This method is also preferred in men with anorectal infection. Tetracycline hydrochloride, 0.5 gm by mouth four times a day for five days (total dose 10.0 gm), may be used. This treatment has some added advantages. Fewer cases of postgonococcal urethritis result in men on tetracycline. The treatment may also eliminate coexisting chlamydial infections in both men and women, an organism thought to be involved in some cases of urethritis. However, tetracycline hydrochloride is not recommended for pregnant women because of possible toxicity to mother and fetus. Also monilial overgrowth occurs in certain women. A slightly less efficient single dose program is ampicillin, 3.5 gm or amoxicillin, 3.0 gm with 1 gm probenecid by mouth.

Allergic reaction to these drugs should always be considered and measures for proper counteraction must be on hand. Penicillin- or probenecid-sensitive individuals should be treated with oral tetracycline as above. Patients intolerant to tetracycline may be treated with spectinomycin hydrochloride, 2.0 gm, in a single IM injection. Patients with incubating, but not with established syphilis, should be cured by all the above schedules except spectinomycin.

All patients should be recultured from the infected site(s) three to seven days after the completion of treatment. Also cultures should be obtained from the anal canal of all women treated for gonorrhea. Pregnant women should be recultured in the last month of pregnancy. Pelvic inflammatory disease (PID) may be treated with 0.5 gm tetracycline orally four times a day for ten days. However, this treatment should not be used for pregnant patients. Another regimen that may be used is aqueous procaine penicillin, 4,800,000 U IM; ampicillin, 3.5 gm, or amoxicillin, 3.0 gm, each with probenecid 1.0 gm. Either treatment is followed by ampicillin, 0.5 gm, or amoxicillin, 0.5 gm orally four times a day for ten days.

For DGI patients there are several equally effective treatment schedules. Aqueous crystalline penicillin G 10,000,000 U IV per day until clinical improvement occurs, followed by ampicillin, 0.5 gm, four times a day, to complete seven days of antibiotic treatment may be used. Other regimens may include ampicillin, 3.5 gm, or amoxicillin, 3.0 gm orally, each with probenecid, 1.0 gm, followed by ampicillin, 0.5 gm, or amoxicillin, 0.5 gm four times a day, orally for seven days. Other alternative courses are tetracycline, 0.5 gm orally four times a day for seven days; spectomycin, 2.0 gm IM twice a day for three days; or erythromycin, 0.5 gm orally four times a day for seven days. It should be noted that pharyngeal infections are difficult to treat and do not seem to adequately respond to ampicillin, probenecid, or spectinomycin.

Relative resistance of gonorrhea to the various penicillins has seemingly reached a plateau in recent years, and Handsfield has noted it to be closely linked to tetracycline resistance (1978). Thus, penicillin or ampicillin treatment failures should be given spectinomycin, 2.0 gm IM. The more recent emergence of a new form of resistance has caused concern. Penicillinase-producing *N. gonorrhoeae* (PPNG) has been identified in this country although not yet an alarming number of times (Center for Disease Control 1978). However, the future of our past complacency is far from certain. In some areas of the Far East the number of cases with penicillinase-producing gonorrhea organisms has already increased to such a substantial minority (approximately 10%) that penicillin can no longer be used as a treatment of choice (McCormick 1979). It is unrealistic to think that the United States will be permanently spared from this changing resistance picture. The drug of choice in such instances is spectinomycin, 2 gm IM. Gonococci are very rarely resistant to this drug, but if they are, the Center for Disease Control indicates that a treatment with cefoxitin, 2.0 gm IM, with probenecid 1.0 gm, by mouth, may be used (1979).

Infection of the newborn can be prevented by a 1% solution of silver nitrate or antibiotic drops (depending on the state laws) into the baby's conjunctival sac immediately after birth. For further details or treatment of other gonococcal entities, consult the Center for Disease Control pamphlet, "Morbidity and Mortality" Jan. 19, 1979.

Syphilis

In 1978 the total number of reported cases for all ages of primary and secondary syphilis was 21,676 (fig. 7.2) ("Medical News" 1979). It should be emphasized that reported cases of gonorrhea may be considerably fewer than actual, or even diagnosed, cases. Syphilis in the heterosexual adolescent population is said to account for only 0.5% of all

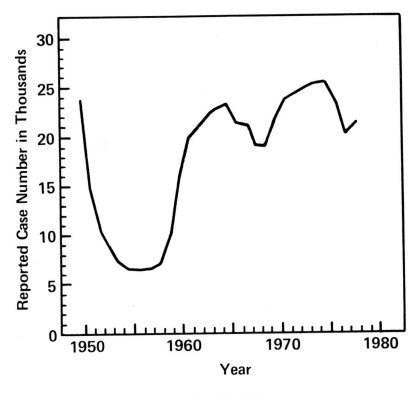

Fig. 7.2 *Primary and Secondary Syphilis,*
United States 1950 – 1978

venereal diseases (Stern and McKenzie 1975). In our random study of
the prevalence of venereal disease in 740 pregnant, indigent adolescents
we found a positive serology for syphilis in 5 (0.7%) (Mumford, Smith
and Goldfarb 1977). The male homosexual may be ten times more
likely to develop syphilis than his heterosexual counterpart. Although
some localities report higher rates, in 1976, 46% of the national cases
of infectious syphilis occurred in homosexual males (Henderson 1977).
If bisexual activity is increasing to the extent that some claim, the female may also face some additional risk as well.

The syphilis spirochetes are slender corkscrew organisms which occur
only in humans. Syphilis can be transferred vertically from mother to
fetus after the third or fourth month of pregnancy (congenital syphilis).

Syphilis can be deduced or detected by dark-field microscopic examination, by an immunofluorescent staining technique and by various ser-

ologic tests. Since serologic testing is most commonly used for screening and follow-up, special attention should be given to these tests and to their ability to elicit "false positives."

Two general kinds of serologic tests for the diagnosis of syphilis are used. The first is a nontreponemal test which uses antigens of normal tissue (e.g., beef heart cardiolipin) to measure nonspecific reagin antibodies which are developed by the patient. Examples of these assays are the flocculation (VDRL and Hinton) tests and the complement fixation (Kolmer, Wasserman) tests. Among these, the VDRL is the most widely employed. False positives can occur in a variety of conditions such as infectious mononucleosis, collagen diseases, malaria, certain febrile illnesses, drug addiction, and perhaps pregnancy.

The most widely used, specific treponemal antibody test is the FTA-ABS assay (the fluorescent treponemal antibody absorption test). This procedure measures the patient's specific antibody response with antigen from killed *T. pallidum*. It is very sensitive and rarely gives false positives. When it does, as in unusual cases of lupus erythematosis or diseases with abnormal globulin formation, another test, the *Treponema pallidum* immobilization (TPI) test, can be used (Rudolph and Duncan 1975).

CLINICAL ASPECTS

Primary Syphilis

In its early stages syphilis may be unrecognized. The incubation period is 10 to 90 days (average of three to four weeks) before a chancre (sometimes chancres) arises. The lesion is usually a painless, superficial ulcer with a clear base and a raised, firm, indurated margin located in the genitalia, pharynx or perianal areas. Chancre locations even on toes have also been reported. In the female the primary chancre may not always be apparent because of its location on the cervix or in the vagina. Regional lymph nodes may be enlarged but nontender. If secondary infection occurs, pain may become prominent. Healing usually occurs without treatment although scarring may develop, particularly if secondary infection has occurred.

The blood VDRL will usually become positive one to two weeks after the primary lesion is noted (primary syphilis). However, Kreutner and Hollingsworth report that 25% of patients with primary syphilis will have a nonreactive VDRL at this early stage (1978). Competent darkfield microscopy or immunofluorescent examination of material from the chancre can demonstrate the offending organisms in over 95% of the cases. Other lesions, such as lymphogranuloma venereum, genital herpes, or neoplasms must be distinguished from the syphilitic chancre.

Secondary Syphilis

Secondary syphilis may follow untreated, or inadequately, treated infections. It has a variable incubation period of a few weeks up to six months. *T. pallidum* may produce systemic signs and symptoms—fever, myalgia, headaches, loss of appetite, a generalized maculopapular skin rash, mucous membrane lesions including patches and ulcers, condylomata lata from weeping papules in moist skin areas, and generalized nontender lymphadenopathy. Meningitis, hepatitis, nephritis, arthritis, alopecia, osteitis, or iritis may occur. Because of the long incubation period and the variety of manifestations, the diagnosis of secondary syphilis may not be associated with the occurrence of the primary lesion. The great variety of possible signs and symptoms also may present a problem. Because of its myriad of symptoms, the venerated Sir William Osler described syphilis as ''the Great Imitator''.

The most common manifestations are those of skin and mucosa. Although skin eruptions may be widely disseminated, skin lesions on the palms and soles of the feet should always arouse suspicion of the diagnosis. Skin and mucous-membrane lesions are highly infectious at this stage, and material from them usually reveals organisms by dark-field immunofluorescent examination.

Blood serologic tests for syphilis are almost always positive in the second state. Cerebrospinal fluid (CSF) may show transient pleocytosis and elevated protein, although only 5% of the fluids examined will elicit a positive serological reaction for syphilis. Laboratory findings associated with hepatitis and nephritis may be prominent.

Latent (hidden) Syphilis

This form of syphilis is the ''sleeping'' phase which occurs after the subsidence of secondary symptoms and before the appearance of tertiary ones. If symptoms recur in the first three to five years after primary infection (so-called ''relapsing'' syphilis), the stage is defined as early latency; if after five years, the latent phase. During the latent phase, positive serology persists. It should be noted that transplacental transmission to the fetus can probably take place at almost any phase in which infectious processes are active.

Late (tertiary) Syphilis

Late lesions may represent, in part, a hypersensitivity reaction of the body. In the "benign" late syphilitic form, there may be a relatively rapid, localized, gummatous reaction of the tissue which usually responds quickly to appropriate chemotherapy.

The second form, however, is more ominous. The clinical picture is one of an insidious, diffuse inflammation, which characteristically involves the central nervous system (CNS) and large arteries. Gummas are most often found in long bones and skin, but can be present in almost any organ. Neurosyphilis represents 15 to 20% of late syphilis lesions which are progressive, disabling and sometimes lethal to the patient. They occur as (1) asymptomatic neurosyphilis in which only laboratory changes of the CSF are noted, (2) meningovascular syphilis, (3) tabes dorsalis, with the typical wide-based gait, and (4) general paresis.

Although late syphilis is not an immediate concern to the adolescent, Luxon, Lees and Greenwood point out that there is still some question as to whether adequate treatment of early syphilis always prevents neurosyphilitic complications (1979). They suggest that despite the best therapy, some persons will develop these late complications for reasons unknown. Perhaps this uncertainty should be made known to the adolescent sexual activist.

PREGNANCY AND SYPHILIS

Needless to say, all pregnant women and girls should have a serologic test for syphilis at the time of the first prenatal visit. In women suspected of being at risk for syphilis, this should always be repeated in the third trimester even if negative initially.

Active syphilis in pregnancy, whether preexisting or acquired during pregnancy, is a serious disease with great potential hazard to the fetus. Some authorities have suggested that pregnancy may decrease the severity of the symptomatic infection for the mother, but the risk to her baby remains very real. As years pass from the time the mother acquired her infection, the likelihood of the infant's showing signs of the disease or a positive serology diminishes.

If active, untreated syphilis is present before conception, the usual result is that of midtrimester abortion or fetal death. If syphilis is present at conception or early in pregnancy, the fetus is usually afflicted, may be aborted, or premature; and if syphilis is acquired late, the infant may be unaffected or be infected, aborted or stillborn. The reason for the relatively delayed (midsemester) abortion in untreated mothers is that for the first 16 to 18 weeks of pregnancy, the fetus is protected from the maternal spirochetes by certain placental cells which atrophy at about four months before allowing transplacental passage of the treponema. Fortunately, adequate treatment, even when administered late in pregnancy, usually prevents congenital syphilis in almost all cases.

A practical clinical consideration should be emphasized when dealing with pregnant adolescents. They characteristically come late for prenatal care. In our large clinic service—we have confirmed the reports of Kreutner and Hollingsworth (1978)—adolescents usually wait 20 to 28 weeks. Thus, the attending medical team must be aware that the time for diagnosis, treatment, and follow-up of pregnant syphilis patients (as well as those with other venereal diseases) is foreshortened.

CONGENITAL SYPHILIS

The fetus or newborn infected with congenital syphilis may present with varied clinical manifestations. Factors which seem to influence the outcome include the time of original maternal infection, the degree and dosage of transplacental treponemal passage, the time of transmission (whether it occurs early—usually transmission does not occur before 16 to 18 weeks—or late in pregnancy), perhaps the immunocompetence of the mother and baby, and the adequacy of treatment, if given.

The classical picture of intrauterine infection is that of an infant with so-called syphilitic pemphigus with large blebs, particularly over the soles and palms, which are filled with seropurulent fluid containing swarms of spirochetes. The skin lesions may also be erythematous or hemorrhagic, and the skin may have a brownish café au lait tint or icteric cast. The mucous membranes can be inflamed with nasal congestion and discharge producing the so-called "syphilitic snuffles." Anemia, enlargement of liver, spleen, and lymph nodes are common in severe cases. Characteristic bony changes may show on x-rays, and abnormalities of the eyes and central nervous system may be present.

Some infants are apparently normal at birth yet may develop early infectious congenital syphilis before two years of age. The symptoms may not develop for weeks, months, or until after a year. The early and late forms of congenital syphilis may be occult and thus missed unless infants at risk are carefully followed. The late, noninfectious, congenital syphilis picture may not become apparent until after two years of age. The clinical picture in this delayed expression may resemble some aspects of the adult disease with neural involvement, deafness and the like. But, because the child is a growing and changing organism, certain classical stigmata appear—Hutchinson's teeth, mulberry molars, frontal skull boss-ing, saddle nose, high palatal arch, and saber shins.

Infants born of mothers suspected of, or shown to have, syphilis should be evaluated immediately after birth, at three to six weeks, monthly until six months, and then every three months until at least a year. If neurosyphilis is present the following should be extended to at least three years with reevaluation, if stable at six month intervals.

Even if the clinical picture appears benign in suspected cases, an in-dication of syphilitic involvement at birth can be gathered if the cord IgM level is 20 mgm/100 ml. If the cord VDRL titer is higher than the mother's, infection should be presumed. If the mother is VDRL posi-tive, the baby's VDRL will also be positive due to transplacental pas-sage of antibody. The FTS-ABS specific treponemal test should also be used for confirmation. Infants from syphilitic-risk situations who have a negative VDRL and no evaluation of cord IgM should be followed with serial serologic determinations. However, because of the dire con-sequences to the baby and the frequent difficulty in following the ado-lescent mother and her infant, most authorities would agree that infants of mothers at risk for syphilis should be treated if the mother's status is unknown, uncertain, inadequately treated, or treated with agents other than penicillin. Thus, even nonsymptomatic infants of syphilitic mothers should probably be treated if adequate postnatal check-ups cannot be assured.

TREATMENT OF SYPHILIS

The drug of choice for all stages of syphilis is injectable penicillin (CDC 1976). It is highly effective in early infections and variably so, in late stages. Hypersensitivity to penicillin should always be determined and preparation to counteract possible reactions always ready. Benzathine penicillin G, 2,400,000 U (given IM one half dose into each buttock), or IM procaine penicillin G with 2% aluminum monosterate (PAM),

117

2,400,000 U first dose, followed by two 1,200,000 U at each of 2 visits at 3 day intervals are recommended (CDC 1976). Procaine penicillin G (aqueous) can also be used but requires daily injections of 600,000 U for 8 days—a total of 4,800,000 U. Patients allergic to penicillin can be given oral tetracycline or erythromycin, 500 mg four times a day for 15 days (total dose 30 to 40 gm), for early forms of syphilis. If the disease is over one year in duration, twice the above-mentioned alternate doses should be given. Moreover, because experience with these alternate schedules is somewhat limited, follow-up should be especially careful.

Latent syphilis can be treated with benzathine penicillin G, 2,400,000 U IM weekly for 3 weeks. With neurological involvement, benzathine penicillin G, 1,200,000 U, IM every 7 days is recommended.

The treatment of congenital syphilis generally follows the recommendations of the Center for Disease Control, although some authorities have made modifications. Without cerebrospinal fluid involvement, 50,000 U of benzathine penicillin G/kg IM in a single dose is given. With neurological disease, an aqueous crystalline penicillin G, 50,000 U/kg, IM or IV in two divided doses a day for 14 to 21 days, or aqueous procaine penicillin G, 50,000 U/kg, IM daily for 14 to 21 days, is recommended. The minimum treatment on these daily schedules is 10 days, and most physicians opt for the two to three week schedules. However, it should be recognized that in newborns the problem of small muscle mass and fragile veins make parenteral administration a formidable task.

The late forms of congenital syphilis should receive 2,400,000 U of benzathide penicillin G IM weekly for four weeks. Alternate treatments range from 600,000 to 2,000,000 U/day of aqueous penicillin G for 10 to 15 days given parenterally.

Treatment for syphilis in pregnancy is determined by the penicillin regimen appropriate for the stage of syphilis of the patient. Treatment of late syphilis is not germane to a discussion of the adolescent's clinical picture because late syphilis does not develop during adolescence.

ADDITIONAL COMMENTS ON TREATMENT

It should be stressed that today's recommended treatment of gonorrhea is 4,800,000 U of IM aqueous procaine penicillin G. However, this dosage will not eliminate established primary syphilis in patients but will ablate incubating syphilis. Clinical follow-up and periodic quantitative

VDRL determinations should be done for at least one year (at 3, 6 and 12 months) in all primary syphilis patients. All other patients should have similar observations for two or more years.

Primary syphilis patients with positive serology, properly treated, should revert to a negative VDRL state within two years. However, 25% of patients with adequately treated secondary syphilis will have a VDRL two years later (Kreutner and Hollingsworth 1978). Patient follow-up in secondary syphilis patients should not be abandoned until there is no clinical evidence of disease activity and the serology reaction is persistently negative or at a fixed, low level (Rudolph and Duncan 1975).

Treatment of local syphilitic lesions is usually not needed. Infants with infectious syphilis should be isolated. Patients at any stage of infectious syphilis should not be sexually active until treatment renders them non-infectious. All cases of syphilis should be reported to the appropriate Public Health officials so that contacts can be identified and investigated. Persons exposed to infectious syphilis three months prior to treatment should be given the antibiotic therapy for early syphilis.

No vaccine for syphilis is yet available although research efforts continue. Condom intercourse, if occlusive, may give some protection to covered parts, but not to unsheathed areas.

Both sexes should wash exposed areas vigorously with soap and water as promptly as possible after sexual intercourse. Since the use of several forms of therapy in the treatment of gonorrhea is increasing, and they may not be effective in eradicating incubating syphilis, patients treated for gonorrhea should have a serologic test for syphilis three to six months after the completion of their gonorrhea treatment.

Although meaningful statistics are not readily available, the following seems to be an acceptable assessment of the course and prognosis of syphilis cases. If no treatment is given, approximately one-third of the persons infected with syphilis may undergo a spontaneous cure, about one-third will remain in a latent phase, and about one-third will develop the serious consequences of late syphilis.

Herpesviruses

The herpesviruses as a group deserve attention and concern. The family of herpesviruses constitutes a group of at least 25 DNA viruses. Although 5 herpesviruses are known to infect humans, herpes simplex virus (types

1 and 2) and cytomegalovirus are the ones which have documented venereal importance. The latter is known to cross the human placenta and may cause damage, frequently severe, to the developing fetus. Some question also exists whether herpes simplex virus, transmitted transplacentally, may in rare cases cause congenital malformations.

The other important human herpesvirus types are the varicella-zoster (chicken pox) and the EB (Epstein-Barr) viruses. The latter has been linked to infectious mononucleosis and perhaps certain human malignancies such as Burkitt's lymphoma and some nasopharyngeal carcinomas.

HERPES SIMPLEX VIRUSES (TYPES 1 AND 2)

One of the more ominous characteristics of the herpes simplex group is that infections may remain latent for a variable—often great—length of time, perhaps even for life. Not uncommonly, acute periods alternate with quiescent ones even though the person has circulating antibodies. Exacerbations may be associated with specific physical or emotional stresses or with immunosuppressive events. Lesions tend to recur in the same areas.

With the use of molecular and serological testing, the herpesviruses have been classified into two distinct groups (types 1 and 2). Type 1 herpesvirus characteristically causes "cold sores" and "fever blisters." In the United States and in many other countries, herpes genitalis is usually caused by a herpesvirus type 2 infection. This affliction is widespread and appears to be increasing so rapidly that it is now considered by many authorities to be one of the major venereal diseases of the world. The true prevalence is unknown but may be as high as 3% of patients in low socioeconomic circumstances. A report on the prevalence of genital viral infections in adolescent girls from a venereal disease clinic indicated that 5 to 12% were afflicted with herpes simplex virus and 10% with cytomegalovirus (Duenas et al. 1972; Jeannson and Molin 1974; Jordon et al. 1973). In another study of 100 sexually active females attending an adolescent clinic for nonvenereal reasons, the prevalence of herpes simplex virus was 3% and cytomegalovirus was 2% (Rauh, Brookman and Schiff 1977). Some reports suggest that adolescent females may account for 25 to 50% of all primary herpes genitalis infections (Nahmias and co-workers 1969; Stern and McKenzie 1975).

CLINICAL PICTURE

Herpes simplex virus type 1 has multiple clinical expressions including (1) acute herpetic gingivostomatitis, aphthous stomatitis, or Vincent's stomatitis, (2) herpes labialis (cold sores or fever blisters), (3) keratoconjunctivitis and (4) truly devastating diseases such as Kaposi's varicelliform eruption and meningoencephalitis—both of which may be fatal.

Herpes simplex virus type 2 is primarily responsible for genital herpes (herpes progenitalis) and neonatal herpes. The latter may cause a severe, generalized, often fatal, illness. Even neonatal survivors of severe infections may suffer permanent brain damage. The newborn is believed to acquire the virus during transit through the birth canal. Thus, women with known genital lesions are now often delivered by cesarian section, although this is not always an effective prophylactic. The relationship of herpes simplex virus type 2 to cervical cancer will be discussed later.

The primary herpes genitalis lesions may be distinct or extensive and involve the perineal area, anus, vagina and endocervix. Generalized reactions such as fever, malaise, pain, dysuria, discharge, vaginal bleeding, and tender bilateral inguinal lymphadenopathy may be present. Individual genital lesions, which may be multiple or clustering, develop as shallow, ulcerating vesicles with edema, especially on mucous membranes or moist areas. The genital lesions are susceptible to secondary infections, particularly by the fungus, *Candida albicans* but also by streptococci and staphylococci. The incubation period may be short (three to seven days), and the acute episodes may last three to six weeks with recurrent exacerbations persisting only about a week and with lesser symptoms.

If genital herpes develops during pregnancy, the problem is serious. The risk to the fetus after 32 weeks is about 10%. If the herpes genitalis is present at delivery, only cesarean section within four hours of the rupture of the membranes can significantly reduce the over 40% afflicication rate for the neonate.

Diagnosis of genital herpes may be presumed by the clinical picture and an examination of smears from lesions appropriately stained and viewed under a regular microscope or by electron microscopy. Scrapings and biopsies may reveal characteristic ''ground glass'' cellular nuclear findings, small intranuclear vacuoles, acidophilic inclusion bodies and small scattered basophilic particles. The only definitive way to diagnose herpesvirus infection is to isolate the virus by tissue culture. Inoculation of specimens into tissue culture allows virus growth which can then be identified by appropriate virological testing. A provisional diagnosis can usually be made in 24 hours. Good culturing technique and fast, careful transport of specimens is necessary for a high culturing-success rate.

Good serologic tests exist for detecting a variety of antibodies naturally developed against the herpes viruses, viral subcomponents or cell by-products. If significant titer changes occur, serial determinations can establish the presence of active infections or reinfections. Perhaps more importantly, such antibody assays allow epidemiologic screening and investigations seeking to link the virus with specific diseases such as cervical cancer.

Herpes simplex virus type 1 is probably more constantly present in humans than is any other known virus. Primary infection appears to occur in infancy or childhood with immunity developing which usually keeps the infection quiescent although in a carrier stage. By adulthood 70 to 90% of persons have antiherpes simplex type 1 antibodies.

Type 2 herpes simplex virus is usually spread venereally and thus infection generally takes place after puberty. Antibody incidence seems to be related to sexual exposure. The prevalence rates of antibodies in normal women range from about 7% to above 20% (Catalano and Johnson 1971; Rawls, Tompkins and Melnick 1969). In women exposed to men with known herpesvirus infection, the prevalence leaps to almost 80% (Rawls and co-workers 1971).

One of the most important concerns about herpes simplex virus infections is its possible relationship with cervical cancer. In this country a variety of investigative techniques from cytology, virology, immunology, genetics and biochemistry have been developed, whose application suggests that herpes simplex virus type 2 infections are important in the etiology of human cervical cancer (Mumford, Kaufman and McCormick 1978). Most of the studies are circumstantial, but the evidence is beginning to be impressive.

American women with cervical carcinoma consistently have a significantly higher prevalence of antiherpes simplex virus type 2 antibodies than do matched controls. Other serological studies of herpesvirus dependent antigens, such as the AG-4 antigen of Aurelian, show a differential positive antibody pattern in cervical cancer patients when compared to control women (Aurelian and co-workers 1973). Recent biochemical and genetic footprinting studies of cervical tumors suggest the presence of the genome of herpesvirus type 2. However, it should be noted that in Japan the oncogenic agent may more often be the herpes simplex virus type 1 than type 2 (Kawana, Yoshino and Kasamatsu 1974). Antiherpesvirus type 1 antibodies are more commonly found in Japanese cervical cancer patients than type 2. Moreover, virologic or biochemical evidence of herpesvirus type 1 in cervical tumor material seems to be greater than in American women.

SPECULATIVE IMPLICATIONS OF HERPESVIRUS INFECTION

Recent findings increase the concern about possible long term effects of herpesvirus infections. Virus shedding by asymptomatic women, or by women who do not reveal any evidence of genital herpes disease despite careful examination, is now known to occur. Adam and co-workers (1979) observed herpes simplex virus shedding in 10% of asymptomatic women for periods up to 111 days after overt disease. A more recent follow-up by the same group (personal communication Adam 1979) has revealed that shedding may be persistent for even longer intervals.

Three women, free of apparent symptoms for periods up to 20 months, were cultured twice daily for one complete menstrual cycle. Herpes simplex virus type 2 was found to be present at one time or another during the cycle in all three women. If confirmed, the implications from this sort of finding could be profound when combined with what is already known about the virus in women. While more, well-controlled investigations are needed, the frequency of asymptomatic genital herpes in women is estimated by some authorities to be between 1 and 6%. It is also stated that approximately one-half of all women with clinical, overt, genital herpes will have recurrent episodes of the disease at regular intervals. The most immediate implication of this kind of persistent virus-host reservoir is for infection via sexual intercourse.

But, there are other concerns as well. If the viral shedding finding is a common one, it may make more understandable the important epidemiologic fact that newborns with herpes infections often have unknown sources of contamination. In one study of 156 newborns with herpesvirus infection, it was found that the source of infection could not be determined in 57% of the cases (Nahmias 1971). Perhaps more importantly, the findings must be considered within the context of some remarks by Rapp concerning the long term consequences of herpes infections and cancer (Rapp 1978). Rapp points out that the number of genital herpes cases is increasing dramatically, and that at the present time, the disease is incurable. This means the prevalence of the disease is cumulative in the population. The population harboring and spreading the disease continues to increase each year. Moreover, Rapp adds that in contrast to most venereal diseases, especially syphilis and gonorrhea in which cures are possible and adequate treatment removes the individual contagious element, the pattern of herpes infection is developing into a unique biomedical experiment. While Rapp mentions the importance of the phenomena to potential infections for neonates, he also adds another sobering thought:

> The human population is now engaged in a large scale program of venereal transmission of herpes simplex virus type 2, a study that no scientist could ethically conduct. An increase in cervical cancer in 15 to 20 years would strongly implicate this virus as the causative agent of this disease and would catalyse research designed to prevent or limit infection due to these viruses.

Thus, if these conjectures have merit, we may be fostering a biological time bomb—defusing it may be impossible after the fact. Since we know the disproportionate prevalence of herpesvirus infections in the adolescent and also have reason to believe that early initiation of intercourse (and perhaps multiple partners) may increase cancer risk, it is the young who may unknowingly be conducting this potentially tragic experiment. The repercussions from the possible interaction in the adolescent female of the events described above may have implications, not only for the medical community but for the educational, public health, and welfare sectors as well.

TREATMENT

The treatment of herpes genitalis is uncertain and often unsatisfactory and usually directed toward symptomatic relief. The time-honored remedies of sitz baths and astringent solutions give some comfort. Local analgesic ointments such as 2% lidocaine may limit intense pain, but should be used sparingly and for short periods (i.e., less than two weeks) to prevent sensitization. These topical ointments may be necessary during the vesiculation and ulceration stages. Topical (or systemic) corticosteroids should not be used. Local antibiotic application to prevent secondary infections are of questionable value. Since *Candida albicans* is a common secondary invader, some authorities recommend nystatin vaginal suppositories, prophylactically or therapeutically. A 10% solution of povo-dine iodine every 48 hours painted on the vagina, cervix, and unroofed vesicles on the vulva may be helpful. Twice daily douching with a po-vodine iodine solution followed by the same medication in a vaginal suppository at bedtime is sometimes recommended. However, it should be noted that some investigators believe douching may tend to spread the lesions. In vitro studies show povodine iodine to be lethal to this virus and provides the rationale that this approach might decrease the duration of the disease and prevent secondary infection. However, good clinical control studies are needed.

A variety of more exotic treatments has been tried. None has yielded excellent results despite some early promising reports. Perhaps the most publicized treatment has been the use of photodynamic dye inactivation of herpes virus by fluorescent or incandescent light after painting the lesions with compounds such as proflavin or neutral red dye (Wallis, Melnick and Kaufman 1972). The earlier positive results have been challenged and the current feeling is that this regimen may not be effec-tive (Myers and co-workers 1975). Moreover, there is the unsettled question as to whether the therapy might alter the virus-cell interaction in such a way as to enhance carcinogenesis. The novel approach of Myers and co-workers advocates direct applications of ether, known to be toxic to complete herpesvirus, to new lesions. Local BCG vaccine sensitization, topical antimetabolites, interferon, and substances known to stimulate interferon are currently being evaluated. Condom usage and postsexual washing may be somewhat helpful in avoiding virus transmission.

CYTOMEGALOVIRUS (CMV)

Cytomegalovirus, another member of the herpes family, appears to be sexually transmitted (Jordan 1973). It is responsible for the severe, and often fatal, disease of the fetus and newborn called cytomegalic inclusion disease. It is estimated that about 10,000 infants a year are afflicted.

Over 80% of adults over 35 years of age in this country have antibodies against CMV. Yet, cytomegalovirus is apparently another virus which is frequently found to exist in a carrier state in women. It is said that 6 to 8% of sexually active young females may have cytomegalovirus in their cervix (Montgomery, Youngblood and Mediaris 1971).

Cytomegalovirus has also been implicated in some cases of endometritis, cervicitis, pelvic inflammatory disease, and in the male, nonspecific urethritis (Eschenbach and Holmes 1975; Jordan and co-workers 1973; McCracken and D'Angostino 1974). No specific therapy is yet available, although experimental trials to search for effective remedies are continuing.

Beta-hemolytic Streptococci

GROUP B STREPTOCOCCUS

It has been recently appreciated that group B streptococcus infections may have venereal aspects. The genital locations of the bacteria can be important in its transmission. The organism is important because it is a rising cause of serious neonatal and young infant infections in the United States. Barton, Feigin and Lins (1973) have estimated that in this country 12,000 to 15,000 babies per year develop this disease. The infection in babies often takes severe, life-threatening forms: specticemia, pneumonia and meningitis. The mortality rate is believed to be about 50% of those afflicted. Of those who survive, as many as 50% may develop neurological sequelae.

Two forms of the disease are noted in infants, an early onset of less than five days and a late onset from ten days to four months of life (Baker and Kasper 1977). The rate of infections for the former is 3.0 to 4.2/1,000 live births and 0.5–1.0/1,000 live births for the latter. Twenty-five to 30% of pregnant women at delivery are said to be colonized by group B streptococcus. However, this situation is usually asymptomatic (Baker and Kasper 1977). Similar rates have been found for nursing personnel attending babies in the hospitals. However, in one study of nonpregnant college women reported by Baker, the prevalence of group B streptococcus was 7% in women with no history of sexual intercourse (1977). As in the babies, there appears to be an interaction in women of host-organism events which may determine not only colonization by the organism once exposed, but also susceptibility to infection by the bacteria. Presumably this interplay is largely dependent on host immune factors.

Increasing numbers of sexual partners and a history of venereal disease do not seem to be positively associated with colonization by group B streptococcus. Baker and Kasper (1977) state, ''Factors that appear to enhance vaginal colonization of group B streptococcus among nonpregnant women are the presence of an intrauterine device, cultures obtained during the first half of the menstrual cycle, and an age of less than 21 years.'' However, as yet, definitive studies among adolescents do not appear to have been undertaken. Studies of the influence of oral sexual practices on colonization are also not available.

Group B streptococci have been isolated from urethral cultures of sexual partners of pregnant women colonized by the bacteria. One study suggests that up to 50% of male partners of colonized pregnant women may be positive (Franciosi and co-workers 1973). A high reappearance rate has been noted for colonized pregnant women who have been treated. When the male partners of the pregnant women were also treated, Baker and Kaper (1977) found that the organism disappeared. Thus, as in so many other venereal situations, the possibility of microbial ''ping-ponging'' between sexes remains strong.

With the apparent susceptibility of the younger female to this organism, future investigations hopefully will be directed toward its impact in the sexually active and pregnant adolescent.

Condyloma Acuminatum

Condyloma acuminatum (venereal or genital warts) are known to be caused by a papilloma virus. Transmission is considered to be primarily sexual. The exact incubation period is unknown, but it may be 2 to 3 months. Hart found that the risk of developing the disease following sexual activity appears to be over 50% (1977). Adolescents are not commonly victims.

The lesions are usually perineal, vaginal or cervical, but can, in unusual circumstances, develop elsewhere. Kreutner and Hollingsworth have found condyloma to be commonly associated with other infections such as moniliasis and trichomoniasis (1978). The individual lesions are fleshy, pointed, soft, moist, excrescences which seem to become less infectious with time. In moist areas the growth may readily spread to adjacent regions. Small lesions may not itch, but large ones do. Some lesions become so extensive that problems with defecation or voiding occur. Spontaneous remission of lesions is possible but so too are recurrences. Pregnancy often encourages exuberant growth. Rectal intercourse may result in perianal or rectal warts. The diagnosis can be made by clinical observation in most instances. For unusual cases, pathologic examination of tissue may be required. Treatment results for condyloma acuminatum vary and seem to depend somewhat on the individual's immune competence, size of lesions, pregnant or nonpregnant status and perhaps whether other vaginal infections coexist. The latter should be independently treated, and, if successful, may enhance the patient's response to the condyloma therapy.

Podophylin, 20 to 25% solution (often in a tincture of benzoin base), may be used on small lesions but not during pregnancy because of potential toxicity to the fetus. Only a small number of lesions per treatment should receive this chemocauterization. Podophylin should not be used intravaginally for fear of anaphylaxis (Powell 1972). Other cauterizing chemicals have been suggested, as have topical antimetabolites such as 5–Fluorouracil. The latter is contraindicated in pregnant patients. During pregnancy, condyloma should be treated relatively conservatively unless they are apt to cause complications during delivery. Following birth, spontaneous resolution is possible. If necessary, cryotherapy, fulguration or surgical excision can be done on pregnant or nonpregnant women. Large lesions are the chief indications for surgery. Trials with autogenous vaccine may be attempted in resistant or massive cases. Even if successful, the response may take a month or more.

Molluscum Contagiosum

The virus causing molluscum contagiosum is a member of the DNA pox family. It is particularly prevalent in underdeveloped countries, and Hart has estimated that it afflicts over 20% of the population in some South Pacific regions (1977). Children are its prime target, but adults can be affected as well. Viral spread is presumably by both direct and indirect contact (i.e., person-to-person contact and the common use of such items as bedding and towels). However, the sexual mode seems to be increasing in adults and adolescents.

The characteristic lesions are produced by the virus infecting most of the epidermal cells in an area of epithelium, producing a pearly, spherical papule, 3 to 7 mm in diameter. These lesions usually do not itch and are relatively few, ranging from 1–30 in number (Hart 1977). In the sexually transmitted form, the lesions are generally found in the lower abdomen, genitalia, pubis, and inner thighs. The incubation period is long, 2 to 3 months. Partly because of this fact, the risk of infection to sexual partners may be low.

Diagnosis is made by the clinical appearance and/or from histological examination or electron microscope identification of the virus. The prognosis is good. Spontaneous resolution usually takes place within two years although new lesions may appear for as long as four years (Kreutner and Hollingsworth 1978). If treatment is necessary, incision and removal of the central core is effective. Other therapies include cryosurgery and fulguration. Chemical cautery with compounds such as 0.7% cantharidin solution may be tried.

Chancroid

Chancroid is an uncommon venereal disease in the United States, caused by a small, Gram-negative rod, *Haemophilus ducreyi*. The major early lesion is a painful genital ulcer which may produce tender inguinal adenitis and a characteristic bubo, usually unilateral, which occurs in about 50 to 70% of the cases. The original eruption starts as an inflammatory macule that progresses rapidly to the vesicopustular stage and then becomes an ulcer. The lymph nodes are enlarged in over half of the cases. The disease, although almost always venereal in origin, has been reported as accidentally acquired lesions of the hand. The incubation period is short, 3 to 5 days or less. Occurrence in adolescence is rare.

Culturing of the organism from open lesions or bubos is the most accurate method of diagnosis. Complex mixed flora may be grown and often other venereal disease organisms are present. A skin test (Ducrey's skin test) is available and may remain positive for years after infection.

Treatment of chancroid is with drugs. Sulfonamides (e.g., sulfisoxazole), 1 gm four times daily for 7 to 10 days, is the usual recommendation. Repeat courses are sometimes necessary. Streptomycin and tetracycline hydrochloride are alternative antibiotics.

Granuloma Inguinale

Granuloma inguinale is another rare adolescent venereal disease. It is caused by the bacteria, *Calymmatobacterium granulomatis* (Donovan bodies). The latter are bacteria encapsulated in mononuclear leukocytes.

The incubation period for granuloma inguinale is 8–12 weeks. The essential disease is a chronic ulcerative, sometimes vegetative, lesion(s) of the vulva, perineum and inguinal areas. Rarely, other genital organs such as the cervix, uterus or ovaries may be involved. Spread to the urethra and anus occurs in about 7% of the cases. Diagnosis is usually made by identification with Wright's or other stains so that Donovan bodies in smears or biopsy can be identified. Therapy is with tetracycline, 500 mg orally four times a day for two to three weeks. Occasionally greater dosages are needed. Erythromycin, chloramphenicol and streptomycin have also been used. The recurrence rate is said to be about 10%.

Corynebacterium Vaginalis *(Haemophilus vaginalis)*

Haemophilus vaginalis is thought to be a significant cause of nonspecific vaginitis in women in adolescence. The organism is a small, non-encapsulated, pleomorphic, bacterial rod which Gram-stains variably, usually Gram negatively. Many women are asymptomatic. Others have mild vulvovaginal irritation with scanty to moderate, gray, slightly malodorous discharge. The bacteria often coexist with other virulent organisms in the vagina and hence is often overlooked as a causative agent. Evidence exists for its sexual transmission (Rein and Chape 1975).

Diagnosis is usually made by smears and culture. Exfoliated vaginal cells seen under the microscope on a wet mount, may have small dark particles adherent to them. These are the attached *H. vaginalis* bacteria that give the so-called "clue cell" feature. Bacteriological culture is the definitive method of diagnosis.

Treatment is sometimes uncertain. Ampicillin, 500 mg four times a day for seven to ten days, or tetracycline, 250 mg four times a day for ten days, are the usual treatments of choice. Triple sulfa creams and other local antibacterial regimens do not seem to be as effective. A recent report by Pheifer and co-workers suggests metronidazole, frequently used for trichomoniasis, is a highly effective treatment (1978). Metronidazole, 500 mg twice daily for seven days, was more effective than ampicillin, other antibiotics, or sulfas. In this study *H. vaginalis* was cultured from the urethra of male partners in 79% of the cases, suggesting another possible ping-pong infection exchange between sexual partners. Confirmatory studies on the use of metronidazole in this form of nonspecific vaginitis will be awaited with interest. In the meantime, the advantages of this highly promising therapy should be weighed against the potential risk of the drug. The latter are discussed in the treatment section on trichomoniasis.

Pediculosis Pubis (Crab Lice)

Crab lice *(Phthirus pubis)* are blood sucking parasites which are more apt to be transmitted sexually than from shared contact with clothes or linen. The eggs (nits) are laid at the base of the pubic skin hair shafts. These eggs hatch in seven to nine days and the new lice attach themselves to the skin of the host. The punctate bites may induce an erythematous papule within a matter of hours. Secondary infection is not uncommon.

The usual clinical presenting picture is that of pubic itching or the patient's simply observing lice moving on the skin surface. Diagnosis is facilitated by the use of a magnifying glass to view the lice or eggs on the pubic hair. The lice can be positively identified when seen on a slide under a microscope.

Treatment is with 1% gamma benzene hexachloride (Kwell) cream, lotion, or shampoo for 12 to 24 hours. Treatment should be repeated in four to seven days to catch any eggs missed on the first application. Sexual partners should be concomitantly treated.

Scabies

Scabies is a skin infection produced by the female mite (*Sarcoptes scabies*). The parasite is transmitted by close skin-to-skin contact, often sexual. The itch mite burrows beneath the skin and deposits her ova. Intractable itching and skin excoriation may ensue. This reaction apparently is a part of a hypersensitivity response and symptoms may take one to three months to appear. Hart reports that eosinophilia up to 15% may be present (1977). Secondary infection of burrows may contribute to the symptoms. Poor hygiene and living conditions are frequently associated with the presence of scabies.

Diagnosis can often be made clinically by the presence of the distinctive papular eruptions. Commonly afflicted areas such as the pubis, axillae, thighs, wrists, and flexor surfaces of the extremities may show the characteristic inhabited burrows.

If needed for definitive diagnosis, the parasite can be extracted and viewed under a microscope. One % gamma benzene hexachloride lotion or cream should be applied to the entire body from the neck down, with special emphasis on high risk infection regions such as the anogenital areas, the wrists, and axillae. Treatment should be repeated in 24 hours with no bathing in between. Twenty-four hours after the second treatment, a bath may be taken. Potentially infected bedding and clothing should be sterilized. All contacts, especially sexual partners, should be treated. If new lesions arise, the treatment can be repeated in two weeks.

Candida albicans

Candida albicans is a common saprophyte of humans which is present in the mouth, vagina, respiratory tract and intestines of normal persons. Its presence may be detected from these sites in cultures in 25 to 50% of women. However, mere presence does not necessarily indicate infection. Nonetheless, it is a common cause of vaginal infection in adolescents as well as women of all ages.

Predisposing factors to *C. albicans* infections include the use of broad spectrum antibiotics (an important potential contributor in adolescents who take tetracycline or other antibiotics for acne), oral contraceptives, pregnancy, diabetes, steroids or other immunosuppressive agents or events, general debility, narcotic abuse, perhaps increased carbohydrates in the diet, and heat and moisture. In the tropics the latter may contribute to the occurrence of vaginal yeast infections. In our society the nylon pantyhose effect may be the most significant contributor. Pantyhose retain heat and are not absorbent.

The organism is an oval, budding, gram-positive yeast which has pseudomycelium in culture, exudates and tissues. Although *C. albicans,* in one sense, is not communicable since most individuals harbor the organism, it is now being considered a minor, sexually transmitted disease (Evans 1976; Handsfield 1977; Rein and Chape 1975). The evidence is circumstantial and based on such factors as a concordance of the peak incidence of infection with the age of maximal sexual activity (16 to 30 years); frequent culturing of *C. albicans* from the urethra of sexual partners of infected women; symptoms of urethritis and balanitis in 10% of infected men; and the high prevalence of *C. albicans* in women with other documented venereal diseases (Rein and Chape 1975). The observation that some cases of candidiasis seem to require concomitant treatment of sexual partners to induce a remission is another anecdotal piece of evidence.

Symptomatic candida vulvovaginitis includes a discharge, vulvar itching, pain, or burning often beginning before menstruation. Dysuria and painful intercourse are other possible complaints. The vulva is usually red, edematous, and excoriated. The vaginal discharge characteristically is white, thick and resembles curds of cottage cheese, usually moderate in quantity, but adherent to the vaginal wall.

Diagnosis is based on smears and cultures. Wet mounts may give a rough quantitative estimate of the number of organisms. Smears are usually viewed when mixed with 10 to 20% potassium hydroxide solution. Rein and Chape report that this form of diagnosis may give a positive index in 40 to 80% of the cases (1975). Gram stains may also give a high, diagnostic-positive rate. Papanicolaou smears are less reliable indicators. Cultures on Sabouraud's or Nickerson's media may be needed to confirm the diagnosis. However, it should be reemphasized that women with almost any form of vaginitis may show some *C. albicans* on smears and wet mounts. Mixed infections are common especially in venereal disease patients. Some recent evidence suggests that some of the vaginitis may be associated with altered, local immune reactions or hypersensitivity reactions to the organism. Mathur has noted alterations of vaginal and systemic immunoglobulin E (IgE) levels in some patients (1977). A skin test is available but generally is not helpful. It is positive in most adults and thus is frequently used as a measure of general cellular immune activity. Serologic tests are of some use in following disseminated diseases but less so with simple vaginal infections.

Treatment of *C. albicans* sometimes may be frustrating, for patients and physicians alike. Careful attention to known predisposing factors and possible underlying disease must always be a key step. A careful history of diet, drug, and other medical treatments, as well as hygiene and clothing habits is necessary. Switching to cotton underwear has effected marvelous "cures" in not a few cases of pantyhose origin. Nystatin suppositories or vaginal tablets (100,000 U), 1 to 2 twice daily placed high in the vagina for 10 to 14 days; miconazole nitrate 2%, one bedtime application for 7 to 14 days; propionic acid gel, one vaginal application daily for 21 days; gentian violet 0.25 to 1% aqueous solution to the vulvovaginal mucosa twice weekly for three weeks; or clotrimazole, one tablet vaginally at bedtime for 7 days may be used. Nystatin by mouth to suppress intestinal *Candida* as a source of possible reinfection is advocated by some. Recurrences may be frequent or prolonged and repeated courses of treatment are not uncommon. Concomitant treatment of male sexual partners and/or the use of the condom in intercourse sometimes helps. This is especially important if the man is symptomatic. During the acute phase of the female's infection, abstinence is recommended to allow maximal treatment response.

Trichomoniasis

This flagellated protozoal infection is a common cause of vaginitis in women and appears to be sexually transmitted. Contact with towels, bedding, and other linens as well as common use of bathing or douche equipment may sometimes play a factor. Infection rates may be as high as 40% in some populations where hygiene is poor. Trichomonads are common in cultures from venereal disease patients of all ages including sexually active adolescents. It may be cultured from the lower urinary tract in both sexes.

The incubation period may be 4 to 28 days (Rein and Chape 1975). Some patients are asymptomatic, but vaginal discharge is a common finding frequently with vulvar itching. The discharge may be fetid green to yellow green, frothy and often copious. Menstruation, the postmenstrual period, and occasionally pregnancy seem to aggravate the condition. The vaginal walls may have discrete petechiae, the so-called "strawberry spots." The external genitalia may be red and excoriated. Urinary symptoms sometimes occur as does pelvic aching (Kreutner and Hollingsworth 1978).

Diagnosis is made from wet mounts of vaginal exudates in which the protozoans can be seen to be slightly larger than polymorphonuclear cells. Tests for gonorrhea and syphilis should be made on all female patients with a positive diagnosis of trichomoniasis, although it is recognized that occasionally the protozoans occur in virgins (Kreutner and Hollingsworth 1978).

The current treatment of choice is oral metronidazole, 250 mg orally three times a day for seven days. At four to six weeks a repeat dose can be given in resistant or reinfection cases provided that the white blood count and differential are normal. Metronidazole is contraindicated during early pregnancy or lactation, or if the patient has certain blood dycrasias or central nervous diseases. The male sexual partner should be treated simultaneously. If this is done Rein and Chape claim that the success rate can approach 95% (1975). Vaginal inserts of metronidazole daily have also been used. Other local antiprotozoal treatments are available and may sometimes be effective.

Chlamydiae including Lymphogranuloma venereum (LGV)

The chlamydiae are a group of large, obligate, intracellular parasites closely related to Gram-negative bacteria. Two species exist, *Chlamydia psittaci* (responsible for the disease in birds which may be transferred to humans), and *Chlamydia trachomatis* which has recently been implicated in a variety of infections besides its long known role in trachoma, inclusion conjunctivitis, and lymphogranuloma venereum. Pelvic inflammatory disease, nongonococcal urethritis, and epididymitis have now been attributed to the organism (Berger and co-workers 1978; Holmes and co-workers 1975; Mardh and co-workers 1977).

Lymphogranuloma venereum is a sexually transmitted disease whose incubation period is 7 to 12 days. The organism, passed by coitus, develops in a small papule or vesicle which may ulcerate, but often goes unnoticed in women. The spread is through the lymphatics which accounts for its characteristic lymphoid picture. Regional lymph nodes enlarge, become matted and usually painful. Large bubos may develop in the groins and become exceedingly tender. A hard, cutaneous, red and purplish-blue nodule may develop. Anorectal lymphadenoma may lead to painful defecation and blood-streaked stools. The late stage may bring scarring of the vagina and rectum or systemic symptoms such as fever, chills, and cramps. Lymphogranuloma venereum is not common in adolescents, but a recent outbreak in a college age group has been described by McLelland and Anderson (1976). Historically, the diagnosis has been made by the clinical picture and the utilization of skin tests. More recently, serologic assays have been most commonly used. The Frei skin test has about an 80% sensitivity, is applied intradermally, and becomes positive in 12 to 40 days following a primary infection. It may remain positive for years, perhaps, for a lifetime. A good complement fixation test is now available and is the diagnostic tool most commonly used. Other chlamydial diseases may cause an elevated titer, but a rising titer over several weeks combined with the clinical findings usually confirms the diagnosis. In addition, a sensitive microimmunofluorescence test is also available.

Treatment of lymphogranuloma venereum is fairly effective but quite time-consuming. Tetracycline is the drug of choice. Usually a dose of 2 gm per day is given (depending on individual patient tolerance) for 2 to 4 weeks. Sometimes it is necessary to repeat the dosage with persistent disease. Sulfonamides have been used and appear to suppress the disease but are not curative.

As noted, other chlamydial infections may give symptoms, but are also known to exist in asymptomatic forms. McCormick and co-workers' recent study over a two year period of 439 unselected asymptomatic college women is revealing (1979). In the earlier part of the study 4.6% of the women were found to be infected with *Chlamydia trachomatis,* and surprisingly only two had concomitant gonococcus infection. Reports from other clinics for sexually transmitted diseases have reported rates of 18 to 31% for chlamydia—a percentage higher than for gonorrhea isolations (Hilton 1974; Hobson 1974; Wentworth and co-workers 1973). Some of these women were symptomatic and the findings of Mardh and co-workers are in accordance with the accumulating evidence that *C. trachomatis* may be the cause of some cases of pelvic inflammatory disease (1977).

In McCormick and co-workers' (1979) two year follow-up of a much smaller group of the women with chlamydia, a significant number kept the infection for at least several months; most were asymptomatic. This finding suggests that women may be reservoirs of infection for their male sexual partners who develop nongonococcal urethritis (or perhaps vice versa). Nongonococcal urethritis is the term used for a group of sexually transmitted diseases whose frequency in men in developed countries, Handsfield claims, exceeds that of gonorrhea (1977). One of the prime causes of this form of male infection is now known to be *C. trachomatis.*

It is very important to note that infants may develop conjunctivitis or pneumonia as a result of their relationship with a mother infected with a chlamydial infection.

The recommended treatment for chlamydia—tetracycline 500 mg by mouth four times a day for seven to ten days—is usually effective although longer courses are advocated by some authorities (Handsfield 1978). Women who have the disease, who are associated with sexual partners with nongonococcal urethritis or who are the source of neonatal chlamydial infections, should be treated with this regimen. If a patient cannot tolerate tetracycline, erythromycin, which may be slightly less effective, can be used. McCormick and co-workers suggest that the treatment of chlamydia in females may be appropriate regardless of the absence of symptoms or physical findings if they are deemed to be a source of infection to others (1979).

Tetracycline therapy may also influence the presence of T-strain and other forms of mycoplasma; the role of these organisms in some cases of cervicitis, urethritis and, perhaps, pelvic inflammatory disease is still somewhat uncertain (Handsfield 1978; Kreutner and Hollingsworth 1978).

References

Adam, E. et al. Persistence of virus shedding in asymptomatic women, who have recovered from herpes genitalis. *Obstet. Gynecol.* in press 1979.

Adam, E. Personal communication, 1979.

Altchek, A. Adolescent vulvovaginitis. *Pediatr. Clin. North Am.* 19:735, 1972.

Aurelian, L. et al. Antibody to HSV-2 induced tumor specific antigens in serum from patients with cervical cancer. *Science* 181:161, 1973.

Baker, C. J., and Kasper, D. L. Immunological investigation of infants with septicemia or meningitis due to group B streptococcus. *J. Infect.* Dis. 126:598, 1977.

Barr, J., and Danielsson, D. Septic gonococcal dermatitis. *Br. Med. J.* 1:482, 1971.

Barton, L. L.; Feigin, R. D.; and Lins, R. Group B beta hemolytic streptococcal meningitis in infants. *J. Pediatr.* 82:719, 1973.

Berger, R. E. et al. *Chlamydia trachomatis* as a cause of acute "idiopathic" epididymitis. *N. Engl. J. Med.* 298:301, 1978.

Bhattacharyya, M. N.; Jephcott, A.

E.; and Morton, R. S. Diagnosis of gonorrhea in women: comparison of sampling sites. *Br. Med. J.* 2:748, 1973.

Branch, G., and Paxton, R. A study of gonococcal infections among infants and children. *Public Health Rep.* 80:347, 1965.

Brown, W. J. Trends and status of gonorrhea in the United States. *J. Infect. Dis.* 123:682, 1971.

Catalano, L. W. Jr., and Johnson, L. D. Herpesvirus antibody and carcinoma in situ of the cervix. *JAMA* 217:447, 1971.

Center for Disease Control: gonorrhea: CDC recommended treatment schedules. *Morbid. Mortal. Weekly Rep.* 28:13, 1979.

Center for Disease Control: penicillinase (B-lactamase) producing *Neisseria gonorrhea. Morbid. Mortal. Weekly Rep.* 27:10, 1978.

CDC recommended treatment schedules for syphilis. *Morbid. Mortal. Weekly Rep.* 25:107, 1976.

Crawford, G. et al. Asymptomatic gonorrhea in men: caused by gonococci with unique nutritional requirements. *Science* 196:1352, 1977.

Dans, P. E. Gonococcal anogenital infection. *Clin. Obstet. Gynecol.* 18:103, 1975.

Duenas, A. et al. Herpes virus type 2 in a prostitute population. *Am. J. Epidemiol.* 95:483, 1972.

Eshenbach, D. A. et al. Polymicrobial etiology of acute pelvic inflammatory disease. *N. Engl. J. Med.* 293:166, 1975.

Eschenbach, D. A.; Harnisch, J. P. and Holmes, K. K. Pathogenesis of acute pelvic inflammatory disease: Role of contraception and other risk factors. *Am. J. Obstet. Gynecol.* 128:383, 1977.

Eschenbach, D. A., and Holmes, K. K. Acute pelvic inflammatory disease: current concepts of pathogenesis, etiology and management. *Clin. Obstet. Gynecol.* 18:25, 1975.

Evans, T. N. Sexually transmitted diseases. *Am. J. Obstet. Gynecol.* 125:116, 1976.

Felton, W. F. Contrasting views on the infectivity of gonorrhea. *Br. J. Vener. Dis.* 49:151, 1973.

Fleming, W. L. et al. National survey of venereal diseases treated by physicians in 1968. *JAMA* 211:1827, 1970.

Franciosi, R. A., Knostman, J. D., Zimmerman, R. A. Group B Streptococcal neonatal infant infection. *J. Pediatr.* 82:707, 1973.

Gilstrap, L. C. et al. Gonorrhea screening in male consorts of women with pelvic infection. *JAMA* 238:965, 1977.

Handsfield, H. H. Disseminated gonococcal infection. *Clinc. Obstet. Gynecol.* 18:131, 1975.

Handsfield, H. H. Clinical aspects of gonococcal infections. In *The Gonococcus,* ed. R. B. Roberts. New York: John Wiley and Sons, 1977.

Handsfield, H. H. Gonorrhea and nongonococcal urethritis. *Med. Clin. North Am.* 62:925, 1978.

Handsfield, H. H.; Hodson, W. A.; and Holmes, K. K. Neonatal gonococcal infection I. Orogastric contamination with *Neisseria gonorrheae.* *JAMA* 225:697, 1973.

Handsfield, H. H. et al. Asymptomatic gonorrhea in men: Diagnosis, natural course, prevalence, and significance. *New Engl. J. Med.* 290:117, 1974.

Handsfield, H. H.; Wiesner, P. H.; and Holmes, K. K. Prospective study of disseminated gonococcal infection. Presented at the Thirteenth Interscience Conference on Antimicrobial Agents and Chemotherapy, 19–21 September in Washington, D.C. 1973.

Hart, G. Sexual Maladjustment and disease. Chicago: Nelson Hall, 1977.

Henderson, R. H. Improving sexually transmitted disease health service for gays: a national prospective. *Sex. Transm. Dis.* 4:58, 1977.

Hilton, A. L. et al. *Chlamydia* A in the female genital tract. *Brit. J. Vener. Dis.* 50:1, 1974.

Hobson, D. et al. Simplified method for diagnosis of genital and ocular infection with *Chlamydia. Lancet* 2:555, 1974.

Holmes, K. K. et al. Etiology of nongonococcal urethritis. *N. Engl. J. Med.* 292:1199, 1975.

Holmes, K. K.; Johnson, D. W.; and Trostle, H. J. An estimate of the risk of men acquiring gonorrhea by sexual contact with infected females. *Am. J. Epidemiol.* 91:170, 1970.

Holmes, K. K.; Wiesner, P. J.; and Pedersen, A. H. B. The gonococcal arthritis syndrome. *Ann. Intern. Med.* 75:470, 1971.

Israel, S. L., and Deutschberger, J. Relation of the mother's age to obstetric performance. *Obstet. Gynecol.* 24:411, 1964.

Israel, K. S.; Rissing, K. B.; and Brooks, G. F. Neonatal and childhood gonococcal infection. *Clin. Obstet. Gynecol.* 18:143, 1975.

Jacobs, N. F., and Kraus, S. J. Gonococcal and nongonococcal urethritis in men. Clinical and laboratory differentiation. *Ann. Intern. Med.* 82:7, 1975.

Jeansson, S. and Molin, L. On the occurrence of genital herpes simplex virus infection. *Acta Derma. (Venereol.* Stockh.) 54:479, 1974.

Jerome, E. et al. Gonorrhea at a teenage medical service. *Minn. Med.* 57:245, 1974.

Jordon, M. C. et al. Association of cervical cytomegaloviruses with venereal disease. *N. Engl. J. Med.* 288:932, 1973.

Kawana, T.; Yoshino, K.; and Kasamatsu, T. Estimation of specific antibody to type 2 herpes simplex virus among patients with carcinoma of the uterine cervix. *Gann* 65:439, 1974.

Kellogg, D. S. Jr. Current methods for the laboratory diagnosis of gonococcal infections. In *The gonococcus,* ed. R. B. Roberts. New York: John Wiley and Sons, 1977.

Kohen, D. P. Neonatal gonococcal arthritis: three cases and review of the literature. *Pediatrics* 53:436, 1974.

Kreutner, A. K., and Hollingsworth, D. R., ed. *Adolescent obstetrics and gynecology.* Chicago: Year Book Medical Publishers, Inc., 1978.

Litt, I. F.; Edeberg, S. C.; and Finberg, L. Gonorrhea in children and adolescents: a current review. *J. Pediatr.* 85:595, 1974.

Lucas, J. B. Gonorrhea. In *Communicable and infectious disease;* ed. P. H. Top, and P. F. Wehrle. St. Louis: C.V. Mosby, 1972.

Luxon, L.; Lees, A. J.; and Greenwood, R. J.: Neurosyphilis today *Lancet* 1:90, 1979.

Mardh, P. A. et al. *Chlamydia trachomatis* infection in patients with acute salpingitis. *N. Engl. J. Med.* 296:1377, 1977.

Martin, J. E.; and Lester, A. Transgrow, a medium for transport and growth of *Neisseria gonorrheae* and *Neisseria meningitidis.* *HSMHA Health Rep.* 86:30, 1971.

Mathur, S. et al. Immunoglobulin E anti-candida antibodies and candidiasis. *Infect. Immun.* 18:257, 1977.

McCormick, Wm. M. Treatment of gonorrhea—is penicillin passé? *New Engl. J. Med.* 296:934, 1979

McCormick, Wm. et al. Fifteen-month follow-up study of women infected with *Chlamydia trachomatis. New Engl. J. Med.* 300:123; 1979.

McCracken, A. W., and D'Angostino, A. N. Acquired cytomegalovirus infection presenting as viral endometritis. *Am. J. Clin. Pathol.* 61:556, 1974.

McLelland, B. A., and Anderson, P. C. Lymphogranuloma venereum: outbreak in a university community. *JAMA* 235:56, 1976.

Medical News. *JAMA* 241:981, 1979.

Montgomery, R.; Youngblood, L.; and Mediaris, D. N. Recovery of CMV from cervix in pregnancy. *Pediatr.* 49:524, 1971.

Mumford, D. M.; Kaufman, R. H.; and McCormick, N. Immunity, herpes simplex virus and cervical carcinoma. *Surg. Clin. North Am.* 58:39, 1978.

Mumford, D. M.; Smith P. B.; and Goldfarb, J. L. Prevalence of venereal disease in indigent pregnant adolescents. *J. Reprod. Med.* 19:83, 1977.

Myers, M. G. et al. Failure of neutral-red photodynamic inactivation in recurrent herpes simplex virus infections. *N. Engl. J. Med.* 293:945, 1975.

Nahmias, A. J. et al. Antibodies to herpesvirus hominis types 1 and 2. II. Women with cervical cancer. *Am. J. Epidemiol.* 89:547, 1969.

Nahmias, A. J. et al. Perinatal risk associated with maternal genital herpes simplex virus infection. *Am. J. Obstet. Gynecol.* 110:825, 1971.

Pheifer, T. A. et al. Nonspecific vaginitis, role of *Haemophilus vaginalis* and treatment with Metronidazole. *N. Engl. J. Med.* 298:1429, 1978.

Pierog, S. et al. Gonococcal ophthalmia neonatorum: relationship of maternal factors and delivery room practices to effective control measures. *Am. J. Obstet. Gynecol.* 122:589, 1975.

Portnoy, J. et al. Asymptomatic gonorrhea in the male. *Can. Med. Assoc. J.* 110:169, 1974.

Powell, L. C. Condyloma acuminatum. *Clin. Obstet. Gynecol.* 15:948, 1972.

Rapp, F. Herpesvirus, venereal disease, and cancer. *Am. Sci.* 66:670, 1978.

Rauh, L.; Brookman, M.; and Schiff, G. M. Genital viral surveillance among sexually active adolescent girls. *J. Pediatr.* 90:844, 1977.

Rawls, W. et al. Genital herpes in two social groups. *Am. J. Obstet. Gynecol.* 110:682, 1971.

Rawls, W. E.; Tompkins, W. A. F.; and Melnick, J. L. The association of herpesvirus type 2 and carcinoma of the uterine cervix. *Am. J. Epidemiol.* 89:547, 1969.

Rein, M. F., and Chape, T. A. Trichomoniasis, candidiasis, and the minor venereal diseases. *Clin. Obstet. Gynecol.* 18:73, 1975.

Rigg, C. A. Venereal disease in adolescents. *Practitioner* 214:199, 1975.

Rudolph, A. H., and Duncan, W. C. Syphilis—diagnosis and treatment. *Clin. Obstet. Gynecol.* 18:163, 1975.

Stern, M. S., and McKenzie, R. G.

Venereal disease in adolescents. *Med. Clin. North Am.* 59:1395, 1975.

Tronca, E. et al. Demonstration of *Neisseria gonorrheae* with fluorescence antibody in patients with disseminated gonococcal infection. *J. Infect. Dis.* 129:583, 1974.

Wallis, C.; Melnick, J. L; and Kaufman, R. H. Herpes genitalis: management—present and predicted. *Clin. Obstet. Gynecol.* 15:939, 1972.

Wentworth, B. B. et al. Isolation of viruses, bacteria and other organisms from venereal disease clinic patients; methodology and problems associated with multiple isolation. *Health Lab Sci.* 10:75, 1973.

Wiesner, P. J. et al. Clinical spectrum of pharyngeal gonococcal infection. *New Engl. J. Med.* 288:181, 1973.

Wiesner, P. J. Gonococcal pharyngeal infection. *Clin. Obstet. Gynecol.* 18:121, 1975.

8

Issues Surrounding Adolescent Pregnancy Terminations

Alfred N. Poindexter, M.D.

Raymond H. Kaufman, M.D.

Few issues elicit as fervent a response as abortion. The mention of abortion causes an immediate polarization of opinion, each side arguing its point with almost fanatical intensity. The Supreme Court decision of January 1973 made it easier for a woman to obtain an abortion, but certainly did not quiet the debate. The question of abortion, although not always openly discussed, has been with us as long as the first unwanted pregnancy and most likely will continue to be an intruder in a society that traditionally would just as soon not talk about sex. First the proabortion forces gain support, then there is a wave of antiabortion response. The net result is a kind of fragile equilibrium regarding this important issue.

Abortion should not be allowed to become a replacement for preventive care, the definitive answer to unwanted pregnancy. If one-half of the fervor expressed by the abortion forces were applied to finding ways to prevent unwanted pregnancy, the emotional conflict of abortion might be avoided. This conflict is particularly hard on one segment of the population, teenagers 15 to 19 years of age. More than one million teenage girls become pregnant every year, and adolescents 17 years or younger account for one-third of all those who have abortions (Hale 1978). In 1976 girls less than 15 years old had the highest abortion ratio (Center for Disease Control 1978). Contrary to the U.S. birthrate drop, the incidence of adolescent pregnancy among younger teens is on the rise.

Equipped with incompletely developed emotional and intellectual skills, the pregnant teenager, still socially and legally considered half-child, half-adult, must face a decision of whether to abort or carry to term.

The risks or complications of abortion for teens are procedure-related and gestational-age dependent. The rate of complications for all methods is about 12%. The most common complications are hemorrhages, infection, perforation of the uterus, retained tissue, failure to terminate and laceration of the cervix. This decision can drastically and permanently alter the rest of her life and the life of the adolescent father. The mortality rate for infants born to mothers younger than 15 is twice that for infants born to mothers in their early 20s (Hale 1978). The young mothers themselves are at greater risk for toxemia, anemia and maternal death. Equally important, involved teenagers drop out of school and enter dismal patterns of economic hardships and welfare dependence, unstable family life and divorce. Salary at age 24 directly correlates with the mother's age at first birth (Hale 1978). Adolescent marriages are two to three times more likely to end in divorce than those between adults.

There is no risk-free solution to the problem of unwanted pregnancy. The question is: Can this particular human struggle be avoided? This question can be answered yes if two major tasks are undertaken. The problems teenagers bring with them when they present with an unwanted pregnancy must be closely examined. A continuum of preventive measures must be designed which are streamlined to the reality of adolescents' lives today, not to society's wishful thinking about what they should be.

In this chapter we ask several questions, the answers to which may help provide solutions to the problem. Who is this teenage girl who presents for abortion; and what is the nature of her knowledge about abortion? How did she become pregnant in this era of supposed sexual frankness and contraceptive availability; i.e., how does she reflect the state of adolescent sexuality? How can a second pregnancy be avoided; moreover, how can all unwanted pregnancies in adolescents be avoided?

Teenagers Presenting for Abortion

Sometimes, sociological literature and oftentimes, rumor describe adolescents who elect termination of pregnancy as sexually promiscuous, emotionally unstable girls from poor, broken homes who take a casual and uncaring attitude toward abortion. Some sources say that they are mostly white; others, predominantly black. The rumors are supported by the hope that this problem, too, can be categorized as "problems of the poor" or "manifestations of the morally bereft." Then the adult community would not have to face a very unpleasant thought: abortion is a problem of the *average* adolescent.

The pregnant adolescent comes from a wide variety of socioeconomic backgrounds. She is white two-thirds of the time and black or from another minority in the other one-third of cases (Center for Disease Control 1978). She is unmarried and financially dependent on her parents (Evans, Selstad, and Welcher 1976). Generally, she does well in school and has never before been pregnant. Frequently she presents herself to the physician later in pregnancy than her adult counterpart, probably because she does not understand the consequences of late abortion. She often is unsure of when she conceived, because of an irregular menstrual cycle or because she simply does not know the relationship between coitus and pregnancy. She has not acted to prevent conception. Almost always she is anxious and ambivalent about her pregnancy and comes to the doctor's office alone, because she is afraid to tell her parents. She often feels worthless and afraid of rejection. She does not know what to do and does not view abortion as an easy substitute for contraception.

In the U.S. 10% of girls 15 to 19 become pregnant each year (Bracken, Klerman, and Bracken 1978). In 1976 over 300,000 adolescents had abortions (Center for Disease Control 1978). Although the majority of these abortions were obtained by white teenagers the Center for Disease Control reports that the percentage obtained by black women continued to increase each year (1978).

The problems confronting every teenager seeking an abortion are magnifications of the complexities that an adult woman faces in the same situation. Although these may be quantitative as well as qualitative differences, some of these are dependent on adolescent mind sets. Young concluded that the fact that the young woman is unmarried is secondary in importance to the fact that she is also an adolescent (1954). According to several reports in the literature (Wolfish 1973; Freeman 1978; and Nadelson 1974) most pregnant adolescents feel that abortion is a difficult solution to an impossible problem. For most teenagers this is the first major decision they have had to make.

Teenagers appear to be somewhat more conservative in their attitudes toward abortion than adults (Zelnik and Kantner 1975). They feel that abortion is all right if the pregnancy is the result of rape; if the mother is in physical danger; if the child might be defective; if the infant's birth would be an economic hardship; or if the birth would destroy family relationships (Evans, Setstad, and Welcher 1976). Girls favorably disposed to abortion tend to be older and higher in socioeconomic status than those against it, and, they tend to be without religious affiliation (Gabrielson and co-workers 1971).

The pregnant teenager, however, is overwhelmed by a complexity of cultural and social pressures and is typically torn between positive thoughts regarding conception and pregnancy and sadness about having to make a choice to terminate the pregnancy (Nadelson 1974). Martin reported that only 5 of 52 girls seeking abortion had no moral conflicts (1973). The rest were concerned because they thought abortion was murder; because they felt guilty for becoming involved in premarital sex and getting pregnant; or because they felt sinful in the eyes of the church.

For most adolescent girls the sexual partner plays a prominent role in the decision to abort (Cobliner, Schulman, and Romney 1973). The boy's reaction to the girl's announcement that she is pregnant can determine the decision to carry to term or to abort. A refusal to marry or sudden desertion may cause the pregnant adolescent to seek abortion immediately. However, sometimes the only difference between an adolescent carrying to term and one seeking an abortion is that the girl carrying to term is able to deny her condition long enough to avoid making a conscious decision.

When comparing young black women (including many teenagers) choosing abortion to other black women deciding to deliver, Bracken, Klerman, and Bracken found that the outcome of each pregnancy was more related to the circumstances of each pregnancy rather than to any particular characteristic of the woman herself (1978). They concluded that the same woman may experience both aborted and term pregnancies. Any preconceived notion about the choice of abortion is very likely to be considerably revised from one pregnancy to the next.

Intense anxiety during the 24-hour period before the abortion is typical (Nadelson 1974). The adolescent patient is afraid to ask questions about pain, anesthesia or side effects. She is often extremely sensitive to the hospital environment, her roommate, doctors and nursing staff (Lipper and co-workers 1973). Most girls do, however, think that abortion in a good hospital is safe (Gabrielson and co-workers 1971).

Contrary to early conservative reports of psychotic-like aftereffects, there is minimal emotional trauma associated with abortion and the majority of adolescents can cope with the stress (Jacques 1973). A follow-up study of 50 girls who had an abortion revealed that most had mild reactions that included guilt, fear and self-reproach, but that their life styles did not change nor did they become emotionally unstable (Lipper and co-workers 1973).

Adolescent developmental conflicts are the same preabortion as post-abortion, and depend on the adolescent's level of psychological maturity (Schaffer and Pine 1972). Therefore, researchers find a range of reactions to abortion from passive behavior to conflict which actually becomes a

145

basis for growth (Schaffer and Pine 1972). Responses of the girl's family and her sexual partner seem crucial to her emotional adjustment following abortion (Martin 1973). Dvejic and co-workers reported that the majority of 38 adolescents who had an abortion did not regret their decision, but said that they would not have another (Dvejic and co-workers 1977). The Center for Disease Control reports that the number of repeat abortions, though, has increased (1978). The reason for this is unclear. Some investigators report that abortion does not create lasting motivation to use contraception (Schneider and Thompson 1976), while others conclude that abortion leads to more effective fertility control in adolescents (Evans, Selstad, and Welcher 1976; Tietze 1975).

Precluding the Need for Abortion

The fact that annually thousands of adolescents naively become pregnant seems paradoxical in this era of supposed sexual frankness. How can any teenager miss the explicit sex that today is an intrinsic part of the television-movie-advertising conglomerate? He or she cannot. But the media message is not one of sexual information; instead it is an advertisement for SEX AS STATUS or for SEX NOW, PAY LATER. The real issue adolescents face, that of being able to move into sexuality cognizant of possible consequences and armed with the beginnings of responsibility, is not discussed in the media. The guilt, ambiguity and awkwardness surrounding the introductory phase of sexual activity is rarely presented or discussed.

So the message is be cool and be sexy, but the message does not come with instructions nor with warnings of the possible side effects of sexuality, that is, pregnancy and abortion. The adolescent comes away with an appealingly glossy, but unreal, view of sex. Most unwed mothers enter a sexual relationship with little thought about what will happen. Once pregnant they fail to imagine the unhappy experience ahead and often simply set the problem aside for a few months (Friedman 1972).

An increasingly permissive and mobile society encourages, and even pressures, adolescents to become sexually active at the earliest possible age. This problem is compounded by one other fact of life; adolescents mature earlier than ever before. On the average, menarche occurs six months earlier than in the last generation (Jekel 1977). Fourteen percent of all 15-year-old females in the U.S. are sexually active; 21% of 18-year-olds, and 46 percent of 19-year-olds are sexually active (Jekel

1977). Fifty-five percent of all adolescents have had sexual intercourse by the time they are 19 (Jekel 1977). Only 45% of those who are sexually experienced have used contraceptives, including those who only occasionally use them.

A dramatic change in the clientele of Planned Parenthood reflects growing sexual precociousness. Prior to 1965 one branch of this community organization in Minnesota (Veerhusen, Cooksey, and Fredlund 1972), typical of branches across the country, served primarily married, or about-to-be-married women of low income. By 1970, 74% of all new patients were unmarried. Fifty-six % had had at least 13 years of education. In 1971 the age of the clientele started dropping. In one year the percentage of adolescents 18 years old or younger increased from 5.4% to 12.2% and has continued to climb.

To aggravate an already awkward situation, adolescence has been extended in the other direction, past high school, through four years in college. One generation ago the adolescent had concrete rites of passage to signal the successful completion of his or her adolescence: physical maturity, financial independence and freedom to marry and support children. Two of these three have disappeared. Because of child labor laws, it is hard for anyone under 20 to get a job. Incredible rates of divorce, a zero population campaign and the cry to get a college education have pushed the average age of marriage from the teens to the twenties.

Only one rite of passage remains, sexual maturity. Regarding sexual expression social messages are clearly contradictory. One message is to delay sexual relations until after college. However, in colleges and universities the men are no longer as a rule segregated from the women. Having reached sexual maturity, they spend most of the day and evening together. Furthermore, restraints on women, historically supposed to be the resisters of sexual advances, have been relaxed, largely as a result of the women's movement of the 1970s. Society also makes it clear that sexual prowess is a benchmark of social maturity; it then insists that teenagers not put this message into practice until years after sexual maturation. A more extensive discussion of this subject can be found in chapter 1.

On the whole, adolescents are not very good about delaying gratification of any kind. Their emotional age often precludes it. The adolescent population continues to get larger and the adult community still does not recognize the gap between what is and what they think it should be. They do not admit that the ideal image of their generation, the virginal girl-wife, has been replaced by an image of sexual experience.

This attitude which is a rift with reality is also assumed by the average teenager. Often the expressed sexual feelings and drives of the teenage girl who becomes pregnant have been unrecognized or ignored (Wolfish 1973); yet the responsibility for avoiding pregnancy is still left to her. According to a New York study (Hausknecht 1972), 95% of girls seeking abortion have never used a contraceptive. In issues of contraception, pregnancy, and abortion, the adolescent girl is basically ignorant of herself as a sexual being. The course of adolescent sexuality is difficult to change, but the outcome, pregnancy, can be averted. The most urgent question then is why do these girls fail to seek, to obtain, and to use adequate contraceptive methods? Availability of contraception and abortion has not reduced the number of deliveries among teenagers (Hale 1978).

Adolescents must come to terms with the highly charged issue of their own sexuality at a time of their lives when they tend to be emotionally and intellectually awkward and financially dependent. For them today's thoughts and feelings are complicated enough; they seldom can gain the distance from their immediate emotions to think ahead.

Sometimes thinking ahead is even repugnant to the adolescent. A good example of this is the girl who says she is only slightly sexually experienced. She confides that on one or two occasions when she did not control her emotions and her physical responses the result was intercourse. But she is convinced it will not happen again. When she goes out with the same boy, she is determined to be strong. To employ a contraceptive or have one available would be tantamount to admitting defeat, would be *premeditated*.

One group of investigators concluded that teenagers who did not use contraceptives fell into three categories (Cobliner, Schulman, and Romney 1973): those that vowed not to engage in sex activities before marriage; the ones that felt that any kind of contraceptive desecrated pure love; and those that were personally and socially irresponsible, like the adolescent boys who say that they do not use contraceptives because it interferes with pleasure. Some teenagers who say when asked about nonuse, "I didn't think I would get pregnant" or "I only messed around a few times," obviously lack an objective knowledge of sexual details. Often they admit to confusion about the rhythm method.

Fear and embarrassment prevent some girls from seeking a physician, since this person might be punitive or tell her parents; fear of contraceptive side effects, especially from the pill and the IUD, keep some from protecting themselves. Some do not know where to go to get contraceptives, and even if they did, do not have the money to buy them. Some can not because of legal restrictions. But peer pressure wins out, and thousands of girls per year have intercourse without using some method of contraception.

Even if an adolescent girl can break through the social and emotional confusion, legal constraints may present yet another barrier. Legal availability of abortion and contraceptive devices to minors varies from state to state, often depending on an individual ruling determining if the teenager is mature or emancipated, as defined by whatever criteria the court decides, such as living away from parents or self-management of financial affairs.

The problem of parental consent is worrisome, both legally and ethically, to physicians who know that if they must withhold advice and contraceptive supply, many adolescent patients will not have anywhere else to turn for help. In Canada the Society for Adolescent Medicine adopted a statement that parents' knowledge and consent are always preferable when treating a minor, but if denial of medical treatment due to lack of parental consent would expose the patient or community to risk, then self-consent should be allowed (Wolfish 1973). The next question is: Who then pays for self-consent treatment? This issue is still being debated in the courts.

The Solutions

The first step to remedying the situation, to preventing unwanted pregnancy sounds easy, but is not. The adult community needs to accept the reality of the situation: the rule of the day is increased sexual activity among teenagers; and women (girls) need medical care to prevent unwanted pregnancy. There is an obvious lag between sexual practices and society's attitudes toward them. Parents still believe that only promiscuous, young, unmarried women get pregnant and seek abortion. There really is little point in trying to stop a sexual revolution by moralizing or turning your back to reality.

As Veerhusen, Cooksey, and Fredlund (1972) so aptly put it:

> If in a major metropolitan area . . . you gather together all of the figures on out-of-wedlock births, all of the figures on infants born less than nine months after the marriage ceremony, if you add to these the growing number of young people going to New York, California and other states for abortions, and put on top of these

all of the young couples seeking birth control services from a variety of community medical services and finally, if you could get an estimate of the number of condoms sold to high school and junior high school boys (you'd also have to add a figure for the lucky ones who are using withdrawal or a douche and to date have not gotten pregnant), the question of need for education, counseling and medical services is more than academic.

Prevention of abortion is not just a medical matter. It is a much more complex problem that also requires the involvement of those in the fields of politics, law, education, and social welfare. Society must not abdicate its responsibility to help protect teenagers from social pressures created by the adult community. The triad of sex education, contraceptive distribution, and counseling, and when all else fails, sensitive pregnancy and abortion counseling must be thoughtfully activated.

SEX EDUCATION

First on most people's list of ways to circumvent abortion is sex education. An increasing variety of services are now offered to the pregnant girl and to the sexually active girl, but little is done to give the adolescent girl the body of knowledge vital to making a choice *before* she becomes sexually active.

Reichelt and Werley (1975) found teenagers painfully lacking in basic sex facts. These researchers measured teenagers' sex knowledge before and after a ''rap session'' about sex and contraceptive use; the session was a prerequisite to obtaining contraceptive materials. Before the session two-fifths of the questions were not answered correctly by a simple majority. After the one session only two items were incorrectly answered by the majority. The speed of information assimilation certainly can not be counted on and probably would surprise their math teachers, but one thing seems certain: the teenagers were eager for information. They are protected from knowledge of contraceptives, but not from the consequences of an unwanted pregnancy.

The major source of information for most teenagers now is the peer group (Reichelt and Werley 1975). Inexperienced or boastful peers can not be depended on for their accuracy. Many people involved with the problem of unwanted pregnancy feel that an effective curriculum of family life and sex education would help teens to (Hale 1978) understand the consequences of their actions, and (Center for Disease Control 1978) be knowledgeable in use of contraceptives if they must be sexually active.

Who should be the teachers? Parents; the schools; the churches; community agencies? This is about as popular a query as how much shall we raise the tax levy. The fact is that parents in the U.S., primarily because they are embarrassed or judgmental, make ineffective teachers about sex, and often look for outside help in imparting the knowledge on this subject to their children.

Teaching sex in church has major advantages and disadvantages. Parents are generally more comfortable knowing that sex is being dealt with in a religious context, within a value system that they, as church members, have chosen. But a church course on sexuality may largely provide religious dogma. Another major disadvantage is that many adolescents do not go to church.

In school they are a captive audience. Possibly the best approach to sex education would be continuum of teaching, starting in preschool and stopping at graduation: a sequential pattern of topics geared to the grade level of the student. Difficult to envision, however, is what it would take for parents, teachers, principals and a Board of Education to agree on the curriculum. Each school district would almost have to make an autonomous decision as to course content. Even then, who would teach the course? Teachers would have to be specially trained.

Whoever the teacher is, he or she should be aggressive but nonjudgmental and should be neither permissive nor punitive. It is very important that teachers do not transmit their own feelings of discomfort. And whoever the principal instructor is, the course should call for participation of health professionals in order to guarantee accurate information.

Basic sex education should include not only concepts about sexuality and reproduction, but also the risks of pregnancy and abortion, as well as practical aspects of prevention. Cobliner, Schulman, and Romney (1973) found that prevention of unnecessary abortion is clearly linked to preventive care and to intensive study of the abortion issue.

Such educational thrusts do not have to be limited to formal school settings. The media, especially in the area of birth control, possesses powerful motivational potential. However, presently, in spite of the pervasive sexual messages routinely promoted by television and the movies, contraceptive advertising is frowned upon. Yet, advertisements for breath fresheners to "catch that certain somebody," deodorants and

151

douches are widespread. Contraceptive commercials that will capture the teenage girl's attention and imagination like the most creative shampoo advertisement are needed.

A branch of Planned Parenthood in Michigan (House and Goldsmith 1972) making a nationwide survey of 153 Planned Parenthood affiliates, identified what appears to be a particularly effective program of sex education. In this program used by several affiliates, education takes three forms: (1) individual interviews, (2) individual or group instruction on birth control methods and (3) "rap sessions." "Rap sessions," probably the fiber that holds the program together, enables the participating teens to explore aspects of sexuality that they normally would not get to discuss in the course of day-to-day living. Discussion subjects include relationships with parents in regard to sexual activity; decision making: to have or not to have sex; male, female expectations and roles; and communication with boyfriends/girlfriends about sexual feelings. In verbally working out some of these problems with peers who are experiencing the same gamut of frustration and confusion, an adolescent has the opportunity to sort out his or her own feelings and begin to construct a value system on which to base adult decision-making.

An offshoot of this Planned Parenthood study is an unexpected positive note about community resistance to sex education: The survey responses showed overwhelmingly that respondents' original expectations of adverse public reactions to the program were not fulfilled. The crisis of unwanted pregnancy is too important to let small segments of the community silence communication so necessary to young people.

LONG-TERM PLANNING VERSUS IMMEDIATE ACTION

An effective sex education system takes time and money to set up. While program plans and teacher selection and training are going on, what can be done now? *Now* the concerned medical professional can provide dignified medical services to the adolescent, including an opportunity for contraceptive and abortion counseling, pregnancy testing, VD screening, Papanicolaou smear testing and contraceptive distribution. Contraceptive dispensing is a preventive measure that can be put into action now, but it should never become an impersonal or mechanical procedure.

Oral contraceptives and the IUD, the two most efficacious birth control methods, are most frequently the devices given to the adolescent girl. Both methods are accompanied by possible side effects, which should be explained to the patient in detail, but both share an important quality: they require little motivation on the part of the teenager. Some motivation is necessary to take the pill daily, but it is outside the realm of passion. The adolescent girl does not have to exert willpower to stop and insist on a condom or foam while in the middle of a sexual encounter.

The physician must go over all birth control methods, their effectiveness, and practical use and raise the issue of the possible consequences of sexual activity, that is, pregnancy and abortion. An alternative contraceptive method must always be offered if one kind is being discontinued.

Schools, T.V. and radio should be encouraged to give out information about where contraceptives can be found; and free contraceptives should be available to those who cannot afford them. A good service should supersede concerns about the adolescent once she becomes pregnant.

But if she does get pregnant, the teenager must be helped to understand all the options open to her, the significance of her pregnancy and how she can avoid a second pregnancy. One campus-based crisis center mentioned in abortion literature (Kerenyi, Glascock, and Horowitz 1973) provides counseling, referrals and an emergency loan fund. Whatever the program, physicians and clinic personnel must be sensitive to the teenager's emotional stress and recognize the emergency of her situation.

The triad of sex education, contraceptive distribution and pregnancy and abortion counseling only works in certain social climates. Changes in the structure and attitudes of society are needed if we are to avoid slipping into the belief that abortion is a contraceptive procedure. We need to take a hard look at adolescent pregnancy, urging our governmental and educational institutions to do the same.

References

Bracken, M. B.; Klerman, L. V.; and Bracken, M. Abortion, adoption, or motherhood: an empirical study of decision-making during pregnancy. *Am. J. Obstet. Gynecol.* 130:251–262, 1978.

Center for Disease Control. Abortion Surveillance 1976. U.S. Government Printing Office Publication No. (CDC) 78–8205, 1978.

Cobliner, W. G.; Schulman, H.; and Romney, S. L. The termination of adolescent out-of-wedlock pregnancies and the prospects for their primary prevention. *Am. J. Obstet. Gynecol.* 115:432–444, 1973.

Dvejic, H. et al. Follow up of 50 adolescent girls two years after abortion. *Can. Med. Assoc. J.* 116:44–46, 1977.

Evans, J. R.; Selstad, G.; and Welcher, W. H. Teenagers: fertility control behavior and attitudes before and after abortion, childbearing or negative pregnancy test. *Fam. Plann. Perspect.* 8(4):192–200, 1976.

Freeman, E. W. Abortion: subjective attitudes and feelings. *Fam. Plann. Perspect.* 10:150–155,1978.

Friedman, C. M. Unwed motherhood: a continuing problem. *Am. J. Psychiatry.* 129:117–121, 1972.

Gabrielson, I. W. et al. Abortion: adolescent's attitudes. *Am. J. Public Health.* 61(4):730–738, 1971.

Hale, M. Meeting the health needs of the sexually active adolescents. *Contemporary OB/GYN.* 12:80–97, 1978.

Hausknecht, R. U. The termination of pregnancy in adolescent women. *Pediatr. Clin. North Am.* 19:803–810, 1972.

House, E. A. and Goldsmith, S. Planned parenthood services for the young teenager. *Fam. Plann. Perspect.* 4:27–31, 1972.

Jacques, R. Abortion and psychological trauma. *Medical Arts and Sciences,* 27:52–59, 1973.

Jekel, J. F. Primary or secondary prevention of adolescent pregnancy? *J. Sch. Health,* 47:457–460, 1977.

Kerenyi, T. D.; Glascock, E. L.; and Horowitz, M. L. Reasons for delayed abortion: results of four hundred interviews. *Am. J. Obstet. Gynecol.* 117:299–311, 1973.

Lipper, I. W. et al. Abortion and the pregnant teenager. *Can. Med. Assoc. J.* 109:852–856, 1973.

Martin, C. Psychological problems of abortion for the unwed teenage girl. *Genet. Psychol. Monogr.* 88:23–110, 1973.

Nadelson, C. Abortion counseling: focus on adolescent pregnancy. *Pediatrics.* 54(6):765–769, 1974.

Reichelt, P. A. and Werley, H. H. A sex information program for sexually active teenagers. *J. Sch. Health.* XLV:100–107, 1975.

Schaffer, C. and Pine, F. Pregnancy, abortion and the developmental tasks of adolescence. *J. Am. Acad. Child Psychiatry.* 11:511–536, 1972.

Schneider, S. M. and Thompson, D. S. Repeat aborters. *Am. J. Obstet. Gynecol.* 126:316–320, 1976.

Sorrel, W. E. Abortion: its psychodynamic effects. *Psychosomatics.* 8:146–149, 1967.

Tietze, C. Contraceptive practice in the context of a non-restrictive abortion law: age-specific pregnancy rates in New York City, 1971–73. *Fam. Plann. Perspect.* 7:197–202, 1975.

Veerhusen, B. A.; Cooksey, P.; and Fredlund, D. Pregnancy: a crisis in health education. *Am. J. Public Health.* 62:821–823, 1972.

Wolfish, M. G. Adolescent sexuality. *Practitioner.* 210:226–231, 1973.

Young, L. R. Out of wedlock: a study of the problems of the unmarried mother and her child. New York: McGraw-Hill, 1954.

Zelnik, M. and Kantner, J. F. Attitudes of American teenagers toward abortion. *Fam. Plann. Perspect.* 7:89–91, 1975.

9 Parenting Education

Peggy B. Smith, Ph.D.

Parenting, although biologically as old as humanity, has only recently become a recognized academic, behavioral, and social entity, with professionals attesting to the importance of its responsibility. Salk (1974) indicates that parenthood is probably the most important role that people assume in life with the least amount of deliberate training. In his estimation, the emotional aspect of parenthood is the area in which people are least prepared. Lieberman (1971) believes that parenting is probably the most difficult and influential task individuals have. As such, it should be a national priority, costly to do well, but more costly to neglect. Probably one of the most provocative statements about parenting was made by Caplan (1977) of the Princeton Center for Infancy who suggests that there should be "licensing" and training for all prospective parents in our society. Although such statements are obviously extreme, in the final analysis, 85% of the population will be involved in some type of parenting experience (whether it be traditional or not) and the teaching of basic skills and responsibilities of parenthood should not be left to chance. To implement such an educational experience and provide deliberate vocational training in the area of parenting, physicians (Spock 1976), educators (White 1975; Kruger 1975), and academicians (Erikson 1950) have endorsed the development of curriculum for elementary and secondary school populations. Additionally, various cultural and sociologic changes have made the general population aware of the need for some organized presentation of parenting information.

Background

Anthropologic and sociologic studies provide information that supports the need to initiate formal training in the area of parenting skills. Whiting and Irvin (1953) indicate that many child-rearing problems are common to all cultures. Actual parenting and child-rearing styles (Benedict 1934; Sears, Maccoby, and Levin 1957) can be identified in various cultural settings. In American society, technologic factors significantly affect the way individuals parent their children. Forces such as stress, family mobility (Weissman and Paykel 1972), the redefinition of the extended family as a supporting resource, (Turner 1975), and the lifestyle of an urbanized and industrial nation have gradually combined to change the cultural tenets on which traditional parenting activities are based (Solomon 1973).

The development of parenting curricula also reflects the impact of the changing role of women (Friedan 1963) on child-rearing practices. The redefinition of a woman's responsibilities to her family and children has been profound. Increased numbers of professionally trained women and the spiral of inflation have gradually created a massive women's work force. The number of women workers has more than doubled since the early 1940s and the number of working mothers has increased eightfold since that time. More than 50% of wives who worked in 1972 had children under 18 (Seifer 1973). A woman's ability to earn a pay check not only enhances her independence but also forces the issue of who is ultimately responsible for the parenting of the children. The combination of marriage, motherhood, and a career is increasingly being chosen by college freshmen (Epstein and Branzaft 1972). Elective absence from the home usually redistributes the responsibility of raising the children between the parents in a more egalitarian way. This new division of labor in caring for children has initiated a reassessment of the various skills and abilities necessary to raise a family competently. Reevaluation also underscores the need for the development of parenting curricula that portrays childrearing as a joint venture by both the father and mother.

Studies of early childhood learning patterns have also influenced the development of parenting curricula. In the academic area, numerous authors have stressed the significance of early childhood development (Bruner 1968; Brackbill 1967; White 1975), some asserting that it is the prime period to establish learning foundations. Bloom, Davis, and Hess (1965) indicate that with early learning experiences many young children are able to more readily acquire language and reading proficiencies. Motor abilities are known to profit from early stimulation (Johnston 1966) and the importance of this stimulation through trained interaction has been recognized. It is apparent that parents should have an opportunity to learn as many techniques as possible that might maximize their children's development. Parenthood education as a part of a general curriculum is considered by some to be the vehicle to convey such information before a pregnancy occurs.

The media has indirectly contributed significantly to the education for parenthood movement. Television programs such as ''Sesame Street'' developed by Children's Television Workshop recognize that environmental influences have their greatest impact on childhood development prior to school entrance and that early cognitive development of preschool children is often depressed by poverty or discrimination. Using a magazine format, the series presented cognitive concepts to preschoolers through novelty, variety, and lively delivery. It should be noted that recent evaluators believe that parental effort and influence may strengthen the power of programs like Sesame Street to bridge the gap between socio-economic populations (Cook and co-workers 1975). They also suggest that parental encouragement accompanying television watching will materially affect early learning. Evaluation of the series found that, in the presence of such encouragement, three-year-old children were capable of learning concepts not usually introduced until the three-year level.

The abundance of popular literature on the subject of parenting has helped to create an awareness among the general population of the importance of prior training for parenthood, whether it be during adolescence or adulthood (Salk 1974; Caplan 1977; White 1975). Approaches to parenthood responsibilities are quite diverse. Some authors reemphasize Piagetian stages of learning and their importance in cognitive development (Braga and Braga 1975). Others stress the practical side of parenting with cookbook solutions to specific problems (Corsini and Painter 1975; Dreikurs 1972).

Educators have recently attempted to apply classical child growth and development theories to child-rearing techniques appropriate to a changing technologic culture. Some writers interpret child-rearing techniques in terms of the Skinnerian model and its off-shoot therapy of behavior modification (Bird and Bird 1972). They suggest that by adapting the classical stimulus-response learning model to guidelines for raising children, behavior can be molded into the appropriate outcomes. Others concentrate on the affective domain of parenting (Gordon 1970). One school of thought emphasizes the development of communicative skills which sensitize parents to their child's needs as well as teach techniques to diffuse anger through the use of descriptive language (Ginott 1965; Faber and Mazlish 1974).

Despite the variety of attempts to apply theory to everyday parenting behaviors, there is still the question of how soon organized parenting skills should be applied to enhance educational development. There is concern that educational enrichment stimulation, now being advocated, is not being initiated early enough. Some researchers (White 1975) have proposed that intervention, to be truly effective, must begin by the first three years of life. Adapting such a hypothesis to parenting training opportunities means that school curricula should incorporate basic parenting concepts into a variety of elementary and secondary experiences so that potential parents will be reached soon enough to bring about change.

In addition to providing information and training that refine parenting skills and practices, parenting education is often considered a possible prophylactic or remedial step in the amelioration of a variety of social problems, one being child abuse and neglect. Although children have been mistreated and killed by ritual, accident, or malicious intent from the dawn of the human race (Solomon 1973), identification of these phenomena and their possible prevention through education are of recent origin. Interestingly, most of the early efforts came from specialists in pediatric radiology (Caffey 1946; Silver and Kempe 1959) who were concerned initially about medical treatment (Elmer 1963). The concept of the "battered child" was established in the 1940s and has remained a verbal stimulus for societal action aimed at the protection of dependent children.

Widespread interest generated from those reports has brought about initial affirmative action, one phase of which is parenting education. Documentation of the incidence of child abuse has increased in reliability because of legal reporting requirements (Isaacs 1973) and organization of central registries (Gil 1975). Broad identification guidelines for the abused child (Zalba 1967), the abusive parent (Wasserman 1967), and the family dynamics involved (Isaacs 1973) have also developed.

The analysis of parent-child relations in child abuse cases reveals patterns that reaffirm the need for parenting education. The evolving profiles of the parents show that they may be sensitive to stressful situations (Solomon 1973), may possibly lack good parent models themselves (Rubin 1966), and may have inappropriate behavioral expectations of their children (Broeck 1974). Since true pathologic personalities were not identified, the individuals profiled seem to, in the main, have mislearned the parental role. These persons, whether biologic or surrogate parents, had distorted perceptions of the meaning of parenthood as well as misconceptions of the basic needs and behaviors of their progeny. For example, such parents often expected too early milestones in the child's emotional and psychological development. When the child fails to fulfill such expectations, these parents frequently become frustrated and angry. These reactions, rooted in ignorance, result in child abuse and neglect.

Moreover, parental love and child abuse and neglect, while seemingly a bizarre combination, are not mutually exclusive. Various sources revealed that some reasons for abuse and neglect find their basis in "love" (Delsordo 1963). Punishment may be conducted for the child's own good or considered a lesson needed for character development. Parents have inappropriately physically confined children to protect them from harm. Thus, actions which may appear cruel and unusual to the objective eye are considered by the instigators as acceptable and "loving" parenting behavior.

In order to prevent child abuse and neglect, various educational programs are recommended to teach appropriate parenting skills, attitudes, and behaviors according to the needs of a selected target audience. Such parenting education measures can provide academic and effective information relevant to the task of child rearing. Insight into communication styles and interpersonal interaction is especially helpful to parents who are predisposed toward perpetrating abusive and/or neglectful acts toward their children.

A similar growing social problem that could benefit to some degree from the introduction of training in parenting skills is teenage pregnancy. Many disciplines have worked with the pregnant adolescent and have affirmed her high-risk status in a variety of ways. As indicated in discussions in previous chapters, the medical, emotional, and educational difficulties of this population are significant. Professionals who initially focused attention on the "at risk" adolescent mother are gradually extending their attention to the child as well. Although extensive assessment of child-rearing techniques of young parents has not been done (Williams 1974), available information indicates a recent shift from a heavy emphasis on the adoption alternative to child rearing as a single parent. Studies indicate that the girl who elects not to terminate pregnancy does so with the basic intention of raising her child to maturity (Smith 1975). Whereas single parenthood status has in the past been more prevalent among some minorities, this behavior is now becoming visible across all racial groups. Obviously single parenthood status affects not only the mother's future education and sociologic alternatives, but also the future of the infant. Thus, programs that initially treated the pregnant adolescent solely in a medical context have expanded to include preparation for her ongoing education and future vocation as a wage earner. Continuing in this direction, the next step that many see as logical and necessary is provision of training for her competent parenthood (Braen and Forbush 1975). In fact, the plight of the adolescent parent appears to be a significant factor in facilitating the development of the parenthood education movement. As Kruger (1975) points out:

> A basic concern must move beyond the pregnant girl for whom prevention is too late, to the universe of young people who are potential school-aged parents. Experience has shown that this phase of education must concentrate not only on assuring an understanding of biological factors of human reproduction and of responsible sexual behavior, but also must concentrate on assuring an understanding of the responsibilities and demands—yes the joy as well—of the parent role.

Programs from the Private Sector

The majority of programs in parenting education developed by the private sector for school use are fairly consistent in content. The issues usually covered are: perinatal development, baby care, personal hygiene, money management, child development, family and peer relationships, and in some cases information on human sexuality. The primary variances among developed packages are the target audiences, reading level, creativity in presentation, areas of emphasis, and selection of teaching techniques.

For the pregnant girl or teen mother, several curricula have been developed that directly address issues surrounding the pregnancy and the care of the child. The Consortium on Early Child Bearing and Child Rearing, Child Welfare League of America (1974), has devised six workbooks for this audience which, in a multi-ethnic format, focus on the needs of the teen mother. Detailed information is given on the actual birth process and on the specific needs of the newborn. Early child development and child care are also emphasized. Relationships with family members and with the father of the baby are also discussed. The issues of marriage, especially for the single parent, are covered in a workbook volume. Some included aspects, however, would not be appropriate for nonpregnant school age students or for families of students who live in conservative and/or sheltered communities.

Another parenting curriculum developed for utilization with pregnant adolescents is *Teenage Pregnancy: A New Beginning* (Barr and Monserrat 1978). Developed and pilot tested primarily with teenage parent audiences, the format, reading level, and approach reflect the needs of teenage parents specifically in the southwestern part of the United States. The curriculum is quite sensitive to the cross-cultural issues that affect individuals of Spanish and American Indian origin. Included in the curriculum package are supplementary materials on exercises and breast feeding, with Spanish editions available. School usage of this curriculum is facilitated by a student study guide and by a preliminary and follow-up test. As with the other curricula for teen mothers, the specific focus is on the pregnancy, and the explicitness of included information may limit its use for the general adolescent population.

A third curriculum for the pregnant adolescent has been developed by Bank Street College of Education and focuses on issues of good nutrition for both mother and child and the emotional and physical aspects of pregnancy. This package utilizes a comic book format for some components. Two examples, "The Junk Food Blues" and "Days of Change" are accompanied by fact books providing more in-depth material. A teacher's guide, flash cards, pregnancy weight charts, and posters are also provided.

The format of other parenting projects focuses on the needs of the nonpregnant girl and boy. "Starting a Health Family," designed by the Educational Development Center, provides course materials that discuss the responsibilities of pregnancy in parenthood and the association between adolescent pregnancy and birth defects. This latter emphasis may be attributed to the fact that the National Foundation-March of Dimes is one of the primary funders of this project. The materials are developed for students in both junior and senior high schools and their parents. A teacher guide also accompanies the material. A unique aspect of this curriculum series is tape cassette interviews with teenagers and older parents who talk about their experiences with pregnancy and parenthood. The material and content are augmented by a discussion guide that focuses on the issues of responsibility, values, clarification, and decision making.

The Boys Club of America, Boy Scouts of America, Future Homemakers of America, and Girl Scouts of America have all been actively involved in developing parenting curricula. Some of these projects move beyond the issue of parenting to the specifics of infant care and play. The Johns Hopkins Hospital prepared a series entitled "Infant Play and Learning" that attempts to help parents and other child caretakers make better selection and use of play materials for infants. The focus of this curriculum is primarily for infants from one to 12 months of life.

The mass media has also become involved in the area of currriculum development and parenting education. A series entitled "Middle Road Traveler" consists of 12 video tapes and/or 16mm films with instructor's guides to be used for the junior high school group. Developed by Baylor College of Medicine-Population Program, Texas Child Care 76, Inc., Gulf Region Education Television Affiliates, and the Houston Independent School District, this presentation uses a magazine format similar to Sesame Street to dramatize the basics young people need to know about children before they decide to become parents. One of the segments in the film series repeated in each tape is of a soap opera entitled "Third House From the Corner." It tells of the problems of a young couple who decide to marry and live with the wife's family. Some of the topic areas addressed by the couple are parental expectations, economics, nutrition, health, safety, discipline, legal rights and responsibilities, family living styles, communication, interpersonal relationships, and child development. Three or more of these topics are built into each of the first 11 segments and are reinforced through repetition. The twelfth tape summarizes the entire series.

The National Foundation-March of Dimes has also been instrumental in developing a variety of audio-visual resources that can be used in the context on parenting education. Reflective of this developmental source, most of the material focuses heavily on medical issues involved in parenting. However, within this focus a wide range of topics is covered. Nutrition, sickle cell, venereal disease, rubella, drugs, and genetics are all addressed in a media format. In addition, a general discussion of parenting featuring Dr. Lee Salk looks at practical and positive issues of being a parent. This information is suitable for both junior and senior high school students.

Audio-visual material has also been developed that focuses on the special needs of adolescent parents. Parent Magazine Films, Inc. has developed a variety of filmstrip sets on child development and family relationships that look directly at the problems faced by the adolescent parent. Issues such as daily routines and problems, planning for the future, and the realities of parenthood are handled in an appealing and insightful manner. Each of the sets contains five colored filmstrips with audio record or cassettes, audio script booklets, and accompanying discussion guide.

Federal Initiatives in Parenting Education

The Federal Government has also initiated efforts to endorse and encourage endeavors and instruction in parenting education. In 1972 the Department of Health, Education and Welfare created the interagency Task Force on Comprehensive Programs for School Age Parents; primary responsibility for its activities was given to the Office of Education under the directorship of W. Stanley Kruger. Although the Task Force primarily encouraged the establishment and expansion of comprehensive services for teen parents, its effort facilitated the development of parenting projects for nonpregnant girls and teenage boys. In 1973 the Office of Education, in cooperation with the Office of Child Development, initiated the Education for Parenthood Projects. The major feature of this project is the Exploring Childhood Curriculum developed by the Educational Development Center in Newton, Massachusetts. By 1978, student participation in this project had surpassed 200,000. This educational experience offered high school boys and girls the opportunity for field placements where they could interact with young children and have experiences in the vocation of child care. Adolescents had an opportunity to obtain practical information on child development that was applicable to their present and future vocations. Voluntary youth service agencies have been significantly involved in developing the Exploring Childhood Series. Agencies such as the Boy Scouts, Girl Scouts, Boy's Club, and the Salvation Army have developed supplemental materials concerning various aspects of child care.

Federal initiatives have also encouraged the development of training material for individuals interested in entering occupations related to child care. The teaching module "Child Care and Development Occupations" was designed by the Atlanta Public Schools to assist in these training activities. The curriculum was developed primarily for use by teachers in vocational and technical education, secondary and post-secondary schools, and adult programs. The format consists of 25 self-contained nonsequential units easily adaptable to a variety of training programs, both in the public and private sector.

The federal government has also encouraged the development of parenting materials that focus on the needs of special interest groups. Educational materials have been developed directed to the needs of the physically and mentally handicapped and, although not appropriate for the needs of the general population, provide specialized information and support to families with special problems.

Emerging Issues of Parenting

For a variety of cultural, economic, and traditional reasons, when one speaks of the vocation of parenthood, the emphasis is tacitly placed on the mother. Through some covert process of biologic predestination, parenthood often appears to be synonymous with motherhood. Growing concern, however, has been expressed for the role of the father, with some professionals suggesting that more attention should be added to the fathering process. Dodson (1974) stresses the importance of the male role model and of the needed interaction of the father to formulate a strong emotional bond and well-developed sexual identity. The importance of the father is also stressed by Biller and Meredith (1974) who emphasize through a variety of examples that child caring and rearing behaviors in no way contradict the masculine role. In the text, Biller and Meredith not only emphasize the contributions of the father but also demonstrate his role in the development of the child's learning style and analytic behavior. Throughout their work, heavy emphasis is placed on the importance of the male role and his integral part in all aspects of parenthood.

Another emerging trend in the area of parenting is specialization of information concerning the raising of minority children. Based on the fact that most books on child care are written for middle class white families, several authors have indicated that the developmental needs of minority children include special problems specific to their race. Such works emphasize the importance of children growing up secure in their identity and comfortable with the relationships with individuals from all racial backgrounds. Comer and Poussaint (1975) focus on race related issues of childbearing and rearing in lower income families. Other works written on black child rearing also examine the affective messages transmitted interracially and how these attitudes affect the role of parenting in black families (Harrison-Roth and Wyden 1973).

As the field of parenting moves out of the developmental stage and emerges into the area of scientific documentation, it must face the issue of evaluation. In order to establish credibility as an independent entity, the science of parenting must demonstrate that the presentation of appropriate information on how to raise children will bring about positive change that can be measured in a valid and reliable manner.

In order to insure effectiveness, several preliminary prerequisites for a parenting curriculum are mandatory. Probably the most important criterion is a level of information that appeals to the particular audience. The ability to make the content interesting to a pre-parent audience is a huge challenge in itself. For the never-pregnant teen, the specific content on child caring and rearing may not be relevant. These adolescents for the most part have had limited exposure to infants and children outside of their own family, usually confined to baby sitting. Such superficial contact with infants does not provide a realistic picture of parenthood. Moreover, because most adolescents are not pregnant, the need for information on parenting is not immediate and therefore may be emotionally disregarded by the adolescent as ''excess learning baggage.'' Some developers of parenting projects have been able to circumvent this issue. They have succeeded by providing material of high interest in a lively manner. Delivery becomes as important as content. In this way, the adolescent's attention is directed toward the content of parenting and child rearing.

A second prerequisite is the reconciliation of materials on parenting with the developmental process of adolescence. As a part of their transition from childhood to adulthood, adolescents in general manifest very little interest in future issues, even though those issues may be affected by immediate activities. Therefore, the consequences of the adolescent's actions may not be realistically perceived and evaluated prior to initiation of behavior. This typical adolescent thought process is especially relevant to the issues of childbearing and rearing. Many adolescents have difficulty reconciling the cause and effect relationships between intercourse, pregnancy, and parenthood. This normal consequence of action may not, in their estimation, apply personally. The fact that sometime in the future they may become parents is not a strong enough reason for them to generate active and enthusiastic involvement in such curricular programs. Such lack of perceived need on the part of adolescents was documented in the evaluation of the Education for Parenthood curriculum (1978). In response to the query that parents should become parents only after they know a lot about raising children, a substantial minority of the sampled youth did not believe or were not sure that it was necessary to have this knowledge. The evaluators conclude that ''the need for education for parenthood is apparently not evident to a fairly large group of young people in the country and . . . that the Education for Parenthood Program appears to have minimal influence in changing opinions on this issue'' (Morris 1977).

Fortunately, most successful parenting projects are able to make the material appealing to the adolescent while presenting substantive content. With this task accomplished, these projects have attempted to measure the effects of such content on target audiences. The decision as to what to measure should be predicated on the stated goals and objectives. Although the specifics among projects may vary, most evaluation provides descriptive data on participating populations, programmatic specifics, administrative effectiveness, and the degree of parental involvement. In addition, evaluation of parenting projects should include assessment of changes in these three areas: knowledge, attitudes, and behaviors in the target group as a result of participation in the parenting project. It should be pointed out that two of these three components can be easily evaluated. By means of a preliminary and follow-up written test, changes in knowledge and attitude can be ascertained. However, measuring behavioral change as it relates to parenting is fraught with difficulties. For the nonpregnant adolescent the assessment of behavioral change requires long-term monitoring of the adolescent's reproductive and childrearing behavior. This process demands identifying those adolescents who are sexually active and who elect to use birth control or abortion. Accurate assessment must also concern itself with those adolescents who find themselves pregnant and who elect to carry the pregnancy to term. Other monitoring problems include ethical, political, and pragmatic aspects. Even if one gets beyond the invasion of privacy aspect, following individuals over a five to ten year period is a difficult research project at best. Moreover, such an effort may not be sensitive to intervening experiences that may drastically affect parents' childrearing behaviors for better or worse.

Some projects, in order to provide a behavioral outcome assessment, have been able to circumvent the problems of long-term follow-up by evaluating parenting skills through the assessment of on-site performance. Several projects have built-in nursery components which allow adolescents to apply their learning by actually working with children. Given the availability of appropriate supervision of these activities, such an evaluation can provide valuable information. However, one should be aware that the nature of such child care nurseries may be stilted and artificial, not representing ''real life'' parenting situations.

Even when curricular objectives are clearly and specifically delineated within the areas of knowledge and attitudes, the mechanics of evaluation are often a significant task because of the absence of already existing parameters. Innovative projects by definition lack the documented track record of success; no single standardized instrument can adequately measure the effects of new curricula on target audiences. Projects that attempt to assess their accomplishments in terms of learning and attitude change are therefore often faced with the additional challenge of developing valid and reliable evaluation instruments. In order to shorten this sometimes tedious and time-consuming task, some projects have developed new questions and combined them with already existing evaluation materials that have been standardized with similar audiences. One should be cautioned, however, that items taken out of context often shortchange the total impact of new and innovative programs.

In spite of the variety of obstacles encountered in the implementation of evaluation design, a number of projects have been able to document either empirically or descriptively the effects of the parenting curriculum. The project entitled "Education for Parenthood" was a parenting project whose target audience consisted of the youth in national voluntary organizations. Evaluation focused not only on demographic and related information, but also on participants' attitudes concerning children, parents, careers, and child care skills. Basic knowledge about prenatal development, child development, social and medical needs of children, family and adult-child interaction, adolescence, and sexual behaviors were also assessed. The overall evaluation of the program by participants was also obtained. In general, the most significant change was a movement from the traditional family definition to shared parenting. Predictably, differences were noted between male and female responses. Positive changes were also found in participants' self-esteem and their perception of their own care for children. One area of note was the response indicating that participants did not feel that they could influence or improve the intelligence of their children through stimulation. In the category of knowledge, some gains were noted, but they were small. However, the general opinion of participation in the projects was quite positive, with only 3% indicating that the experience was negative.

An empirical assessment was also conducted on the video parenting series entitled "Middle Road Traveler." The junior high school boy and girl were the target audience for this series. Utilizing a magazine format, this audio-visual parenting project was evaluated on several dimensions. Formative and summative evaluation were conducted during a 15 month

167

contract with attention focused on measuring change brought about by student attitudes and knowledge as a result of viewing the series. By developing a pilot trial evaluation instrument, the evaluation staff was able to assess baseline data on parenting knowledge, student attitudes concerning commercial and instructional television, and child-rearing experiences at the target age group. After viewing each of the 12 tapes, measurement of knowledge and attitude were obtained. In general, the participating students made significant gains in various curriculum objectives. The strongest cognitive gains were made in the areas of expectations, child development, discipline, and economics. The gains in the affective domain were even more striking. The evaluators (Will and Hotvedt 1977) pointed out that more than one-half of the standard deviation was obtained in the area of communication objectives. The viewer appeal of this series was also positively evaluated. In general, the series's effectiveness exceeded both commercial and instructional television in a variety of measures. As in the Education for Parenthood series, significant differences in learning between the sexes were observed. The most significant observed difference for the male was the gain made in attitudes concerning the economics of parenting. As might be expected, the females who participated in the project showed the greatest overall gains.

Problems in Parenting Education

The implementation process of massive programs in parenthood education must address a variety of difficult problems. One of the most pervasive problems is the general lack of awareness and, in some cases, apathy concerning the prerequisite skills for parenthood. The parenting/nurturing role has erroneously been thought to be species-specific behavior not affected by the learning process. For many years the possibility that parents were inadequate because of innate deficiencies was not even considered. Nurturing behavior was considered specially indigenous in the female. The mother was seen as equipped with instinctive maternal behavior that provided her a complete repertoire of mothering skills. Recent findings implicate the mother as perhaps playing a primary role as perpetrator of child abuse and neglect and underscore the fallacy of the "innate" belief (Gil 1975).

Research has shown that roles are learned phenomena, and parenting behaviors are no exceptions (McNeil 1973). Parenthood is biologic only in its most limited sense. Some research has gone so far as to suggest that emotional bonding, if not established early in the infant's life, will not positively develop in the parent-child relationship (Klaus and Kennell 1970). Conscious subsequent levels of parenting have cultural and sociologic implications that are affected by covert processes of learning and vocational training.

After the need for parenting instruction has been recognized, implementation problems must also be resolved. A primary issue is to select specific curriculum content. Philosophical focus, therefore, must be defined. The curriculum may be primarily child-oriented, emphasizing the physical, emotional, and psychologic needs of the newborn, or it may pertain primarily to the development of skills in the parent population. Usually a compromise is struck between these approaches; then decisions must be made to achieve an appropriate balance between these two approaches. Because of this lack of consensus over content objectives, evaluation of leadership in the field has sometimes been in conflict. Diverse disciplines converging on parenting education as a common cause must resolve or at least neutralize issues of territoriality and turf. Many educational institutions are unable to deal with this conceptual and curricular conflict and are therefore immobilized in the implementation process.

Parenthood education like sex education, in the school setting, must also attend to the semantic name game. Since the school has become the logical vehicle for disseminating parenting curricula to the school-age population, preexisting sensitivities to certain words in the educational area become issues in parenting education. One such often confused issue is the equation of sex education with parenting curricula. While some authors (Gordon and Wollin 1975) find significant content overlap between the two topics, some professionals believe that parenting curricula is distinct from human sexuality. As Francis J. Roberts (1976), President of Bank Street College of Education indicates that

> just as parenthood is more than child care, it is important for schools thinking about curriculum to help communities understand that preparation for parenthood is not primarily "sex education." Unfortunately, the reason why so many communities get nowhere on parent preparation is that adults get great gratification in debating the pros and cons of sex education and seldom get beyond this point of beginning.

It appears that in light of possible retaliation by opponents in the community the political fears stimulated by the pairing of sex education and parenting curriculum seem well founded.

This approach to parenting education, however, is not universally accepted. Critics feel that the educational materials available are too limited in scope, and in some cases, unrealistic. Ambrose (1978) states that in a number of publications concerning parenting:

> There is no suggestion that in real life, the consequences of childbirth for the teenager may include curtailed schooling, limited job opportunities and a life of poverty for the mother and her child. Given its rosy view of teenage pregnancy outcome, (there is) no need to discuss the alternative of abortion, or the risk of future unplanned pregnancies or the need to use contraception to avert them.

While such presentations may mollify individual sensitivities to issues of human sexuality, the unrealistic nature of the content may lull the adolescent into false security, thereby dulling her perception of consequences to her actions.

References

Ambrose, L. Misinforming pregnant teenagers. *Fam. Plann. Perspect.* 10:51, 1978.

Barr, L., and Monserrat, C. *Teenage pregnancy: A new beginning.* Albuquerque, New Mexico: New Futures, Inc., 1978.

Benedict, R. *Patterns of culture.* Boston: Houghton Mifflin Company, 1934.

Biller, H., and Meredith, D. *Father power.* New York: David McKay Company, Inc., 1974.

Bird, J., and Bird, L. *Power to the parents.* New York: Doubleday and Company, 1972.

Bloom, B. S.; Davis, A.; and Hess, R. *Compensatory education for cultural deprivation.* New York: Holt, Rinehart and Winston, 1965.

Brackbill, Y. *Infancy-early childhood, a handbook to human development.* New York: The Free Press, 1967.

Braen, B. B., and Forbush, J. B. School-age parenthood—A national overview. *J. Sch. Health* 5:45:256–267, 1975.

Braga, L., and Braga J. *Learning and growing.* Englewood Cliffs, New Jersey: Prentice-Hall, 1975.

Broeck, E. T. The extended family center. *Children Today* 3:2–6, 1974.

Bruner, J. S. *Cognition and learning in human development*. Symposium at St. Christopher's Hospital, Temple University, Philadelphia, 1968.

Caffey, J. Multiple fractures in long bones of infants suffering from chronic subdural hematoma. *A.J.R.* 56:163–173, 1946.

Comer, J. P., and Poussaint, A. F. *Black child care*. New York: Simon and Schuster, 1975.

Cook, T. D.; Appleton, H.; Conher, R.; Schaffer, A.; Tamkin, G.; and Weber, S. J. *Sesame street revisited: a study in evaluation research*. New York: Russell Sage Foundation, 1975.

Corsini, R. J., and Painter, G. *The practical parent*. New York: Harper and Row, Publishers, 1975.

Delsordo, J. D. Protective case work for abused children. *Children* 10:213–218, 1963.

Dodson, F. *How to father*. Los Angeles: Nash Publishing Company, 1974.

Dreikurs, R. *The challenge of child training*. New York: Hawthorne Books, 1972.

Elmer, E. Identification of abused children. *Children* 10:180–184, 1963.

Epstein, G. F., and Branzaft, A. L. Female freshmen view their roles as women. *J. Marriage and Fam.* 34:671–672, 1972.

Erikson, E. H. *Children and society*. New York: W. W. Norton, 1964.

Faber, A., and Mazlish, E. *Liberated parents, liberated children*. New York: Grossett and Dunlap, 1974.

Friedan, B. *The feminine mystique*. New York: W. W. Norton, 1963.

Gil, D. G. Unraveling child abuse. *Am. J. Orthopsychiatry* 45:346–356, 1975.

Ginott, H. *Between parent and child*. New York: Macmillan, Inc., 1965.

Gordon, S., and Wollin, M. *Parenting: a guide for young people*. New York: William H. Sadlier, Inc., 1975.

Gordon T. *Parent effectiveness training*. New York: David McKay, Co., Van Ree Press, 1970.

Harrison-Ross, P., and Wyden, B. *The black child, a parent's guide*. New York: Peter Wyden, Inc., 1973.

Isaacs, J. L. The law and the abused and neglected child. *Pediatrics* 51:783–792, 1973.

Johnston, M. K.; Kelley, C. S.; Harris, F. R.; and Wolf, M. W. Application of reinforcement principles to development of motor skills of a young child. *Child Dev.* 37:379–387, 1966.

Klaus, M. H., and Kennell, J. H. Mothers separated from their newborn infants. *Pediatr. Clin. North Am.* 17:1015–1037, 1970.

Kruger, W. S. Education for parenthood and school-age parents. *J. Sch. Health* 5:292–296, 1975.

Lieberman, E. J. Informed consent for parenthood. In *Abortion and the unwanted child,* ed. C. Reiterman. New York: Springer Publishing Co., 1971.

McNeil, E. B. *Being human, the psychological experience*. New York: Harper and Row, 1973.

Morris, L. A. ed. *Education for parenthood: a program, curriculum and evaluation guide*. Washington, D.C.: H.E.W. Publication No.

(OHDS) 77–30125, 1977.

Princeton Center for Early Childhood, The first twelve months: your baby's growth and development in the first year of life. New York: Grossett and Dunlap, 1977.

Roberts, F. J. An educator's view of parenthood preparation in the schools. Speech given at Parenting—PTA Priority, March 25–27, 1976.

Rubin, J. The need for intervention. *Public Welfare* 24:230–235, 1966.

Salk, L. *Preparing for parenthood.* New York: David McKay Company, 1974.

Sears, R. R.; Maccoby, E. E.; and Levin, H. *Patterns of child rearing.* Evanston, Illinois: Row, Peterson and Company, 1957.

Seifer, N. *Absent from the majority: working class women in america.* New York: American Jewish Committee, 1973.

Silver, H. K., and Kempe, C. H. Problems of parental criminal neglect and severe physical abuse of children. *J. Dis. Child* 95:528, 1959.

Smith, P. B.; Mumford, D. M.; Goldfarb, J. L.; and Kaufman, R. H. Selected aspects of adolescent postpartum behavior. *J. Reprod. Med.* 14:159–165, 1975.

Solomon, T. History and demography of child abuse. *Pediatrics*

51:4, 773–776, 1973.

Spock, B. *Baby and child care.* New York: Pocketbooks, 1976.

Turner, J. G. Patterns of intergenerational exchange. A developmental approach. *Int. J. Hum. Dev.* 6(2):111–115, 1975.

Wasserman, S. The abused parent of the abused child. *Children* 175–179, 1967.

Weissman, M. W., and Paykel, E. S. Moving and depression in women. *Society* 9(9):24–28, 1972.

White, B. L. *The first three years of life.* Englewood Cliffs, New Jersey: Prentice-Hall, 1975.

Whiting, J. W. M., and Irvin, L. C. *Child training and personality.* New Haven: Yale University Press, 1953.

Will, E., and Hotvedt, M. O. Parenting education through television: an evaluation of the middle road traveler series for adolescents. Program for Health Management, Baylor College of Medicine, 1977.

Williams, T. M. Child-rearing practices of young mothers: what we know, how it matters, why it's so little. *Am. J. Orthopsychiatry* 44:70–75, 1974.

Zalba, S. R. The abused child. A typology for classification and treatment. *Soc. Work Health Care* 1967.

10 Legal Aspects of Adolescent Pregnancy

Carla W. Dowben, J.D.
Peggy L. Bunch, J.D.

Minors' Consent to Medical Treatment

In the last decade the legal community and legislators have given much attention to the adolescent's right to exercise control over her body. Significant legal changes have occurred that affect sexually active minors, pregnant adolescents, and adolescents who have become parents. Historically, children were considered property of their parents, and parental consent was an absolute requirement for providing medical treatment to minors except in very unusual circumstances. If a physician treated a minor child without parental consent, he risked being charged with assault and battery because the minor was regarded by the law as unable to consent to medical treatment. Because of the threat of criminal charges or civil suit, physicians were reluctant to treat adolescents without parental consent. Adolescents were reluctant to ask their parents for consent for treatment when it involved telling them about sexual activities.

These legal rules have begun to be altered in recognition of significant changes in the social and life styles of young adults. Larger numbers of adolescents are living away from their families before they reach the legal age of majority. Sexual activity of young persons is increasing and the age at which sexual intercourse begins for young males and females is steadily dropping. As a result larger numbers of pregnancies as well as venereal disease and other sex-related medical problems are occurring in an increasingly younger population. It was apparently the recognition of an epidemic of venereal disease in sexually active minors in the 1960s that led many states to either remove the age limit or significantly lower the age at which minors could consent by themselves to medical treatment without the requirement of parental consent.[1] While it is still the general legal rule in the absence of specific state laws that minors need parental consent to see a physician or to receive medical and surgical care before the age of majority in their state of residence, there are at present at least four possible circumstances (depending on the law in the particular state where the young person lives) that may permit her to receive medical care without parental consent.

First, by legislation many states permit minors to consent on their own to medical treatment at a lower age (at 16 or 14) than the age of majority, and a few states have no minimum age at all. It is important for health providers to check the "minor treatment law" of their state.[2] Many states specify medical conditions (such as venereal disease or pregnancy) for which a minor of any age does not need parental consent to receive medical treatment, or the age or circumstances at which a young person may consent to medical treatment on their own.

Second, in a genuine medical emergency which poses an immediate threat to a minor, the law implies consent when the consent of a parent or guardian cannot be easily obtained.[3] In an emergency situation doctors can proceed to treat young persons without fearing liability for not having obtained parental consent.[2] Some states have now broadened the definition of a medical emergency to include not only an immediate danger to life but also the health or mental well-being of a child.[3,4]

Third, emancipated minors also are given the power to consent. A precise determination of when a minor is emancipated depends on the statutory definition in the particular state. Ordinarily, an emancipated minor is one who is emancipated from parental control by living apart from their parents and by financially supporting themselves at least in part or by managing their own financial affairs regardless of the source of income. They also may become emancipated for purposes of consent to medical treatment by marrying, or by having a child, or by entering the armed forces. If the married minor is later divorced, the minor remains emancipated. It is also possible to emancipate a minor through a judicial order of a court of law. A large number of states expressly state by law that an emancipated minor may consent to any medical care and treatment without permission of her parents.[2]

Fourth, in recent years yet another legal exception to the requirement for parental consent has been recognized. It is called the "mature minor rule." No cases can be found in the last two decades in which a parent was able to recover damages for treatment of a minor 15 or older without parental consent even when there was no "minor treatment statute." A mature minor is one who has sufficient intelligence and maturity to comprehend and to appreciate the nature of the medical treatment sought or proposed by the physician and to understand the possible consequences of treatment. The mature minor is considered capable of giving an informed consent, but there is no precise guideline for determination of a mature minor. Factors to consider include not only the emotional and mental maturity of the minor, but also the nature and seriousness of the proposed medical treatment.[5]

Financial Responsibility for Medical Care

Ordinarily, parents are required to pay for the necessary expenses of their children. Necessaries are goods or services provided for the health and welfare of a child, such as food, clothing, shelter, and medical care. Medical costs are clearly considered a necessary expense in normal circumstances.[6] However, if an adolescent child claims to be an ''emancipated'' or a ''mature'' minor and consents to her own treatment, she will usually be liable for her own bills. Also, the minor cannot later disaffirm the contract she made with the doctor or hospital for medical care; this constitutes an exception to ordinary contract law according to which a minor may disaffirm a contract she enters into until she reaches the age of majority. Therefore, if consent is obtained on the basis of the minor's claiming to be emancipated, the parent is not liable for the medical expenses incurred; but the minor will be if she has money to pay for them. If the minor has no money, it is usually not worth the expense involved to sue for them.[5]

Unfortunately, many minors who are legally recognized as capable of consenting to their own medical treatment are nonetheless required, in the experience of the authors, to obtain parental consent by health agencies. This is particularly true in the case of pregnant minors. Hospitals, clinics, and physicians often require pregnant minors to obtain parental consent for prenatal care on the ground that the minor probably has insufficient funds to pay the medical and hospital bills for the pregnancy and delivery. Thus, the well-intended state laws to allow adolescents to receive necessary medical care without parental consent are often ignored by health providers who are concerned that they will be unpaid for the services provided.

A serious constitutional challenge might well be raised to the fairly common practice of public hospitals' refusing prenatal care to minors on their own consent as is permitted by most state minor treatment laws. Many city and county hospitals and other publicly supported health facilities continue to refuse to provide medical treatment to pregnant adolescents until a parent of the child also signs consent for the prenatal care and delivery. In 1974 the U.S. Supreme Court in *Memorial Hospital v. Maricopa County*[7] held that an indigent patient had a constitutional right to necessary medical care at a publicly-supported or tax-supported facility, and that failure to admit him or her was a denial of basic necessities for existence. Serious constitutional issues are raised when an indigent adult is treated for the same medical condition for which the minor is turned away when the minor is in fact able to give a knowing consent to treatment. The Supreme Court has held in the area of juvenile offenses that a minor may be treated differently from an adult by a governmental entity only if the difference in treatment is for the benefit of the child.[5,8] Closer scrutiny of the policies of tax-supported health care facilities might lead to a more sympathetic and legally correct policy in providing equal access to health care to adolescents who are in need of such services but cannot or will not involve their parents in order to receive them.

Contraception

Since the adoption of the 26th amendment to the Constitution which grants 18 years olds the right to vote, nearly all states have lowered the age of majority to 18.[9] In addition, many states have enacted statutes expressly lowering the age at which minors can consent independently to any medical care.[2] Today, 31 states and the District of Columbia allow minors to consent to pregnancy-related medical care.[2] Twenty-two states and the District of Columbia specifically permit minors to consent to receive contraceptives.[1] Twenty-two states (though not necessarily the same states) allow minors to consent independently to abortions.[2] Furthermore, in 1968 Congress amended Title IV-A of the Social Security Act[10] to require that family planning services be made available to sexually active minors who request them voluntarily. This and other federal legislation will be discussed later in this chapter when public funding of medical care is considered.

In addition to legislation delineating the extent of a minor's right to obtain sex-related medical care, the issue has come under review of the courts in recent years. Access to abortion and contraception has been an issue intimately related to the legal evolution of the right of privacy. The right of privacy is not expressly mentioned in the Constitution, but the foundation for such a right can be found in several Constitutional amendments. The case of *Griswold v. Connecticut*,[11] was the first specifically concerned with the right of privacy as related to sexual activity. In that case the Supreme Court struck down a Connecticut statute making the use of contraceptives a criminal offense as violating the constitutional right of privacy. The decision was directed toward the right of privacy in the marriage relationship and dealt with the restriction on use of contraceptives only. Distribution of contraceptives remained at issue, as did the question of access to contraceptives by unmarried adults.

Eisenstadt v. Baird,[12] resolved the issue of access to contraceptives by unmarried adults. The Supreme Court stated, "Whatever the rights of the individual to access to contraceptives may be, the rights must be the same for married and unmarried alike." [13] Thus, it was held that unmarried adults do indeed have a right to privacy, and the states cannot prohibit the sale of contraceptives to single adults, circumscribing their right to decide whether or not to bear children.

It was not until 1976 that the issue was decided with respect to minors. In *Jones v. T.H.,*[14] the Supreme Court affirmed a lower court decision to strike down state welfare regulations that required minors receiving AFDC welfare assistance to obtain parental consent as a prerequisite for obtaining family planning services. The Social Security law[15] mandates that voluntary family planning services be made available to AFDC recipients including sexually active minors. The Court noted that the state regulations conflicted directly with these provisions of the Social Security Act. The Supreme Court avoided ruling on the constitutional right of privacy regarding contraception for minors in this case.

In 1977 the Supreme Court ruled that the sale and distribution of nonprescriptive contraceptives (e.g., condoms, creams, jellies, and foams) to minors, cannot be prohibited or even limited by state laws. *Carey v. Population Services International*[16] challenged the New York law prohibiting sale of nonprescriptive contraceptives to anyone under 16 years of age and proscribing distribution of such contraceptives to those over the age of 16 by anyone other than a licensed pharmacist.

In overturning the New York law, the majority of the Court held that because no blanket prohibition or blanket requirement of parental consent could be imposed regarding a minor's decision to terminate her pregnancy, the Constitution did not permit a blanket prohibition of the distribution of contraceptives to minors.

This confusion is reflected in the case of *Doe v. Irwin*[17] where parents sued a state-operated family planning clinic which had been dispensing contraceptives to any minors requesting them. The District Court initially held that without a showing of compelling state interest or of superior rights of minor children, the state could not totally exclude parents of unemancipated minors from decision-making regarding consent to risks of prescribed contraceptive devices and medications. The court stated that parents have a constitutional right to notice and a right to participate in their children's decisions regarding the use of contraceptives. The court explained that parents have a right to privacy in the care and control of their minor children and to free exercise of religion in the spiritual education of their children.

The case later went to the Sixth Circuit Court of Appeals which remanded the case back to the lower court, to review in light of the decision in *Carey v. Population Services International*[16] (see above) that had been decided in the meantime by the Supreme Court. In reviewing its original decision the district court reiterated that parents had a right to notification and involvement with the decision of an unemancipated minor child concerning the use of prescriptive contraceptives, in contrast to non-prescriptive contraceptives decided in *Carey*. Furthermore, the district court held the right of parents to be constitutionally protected under the right of privacy and freedom of religion. In the words of the court: "Even if there is a fundamental civil right among minors to obtain prescriptive contraceptives, that right need not exist to the total exclusion of any rights of the child's parents." This decision is being appealed.

Thus, the issue of whether parental notification can be a constitutionally valid requirement for a minor to receive prescriptive contraceptives when there is no state law which recognizes a minor's right to consent on her own for contraceptives is still an unresolved problem in a number of states. In light of the wide split of opinion by the justices in deciding the *Carey* case,[16] whether minors have the same right to sexual privacy as adults in obtaining all types of contraceptives, an uncertainty will remain for health care providers who offer private, state, or federally funded family planning services to consenting minors without parental involvement. This is particularly true in states with no clear legislative statement on the right of minors to request and receive contraceptives without any involvement of the parents.

The American Medical Association has taken the view that:

> Consistent with responsible preventative medicine and in the interest of reducing the incidence of teenage pregnancy—the teenage girl whose sexual behavior exposes her to possible conception should have access to medical consultation and the most effective contraceptive advice and methods consistent with her physical and emotional needs.

The American Academy of Pediatrics, The American College of Obstetrics and Gynecology and The American Academy of General Practice have taken similar positions.[18] It certainly would seem legally clear that a parent cannot absolutely prohibit the minor's right to ultimately receive contraceptives. However, any legal requirement that parents be first notified or consulted prior to the young adult's either requesting or receiving contraceptives would undoubtedly chill, if not permanently inhibit, some sexually active adolescents from continuing to use professional family planning services as they presently feel able to do, knowing their privacy will be respected.

There continues to be a small but vocal group of citizens who feel that easy accessibility to contraceptives of any kind by young people encourages and increases sexual activity outside of marriage and destroys parental rights of control of the adolescent child. It was such views that led to passage of the New York law later struck down by the Supreme Court in Carey,[16] a law that forbade dispensing nonprescriptive contraceptives to persons under 16 or dispensing nonprescriptive contraceptives to persons 16 or older except by licensed pharmacists. The majority opinion pointed out that the purpose of the law i.e., the state's objectives of preventing sexual activity by young people had demonstrably failed. Until there is a definitive ruling on the minor's right to privacy in obtaining prescriptive as well as nonprescriptive contraceptives in cases of conflicting interest of the parent and child, the issue will remain troublesome. However, there is now no known case in which a physician has been found liable for damages from prescribing contraceptives to minors of any age without parental consent.[4]

The potential for civil liability of physicians who prescribe contraceptives to sexually active minors in a suit brought by parents would not seem great, but certain precautions should be taken by the health professionals to avoid potential problems. The physician has the right to use his medical judgment in prescribing contraceptives when the minor comes to him and presents herself as a person who is already sexually active. The possibility of obtaining parental consent should be asked of the patient by the health professionals involved in her care. A certain number of minors are not reluctant to ask their parents for written consent to receive family planning services. A statement by the physician in the medical record that in his medical judgment pregnancy would be a serious health hazard outweighing possible risks of the contraceptive provided should be noted when consent of the parent cannot be obtained. The minor should be made aware of the risks and benefits of the contraceptive that is decided to be appropriate in her case. Potential side effects of birth control pills, or IUDs should be clearly explained. Any complications that may result should be explained as well as the necessity to return immediately for medical advice or treatment if they occur. The minor must always sign a written consent form for the method of contraception that is decided upon. The necessity for follow-up care must be impressed on the patient. A number of clinics and physicians also have established a policy in which they inform the minor in advance that, in the event of a serious medical problem, they may feel it necessary to inform the parents as well as the minor (e.g. a positive Papanicolaou (pap) test, heart disease, serious kidney disease or other major health problem discovered by the physician or clinic). Finally, an accurate and complete history of the patient must be maintained. Careful medical records of the patient must also be maintained. Discretion is urged as to the detail in which the sexual activities of the patient are recorded in the medical record. There are still a few states, for example Texas, where medical privacy has not yet been legally recognized. A subpoena of the medical records can be obtained that can lead subsequently to serious embarrassment or personal complications for the patient.[19]

Abortion

The decision to engage in sexual intercourse but not to conceive is truly personal. If a woman of *any* age is forced to bear a child for nine months owing to a state law which prevents contraception or abortion, an invasion of privacy—physical, emotional, and spiritual—has occurred. The Supreme Court took the rights enumerated in *Griswold*[11] and *Baird*[12] and extended them to women seeking abortions. In *Roe v. Wade*[20] the Court held that the right of privacy recognized in the contraception cases was "broad enough to encompass a woman's decision whether or not to terminate her pregnancy."[20] The Court stated that criminal abortion laws which allow only those abortions performed to save the mother's life violated the Due Process Clause of the 14th Amendment protecting the right of privacy. The right of privacy *includes* the right of a woman to terminate her pregnancy free from state intrusion.

Specifically, it was held that since a woman's right to decide whether or not to terminate a pregnancy is fundamental, only a *compelling* state interest can justify any state intrusion upon that right.[20] The Court held that prior to the end of the first trimester of a pregnancy, the decision to

180

terminate the pregnancy and to carry out an abortion is a decision that must be left to the woman and her physician. After the first trimester the state may adopt regulations for abortion procedures that are reasonable for the purpose of promoting the health and well-being of the mother. State requirements that abortions be performed only in hospitals or only after other medical opinions have been obtained are not permissible in the first trimester. After the fetus is potentially viable—the determination of viability is a medical judgment—the state interest in preserving a potentially viable fetus becomes compelling and the state may, if it chooses, regulate or even proscribe abortion except in those cases where it is necessary to preserve the life or health of the mother.

A Georgia law restricting abortions only to residents of that state and then only after approval was obtained from a committee of doctors was struck down by the Supreme Court in *Doe v. Bolton*.[21] The law was viewed as an unduly burdensome procedural restriction that interfered with a woman's right to terminate her pregnancy by limiting her access to obtain an abortion. The *Roe* and *Doe* decisions established the right of an adult woman to decide whether or not to bear a child without interference by the state. The issue, however, still remained unresolved concerning the right of a minor girl to consent to an abortion without parental knowledge or consent. A class action suit in Florida provided the first case in which this right was tested.

Prior to the *Doe* and *Roe* decisions, three physicians filed suit in a Florida district court to challenge a state statute requiring unwed minors to obtain parental permission in *Coe v. Gerstein*[22] and requiring a married woman to obtain the husband's consent prior to receiving an abortion in *Poe v. Gerstein*.[22] In response to the decisions in *Doe* and *Roe* the Florida legislature modified the state law, but it still required consent of the parent or spouse. Two pregnant women, an 18-year-old married woman who was unable to obtain consent from her spouse, and another 18-year-old woman unable to obtain parental consent, both in their first trimester of pregnancy, joined in the suit. It was charged by plaintiffs that the statute was an unconstitutional interference with a woman's right to obtain an abortion. The district court agreed, and stated:

> We recognize . . . that the interest of parents within a family unit is qualitatively different, at least in part, from the interest which the pregnant minor daughter may have in her maternal health and the interest which the viable fetus may have in its potential life. . . . (But) a state which has no power to regulate abortions

in certain areas (after *Doe* and *Roe*) simply cannot constitutionally grant power to husbands and parents to regulate in those areas. Therefore, husbands and parents cannot look to the state to prosecute and punish the physician or other participants who perform an abortion against the wishes of husbands or parents.[23]

The Fifth Circuit affirmed this holding on appeal. The court further stated that minors do indeed have a constitutionally protected right to privacy and that *Roe v. Wade* should be applied to unwed teenagers because teenage pregnancies and childbirth involve more and greater risks medically than do those of adult women.[24] It is evident that the decisions made by the courts in *Gerstein* reflect a genuine concern for the many problems resulting from teenage pregnancy and childbirth.

Parts of a Missouri abortion statute were held unconstitutional by the U.S. Supreme Court in *Planned Parenthood of Central Missouri v. Danforth* in 1976.[25] A spousal consent requirement was held unconstitutional because the state could not delegate to a spouse veto power which the state itself could not constitutionally exercise during the first trimester of a woman's pregnancy. The same reasoning was given for not upholding a parental consent requirement. In *Danforth* the court found no significant state interests justifying the consent requirements. The court did rule constitutional the informed consent requirement of the statute. However, it declared the statute's prohibition of saline amniocentesis as a method of abortion after the first trimester was arbitrary and unconstitutional. The Missouri statutory requirement that the physician preserve the fetus' life and health regardless of the state of pregnancy or face civil and/or criminal prosecution was also seen as arbitrary and unconstitutional.

The issue in *Bellotti v. Baird*,[26] also involved a parental consent requirement. A 1974 law passed by the Massachusetts legislature made it a criminal offense to perform an abortion on a minor without the consent of the parents. Suit was brought by a pregnant 16 year old who was afraid to tell her parents of her pregnancy because her father had previously threatened to throw her out of the house and kill her boyfriend if she ever became pregnant. She sought to have the state statute requiring parental consent to abortions performed on minors declared unconstitutional. The U.S. Supreme Court decided that the constitutionality of the law should first be decided by the highest state court before a federal court ruled on the meaning and procedures imposed by the state law. However, the Supreme Court indicated that the Massachusetts law could be interpreted to mean that, although state law requires parental consultation and consent, it will still allow a minor capable of giving informed consent to obtain a court order without parental consultation. Further, the Court ruled that the law permits a minor incapable of giving an informed consent to obtain an abortion order without parental consultation when it is shown an abortion is in her best interest.

Upon rehearing by the United States Supreme Court[27], the judgment of the Massachusetts Supreme Court was affirmed. In the high Court's opinion, it was stated that if a state decides to require parental consent, that state must also provide an alternative procedure by which a minor can obtain authorization for an abortion. It is through this alternative procedure that a minor can demonstrate sufficient maturity to make an informed decision regarding abortion after consultation with her physician, independent of her parents; or if she is not mature enough, or sufficiently informed, an abortion would be in her best interest. It was the Court's concern that parental involvement in the abortion decision does not amount to final and perhaps arbitrary veto.

The Supreme Court's decision, though declaring the Massachusetts law unconstitutional, did leave the door open for states to require parental consent for abortions *so long as* there remains a legal alternative for obtaining authorization in the absence of parental consent. This alternative would presumably be a court hearing. The Massachusetts Supreme Court heard the case on remand from the U.S. Supreme Court. The Massachusetts Supreme Court determined that the state statute was overbroad in its absolute requirement of parental notification before a court could grant a consent order to allow a minor to obtain an abortion. It decided that the statute violated due process and equal protection by providing that a minor's informed consent to abortion can be overridden, even though such consents were valid for other matters. The Supreme Court's final decision on this case is almost certain to have major implications regarding not only a minor's right to consent to abortions, but also a minor's right to privacy in any family planning or pregnancy-oriented services.

What about the pregnant teenager who chooses to keep her pregnancy, but whose parents insist she have an abortion? It would seem that if a minor has a right to consent to treatment, particularly abortions, as a logical extension, the minor should also have the right to *refuse* to consent to an abortion. Only one court decision dealt with this issue and adopted this reasoning.[28] It is clear that a physician who performs an abortion on a minor at the request of her parents, but without her consent, puts himself in jeopardy of a lawsuit for assault and battery when the minor reaches the age of majority.

The Rights of the Father

Often ignored in discussion about the legal problems of teenage pregnancies is the issue of the rights of the unwed father. We have seen that states cannot require the husband's consent for an abortion sought by a woman whether she be a minor or an adult. However, the prospective father has a substantial interest in a woman's pregnancy if the pregnancy is carried to term, whether he is married to her or not. Whatever the marital relationship, a father is legally bound to support his child.[18] If he has custody of his *legitimate* child, or at least shares custody of the child, he is charged with the responsibility of educating and disciplining the child. In addition he has the parental right to the enjoyment of his child as well as eventual support from his child if that is necessary.[29]

What rights does the unmarried father of a child have? The case of *Stanley v. Illinois*[30] was the first to deal with the rights of putative fathers. When the mother of three illegitimate children fathered by Stanley died, the children were placed in the custody of court-appointed guardians without notification to Stanley and without his consent. Stanley had lived with the mother and children for eighteen years and appealed the court's decision. An Illinois statute declared the children to be wards of state upon their mother's death without a hearing to determine the natural father's fitness to retain custody of his children. It was Stanley's contention that the statute violated the Equal Protection Clause of the Constitution. The Illinois Supreme Court upheld the statute and the lower court order. Stanley appealed to the U.S. Supreme Court, which struck down the Illinois statute. The distinction made in the state statute between married and unmarried fathers was held unconstitutional by the Supreme Court, because such distinction created the presumption that unmarried fathers were unfit to raise their children. The Court held that unwed fathers are entitled to the same procedural protection afforded to married fathers. Thus, before a child can be placed by the state in the custody of a court-appointed guardian, the father, whether or not married to the mother, must be shown to be an unfit parent following notice and hearing. Furthermore, a child's illegitimate status cannot automatically give rise to the presumption of the father's unfitness as a parent. Clearly then, natural, though unwed, fathers who "desire and claim responsibility for their children" [30] are entitled to notice and hearing. What is still not clear is whether unwed fathers are entitled to *all* the rights enjoyed by other fathers.

The constitutionality of New York's adoption statute which holds that the consent of the natural father is unnecessary, was upheld by the New York Court of Appeals in *In re Malpica-Orsini* in 1975.[31] Hector Orsini lived with his illegitimate daughter and her mother from November, 1970 until June, 1972. The following September, a judicial order was entered in Family Court, New York County, in which Orsini admitted paternity. He was ordered to pay child support and was granted visitation rights. In February, 1973 the child's mother married another man who sought to adopt the daughter. In the adoption proceeding Orsini moved for enforcement of his visitation rights and for an order to grant him notice and the opportunity to be heard in all proceedings regarding his daughter. Finally, Orsini sought dismissal of the adoption petition. Orsini was granted notice and the opportunity to be heard but was denied the dismissal of the adoption petition. Ultimately, the adoption was approved, and Orsini appealed the adoption order. The New York Court of Appeals upheld the state adoption statute and indicated that the classification within the statute treating unwed fathers differently from other fathers bore a rational relationship to the state's legitimate purpose in promoting the best interests of the child.

The rights of the unwed father have yet to be definitely delineated. It would seem, according to the *Stanley* opinion, that a natural, but unwed, father who has shared in the custody and care of his child does have the right to participate in adoption hearings, but does not have an absolute right to consent or to withhold consent regarding adoption. It will take more higher court decisions to determine the full scope of an unwed father's rights.

Financing the Medical Costs of an Adolescent Pregnancy

As previously discussed, in most jurisdictions pregnant teenagers have the right to consent to pregnancy-related care. An important issue related to this right is to determine who is financially responsible for this care. In actual practice many public and private health professionals and facilities *require* a parent's consent before providing prenatal care to ensure that a legally responsible adult will pay for the prenatal care and delivery of the pregnant child. Some pregnant teenagers are fortunate to have families willing and able to pay the medical bills related to pregnancy, but there are many adolescents who are not so fortunate. There are adolescents who are unwilling to even disclose to their physicians who their parents are, who are too fearful to disclose the fact they are pregnant, who run away rather than confront their parents, who have previously emancipated themselves from their families, or whose families are poor but not on welfare and unable to afford the necessary medical costs. Those teenagers who do work often do not have high paying jobs and may have dropped out of school as a result of the pregnancy. Thus, they are not able to pay the costs and are not eligible for expensive health insurance which would cover their maternity benefits. If their parents do have health insurance, it often may not cover pregnancies of their minor children.

Until the recent enactment by the 95th Congress of the amendment to Title VII of the Equal Employment Opportunities Act of the "Pregnancy Disability Bill"[32] it was not legally required that employers provide pregnancy benefits as part of their health benefits or disability benefits for female employees.[32] Employers will now be required to include health benefits for pregnancy as any other illness or disability in their health insurance and health benefits. Employees who are pregnant will now be entitled to earned sick leave or disability payments as a result of the pregnancy. Employers will be allowed discretion as to whether they will pay for abortion procedures under their health insurance plan. However, they must pay for abortion complications, earned sick leave or disability regardless of the pregnancy outcome. Employers are now prohibited from sex discrimination in employment benefits on the basis of pregnancy of their employees.

There are several federal laws which provide monies for pregnancies and deliveries of indigent women. Unfortunately, the indigent pregnant teenager who has not yet had her first baby is ordinarily not covered by these federal programs until *after* she has delivered her first child. The reasons for this will become clear in the discussion of Title XIX (Medicare funding).

Title V of the Social Security Act[33] was first passed by Congress in 1935 to enable states to extend and improve services to reduce infant mortality and promote the health of mothers and children. In addition the law provides for monies to locate and provide diagnosis, medical, surgical, and other corrective services and facilities for crippled children and those children who have conditions that may lead to crippling. In recent years 6% of all state maternal and child health monies were mandated to be used for family planning services. The emphasis was on rural areas or areas with serious economic problems. From 1945 through 1967, there was also a statutory provision requiring the Secretary of Health, Education and Welfare to approve any statewide plan that provided standards for obstetrical care in accordance with state law.[34]

Most of the Title V monies are given directly yearly to each state's Department of Health, or its designated health agency, although some monies are directly available for projects as either research or demonstration grants with the approval of HEW. Congress now appropriates about 335 million dollars annually for these purposes. At the time this law was passed in 1935, the country was in a severe economic depression with many of the poor families to be served still living in rural areas. Since 1935, this low income population has become significantly more mobile and more urban while the present delivery of medical care is both more sophisticated and oriented to health facilities with the necessary equipment.

Some states develop and make public their state plans and obtain public input before deciding how to spend these categorical maternal and child health monies which the states' Departments of Health receive from the federal government. Unfortunately, the majority of states do not make public their state plans on how these federal monies are spent. Because the federal government does not require a public state plan with public input as to how these monies are spent, it is unfortunately not known how most states spend these funds. Frequently MCH monies are either not given to all parts of a state in an equitable manner or in the most efficient and effective manner to meet maternal and child health care needs appropriate to the 1970s. In most states it is difficult if not impossible to discover exactly how or where the money is used for prenatal care. A State Department of Health may distribute the money through various city or county health departments in a manner which may not be geographically representative or based on current population needs of the state. A pregnant teenager thus may be able to get proper prenatal care if she is fortunate enough to live in an area of the state that has both adequate medical personnel and health facilities and which also receives monies through Title V. The health facility can provide her prenatal services as an eligible low income person through a city or county health service or MCH-funded program. The pregnant teenager may be unfortunate and live in a part of the state that has inadequate numbers of medical professionals, where appropriate medical facilities for her pregnancy or delivery are at an inconvenient distance, and that receives little or no Title V monies. If the pregnant adolescent develops complications during pregnancy, has a complicated delivery, or delivers a low-birth-weight or premature infant, she may indeed have serious problems receiving adequate prenatal care for herself or postnatal care for her infant. She may receive care if she is accepted as a charity patient at a well-equipped teaching hospital, public hospital, or public clinic with adequate staff and facilities. Such facilities are more commonly found in urban than rural areas. In any event the facility may not receive Title V monies to pay for the care provided to the pregnant teenager or her infant.

The authors observe that the Title V Maternal and Child Health monies do not adequately fulfill the intended Congressional purpose. Many state, county and city health agencies are not able to provide directly either the professional staff or facilities required in the 1970s to fulfill the mandate of the 1930s when both the delivery system and the medical care available were substantially less complex.

Congress and the Executive Branch must provide adequate health care for indigent pregnant women regardless of age, and for their children including crippled children, through publicly accountable, auditable, and medically adequate programs. The programs must provide up-to-date medical care and be based on each state's current population needs. Until such provisions are made the inadequate Title V MCH program will continue to be subject to criticism in many states. The title of the law "Maternal and Child Health" has a politically soothing ring. It would be even better if it could provide the services mandated by the title of the law and very much needed in each state to promote maternal and child health needs.

Title XIX of the Social Security Act[35] provides Medicaid funding for medical costs incurred by indigent persons who are receiving, or eligible to receive, AFDC (Aid to Families with Dependent Children) or are receiving, or eligible to receive, federal Supplementary Security Income because they are aged, blind or permanently disabled. Title XIX covers outpatient as well as inpatient hospital services, laboratory, radiological and physician services, and in addition, clinic services, prescriptions, diagnostic, screening, preventative and rehabilitative services. Prenatal services are covered as well as deliveries, but it is a matter of discretion with the state agency which administers the Medicaid programs as to *when* eligibility for Medicaid coverage for pregnancy begins. Many states will not provide Medicaid coverage for an indigent pregnant woman until *after* she delivers her baby. The woman then must present a birth certificate for her baby and be certified as eligible to receive AFDC for her infant. Retroactively she may then be eligible for the Medicaid health coverage which goes with AFDC eligibility which may then pay the cost of her delivery. A pregnant indigent adolescent cannot count on either receiving prenatal health care covered by Medicaid, nor can she expect automatically to receive AFDC or minimal support for food, lodging and clothing during pregnancy, until after she successfully delivers a live baby. In the many states that do not provide either AFDC or Medicaid coverage until after delivery, the pregnant teenager can only be sure of receiving Medicaid coverage if she is already an AFDC recipient or is covered as an AFDC recipient because her parent or guardian is presently on welfare. The Supreme Court has held in *Burns v. Alcala*[36] that states receiving federal financial aid under the AFDC program are not required to offer welfare benefits to pregnant women for unborn children.

Neither can pregnant women (minors or adults) count on Title XIX funds being made available for abortions. In 1977 the Supreme Court decided that the Equal Protection Clause of the 14th Amendment of the Constitution does not require states to pay for nontherapeutic abortions with Medicaid funds, even though such funds are used by the states to pay childbirth expenses.[37] States are given wide latitude in determining the types of medical treatment that will be funded through Title XIX. As long as states provide funds for *necessary medical care,* they are able to determine legislatively or administratively what other kinds of medical assistance reflect the state's objectives of Title XIX. The Supreme Court also has held that publicly funded hospitals need not permit elective abortions to be performed on indigent women although they provide deliveries for indigent women.[38] Thus, at present under the Department of Health, Education, and Welfare appropriations and promulgated regulations, there are only three instances when a pregnant woman of any age may obtain a federally funded abortion under either Title XIX or Title XX of the Social Security Act.[39] Abortion funding is restricted to those instances: (1) when a physician certifies in writing that an abortion is necessary to save the life of the mother; (2) or when a victim of rape or incest resulting in pregnancy has reported the incident promptly to a law enforcement or public health authority or has had someone else report the incident. In no event can the report be later than 60 days after the incident; a form must be filed giving the date of the incident, the name and address of the victim, and the name and address of the person reporting the incident if different than the victim. As of December 1979 only 23 states were funding abortions for indigent women without these restrictive limitations.[40] Seventeen states pay for abortions only under these restrictive federal regulations, and 9 states impose an even greater restriction on paying for abortions with public funds *only* if the mother's life will be endangered if the pregnancy is carried to term. These federal restrictions based on political rather than medical considerations are expected to continue for at least several more years. Congress has, for over three years, engaged in heated debate regarding legislation which would limit federal funding of abortions in those instances where a full-term pregnancy would endanger the life of the mother. The "Hyde Amendment", named for Representative Henry Hyde of Illinois, and similar restrictive language on funding of abortions authored by other members of congress, have been introduced during floor discussions of a number of appropriation bills, social legislation, and health-related bills before Congress. The House has passed legislation carrying restrictive wording on abortion funding, but until recently, the Senate insisted on more liberal language. Most recently, both houses of Congress have agreed to restrictions on financing of abortions in a wide range of bills, authorizing bills from various health programs, Department of Defense health benefits, and in legislation to eliminate discrimination against pregnant workers. Thus, at the present time, monies administered by the Department of Health and Human Services (DHEW), and executive departments, can be used to fund abortions only when necessary to save the life of the mother or in cases of reported rape or incest.

The very restrictive language relative to the funding of abortions—even when they are necessary medically—has come under challenge in the courts. In Illinois, the case of *Zbarraz* v. *Quern*[41] attacked a statute limiting federal funding of abortions in life-threatening situations as being violative of the Equal Protection Clause, as well as contrary to the notion that since *Roe* v. *Wade,* the state may not capriciously interfere with a woman's decision to abort a pregnancy during the first two trimesters of that pregnancy. The federal district court judge ruled the Illinois statute unconstitutional, holding that the state does not have a legitimate interest in preserving the life of a nonviable fetus when the health risk to the pregnant woman could be increased.

The constitutional issue was not examined in the federal district court. The United States Supreme Court has accepted the *Zbarraz* v. *Quern* case for review and has the option of deciding the constitutional question or issuing a narrower decision, which Congress can circumvent, based on welfare law. The issue presently before the Court will be the legality of language allowing for federal funding of abortion when the future health of the woman would be jeopardized by carrying a pregnancy to term. The current law does not contain such language. Only a constitutional decision will the controversy, but in any event, it is unlikely that any kind of ruling will be issued before late 1980.

Legislation for Family Planning

Federal funding for family planning is a very different matter than federal-state funding for pregnancies or abortions. Federal financial assistance for voluntary family planning is available through several different programs. Title IV-A of the Social Security Act[42] mandatorily requires voluntary family planning services be available statewide for recipients of Aid to Families with Dependent Children (AFDC). Included under eligible recipients are minors considered to be sexually active. The states receive federal money on a 90% federal and 10% state match with which such family planning services are provided. Either the state itself can provide family planning services or it may contract with local physicians or agencies for the delivery of family planning services.

The Family Planning Services and Population Research Act, Title X of the Public Health Service Act, became law in 1970.[43] This legislation was intended by Congress to make comprehensive, voluntary family planning services available to low income persons who desired them. Public agencies and nonprofit organizations are given grant money to establish voluntary family planning projects. Under Title X, family planning services are to be made available to anyone, regardless of age, marital or parental status, or income. Funding for this popular program has increased since 1976 in a limited way. However, the funding is still inadequate. There are still many low income girls and women who desire family planning services but do not have easy access to them. Since 1977 emphasis has been placed on creating and expanding accessible voluntary family planning services for adolescents. Up to the present time legislative proposals to require parental notification or consent prior to minors' receiving contraceptives have been defeated.

Title V of the Social Security Act also mandates that 6% of all funds a state receives in MCH be expended for voluntary family planning services.[33] Because of the difficulty of ascertaining how a state spends its Title V monies, it is difficult to determine the extent of family planning services provided by each state with these monies.

Title XX of the Social Security Act[44] is the major source of funding for social services. It includes funding for voluntary family planning services to sexually active minors and adults in a number of states. The federal government provides 90% of the funds against a 10% state or local match for family planning. This program also is a major source of funds for day care programs for indigent or low income working families. These monies are available at a 75% federal and 25% state match. In addition, sometimes innovative and imaginative social service programs in a state are funded by these monies. Each state can use these monies as well to provide funds for child abuse, child protection, emergency care, and foster care under each state welfare department's annual social service plan. These plans are public, and by law require public input in designing the annual plan. The major problem with Title XX is, even with 1978 increased funding by Congress, and increases for 1979, it is not adequate to meet social service needs for all age groups, individual and family needs. Title XX funding for fiscal year 1980 is being considered by Congress as of this writing; but, it can be reasonably stated, there will be no substantial increase in the Title XX monies for the next few years.

The needs of the pregnant adolescent or young teenage mother and father are not presently adequately met by whatever existing programs presently exist whether privately or publicly funded. The recently enacted "Adolescent Health Services, and Pregnancy Prevention and Care Act of 1978" [45] indicates federal awareness that there *is* a problem about pregnant adolescents, adolescent parents 17 and under and their babies. Since there is currently federal executive and legislative reluctance, if not opposition to support abortion, this legislation is designed to provide alternatives through maternity and supportive services. How the recommended 50 million dollars for this Act can adequately provide prenatal and postnatal care, "prevention," "sex education," and a wide variety of counseling, other health and social services remains unclear. The law intends to coordinate and link necessary community services. Unfortunately many of these services do not exist, or are inadequate to meet present or future needs. Many questions were raised about the bill before it was enacted and shall remain as to whether it will approach any real effectiveness in meeting the intended purposes.

Unmet Needs and Future Priorities

An adolescent pregnant girl may well have difficulty in getting adequate medical or social services for which she is either financially eligible or that she can afford. It is likely that her parents will be required to consent for her medical treatment so that they will be held financially responsible for any medical expenses incurred in her pregnancy. A law that would have expanded Medicaid coverage to include pregnant teenagers failed to pass in the 95th Congress, but is now before the 96th Congress. Additionally, the limitation by many states in not providing welfare assistance prior to the delivery of a child poses serious problems of financial survival to pregnant adolescents who are not dependent on their families for financial support during their pregnancies.

After the teenage girl has delivered a baby she may, of course, apply for AFDC for herself and her baby if she chooses to keep and rear the child. The percentage of teenage girls keeping their babies is rising, and they often face serious personal and financial problems in addition to learning the skills of parenting. If the girl wishes to work or return to school she must find adequate day care for her child, as well as the financial means to support herself and her child. The girl's family may support her and help with rearing the baby. She may of course marry the father of the child before or after the pregnancy. Many times one or both teen parents may not be of age to marry without court or parental approval. The financial and social burdens may be multiplied if such a young marriage occurs. If the girl does not marry the father and wishes to apply for AFDC, she is required except in special circumstances by the amended Social Security Act to identify the father who may then be required to help support the child.

The teenager may choose to give the baby up for adoption. Antiabortion advocates urge adoption as a highly desirable alternative to abortion. Unfortunately, adoption is not ordinarily a very realistic prospect unless the baby is white, without handicaps, and has no serious or permanent medical problems. The result is that many children may end up with foster parents or in publicly funded institutions. Adequate foster placement is often not available quantitatively or qualitatively to meet any but the most urgent demands for the most desperate or emergency cases.

There do exist at least 85 federal programs aimed toward assisting adolescent parents and their children. They are often uncoordinated with each other, and may either overlap, or leave gaps in service. In many areas of the country the many necessary services for adolescent parents are either nonexistent, minimal, uncoordinated with each other, or unable to meet many needs of these young persons.

The lot of the pregnant teenager before or after delivery is not an easy one. Aside from psychological and emotional problems she might undergo, the practical problem of obtaining adequate medical care and counseling is very real. Present federal programs are ill-coordinated at best. To get through the red tape of the federal or state system is a monumental task for anyone, pregnant or not. When help is most needed, the bureaucracy can create seemingly insurmountable difficulties adding to the anxiety surrounding the pregnancy. From the time the teenager learns of her pregnancy, prenatal care and counseling should be made available, not only to the mother-to-be, but also to the prospective father and to the families of the teenagers so that intelligent decisions about their future lives can be made. Such services should exist and be available to all pregnant teenagers. As teenage pregnancies are a higher risk than adult pregnancies adequate medical care is a necessity during and after the pregnancy. Accessibility to abortions if that is the decision after proper counseling should also be available.

Once a teenager has delivered her baby, she should be provided an adequate place to live, food, and necessities for the infant and herself. She should have available counseling and programs to help her have a realistic opportunity to finish her education, get a job and remain in the mainstream of society. She needs assistance in parenting education to help her learn the skills of being a good parent to her new child. She should be given job training so that she need not depend on welfare. These kinds of support services are vital to a healthy child and a more loving mother. If her burden is made easier to bear, she is less likely to vent anger and frustration on her child. Unless society provides services and counseling to pregnant teenagers, the result could be perpetuation of child abuse and neglect from generation to generation. This, no society can or *should* tolerate.

There is reason to believe that Congress will finally enact, before 1982, legislation that will cover low income pregnant women before they have their first child, and provide medical care for subsequent children. In December, 1979, the House passed H.R. 4962, which would expand the present Title XIX Medicaid law to provide to all income-eligible pregnant women and children, health care coverage under the higher of two eligibility criterion: The state income level standard for AFDC welfare coverage, even if no application is made for AFDC; or

55% or below national poverty level income-eligible children up to age 18 would be eligible for comprehensive medical care. The House bill would permit pregnant women of any age to receive complete prenatal care through delivery and for 60 days thereafter, even if her income exceeded the eligibility level during this period. However, the House bill totally excludes coverage for abortion *even to save the life of the mother,* at state option.

The Senate version of this bill, S. 1204, is much more restrictive in its medical coverage and does not include any pregnant women or most children over six who are not receiving welfare benefits. Whether the Senate will adopt any version of the House-passed bill with its many amendments is not known. At the same time, amendments to include prenatal care for poor women and medical care for poor children are being considered before Congress. These would provide total national health insurance coverage, under bills that would provide payment for major catastrophic illness.

Most people know that adequate prenatal care for women is inexpensive and is most likely to result in a good outcome for the mother and the baby. The absence of this minimal health care has resulted in births, or subsequent major health impairments in babies and children, that have cost taxpayers millions of dollars for their treatment, which could have been prevented with good health care. Severe retardation, physical and mental handicaps, long hospitalization, medical treatment, and/or resorting to welfare rolls has been the price we all have paid for the neglect and failure to prevent or treat inexpensively the preventable illnesses of infants, children, and adolescents.

Addendum

As this goes to press, significant legal changes on abortion may be occurring. On February 19, 1980, the Supreme Court lifted the Hyde Amendment's injunction against Medicaid expenditures for abortions, and the Court will decide the legal constraints that can be imposed on funding for Medicaid. Whether this will extend to all federal funding for abortions is currently unclear, but with over 72 legal decisions holding that denial of "medically necessary" abortions to Medicaid patients is unconstitutional, it seems likely that the Supreme Court will determine the legal extent of the legislative restrictions.[46] The Child Health Assurance Program (CHAP) is still held in Congress over the abortion riders attached in the House.

Notes

1. AMA News, April 17, 1967, page 4; "Treating a Minor for Venereal Disease" 214 *JAMA* No. 10, Page 1949, December 7, 1970.
2. See appendix compiled January, 1978. As laws of this nature are subject to modification, it is recommended that the laws of the state be examined when questions arise.
3. Prosser, Torts, 103 (4th ed., 1971).
4. Alan Sussman, "The Rights of Young People," 25 (Avon Books, 1977); N.Y. Pub. Health Law sec. 2504 (3) (Supp. 1972); Mass. Gen. Laws Ann. Ch. 112 sec. 12E (1970); Md. Ann. Code Art. 43 sec. 135 (Supp. 1971); Pa Stat. Ann. tit. 35 sec. 10104 (Supp. 1973); Ill. Ann. Stat. Ch. 91 sec. 18.3 (Supp. 1972); Fla. Stat. Ann. sec. 40 458.21 (Supp. 1973); Ga. Code Ann. sec. 58-2905 (1971); N.C. Gen. Stat. Ann. sec. 134-111.1, 90.21.1-21.4 (Supp. 1965).
5. Angela Roddy Holder, "Legal Issues in Pediatrics and Adolescent Medicine," 135–156, (John Wiley and Sons, 1977).
6. See 59 Am. Jur. 2d, Parent and Child sec. 87.
7. *Memorial Hospital v. Maricopa County* 415 U.S. 250, 1974.
8. *In re Gault* 387 U.S. 1, 1967; See also Holder, note 5.
9. States retaining a higher age of majority than 18 for purposes of contract are: Alabama (19), Nebraska (19), and Wyoming (19).
10. 42 U.S.C. sec. 602(a) (15)(A).
11. *Griswold v. Connecticut* 381 U.S. 479 (1965).
12. *Eisenstadt v. Baird* 405 U.S. 438 (1972).
13. Id. at 453.
14. *Jones v. T. H.* 96 S. Ct. 1976.
15. Titles IV-A (42 U.S.C. sec. 601 et. seq.) XIX 42 U.S.C. sec. 1396 and XX (42 U.S.C. 1397).
16. *Carey v. Population Services International* 97 S. Ct. 2010 (1977).
17. *Doe v. Irwin* 428 F. Supp. 1198 (W.D. Mich. 1977)
18. Angela Roddy Holder, "Legal Issues in Pediatrics and Adolescent Medicine" Chpt. 10, 268, 269; Proceedings of the AMA House of Delegates 5556, June 20–24, 1971 quoted in Elizabeth Jordan, "A Minor's Right to Contraceptives," 7 U. of Cal. at Davis Law Re. page 270; 290 1974.
19. Report of the Privacy Protection Study Commission 284 (1977). Forty three states have some form of testimonial privilege regarding physician-patient communication.
20. *Roe v. Wade,* 410 U.S. 113 (1973).
21. *Doe v. Bolton* 410 U.S. 179 (1973).
22. *Coe v. Gerstein* 376 F. Supp. 695 (S.D. Fla. 1973) appeal dismissed for lack of jurisdiction 417 U.S. 279 (1974), denial of injunction affirmed sub nom., *Poe v. Gerstein* 417 U.S. 281 (1974).

23. Id, 376 F. Supp. at 696, 697–699.
24. *Poe v. Gerstein* 517 F. 2d 787 (5th Cir. 1975).
25. *Planned Parenthood of Central Missouri v. Danforth* 428 U.S. 52 (1976).
26. *Bellotti v. Baird* 428 U.S. 132 (1976).
27. *Baird v. Bellotti* 99 S. Ct. 3035 (1979).
28. *In re Smith* 795 A2d 238 (Md. 1972).
29. See *Gomez v. Perez* 409 U.S. 535 (1973).
30. *Stanley v. Illinois* 405 U.S. 645 (1972).
31. *In re Malpica-Orsini* 36 N.Y. 2d 568, 331 N.E. 2d 486, 370 N.Y.S. 2d 511 (1975).
32. 42 U.S.C. sec. 2000 et seq. (1970) as amended in 1978 to include maternity benefits for female employees. See also *General Electric v. Gilbert* 429 U.S. 125 (1976) and *Geduldig v. Arello* 417 U.S. 484 (1974), *Satty v. Nashville Gas Co*. 98 S. Ct. 347 (1977). For a general review of the problem. See: Peg Bunch, Deborah McFarlane, Carla Dowben, ''Pregnancy and the Worker: Who Bears the Burden,'' in press, Vol 4 (4) Women in Health, Winter (1979).
33. 42 U.S.C. sec. 701 et. seq. (1935, as amended).
34. 42 U.S.C.A. sec. 703 (a) no longer in present law.
35. 42 U.S.C. sec. 1396 (1965, as amended).
36. *Burns v. Alcala* 420 U.S. 575 (1975).
37. *Maher v. Roe* 97 S. Ct. 2376 (1977) and *Beal v. Doe* 97 S. Ct. 2366 (1977).
38. *Poelker v. Doe* 97 S. Ct. 2391 (1977).
39. 42 CFR Part 50, 301 et. seq. and 449 100 et. seq. amended by passage of P. L. 96–123 (November, 1979).
40. The states as of the last report are: Alaska, California, Colorado, Connecticut, Georgia, Hawaii, Idaho, Illinois, Louisiana, Maryland, Massachusetts, Michigan, Minnesota, New Jersey, New York, North Carolina, Ohio, Oregon, Pennsylvania, Virginia, Washington, West Virginia, Wisconsin, and the District of Columbia. (Thirteen of these states are under court order to fund abortions without restrictions.) This is obviously subject to change and must be checked after each state's legislative session.
41. *Zbarraz* v. *Quern,* 572 F.2d. 582 (N.D.I. 11. 1979) app'd. sub. nom. *Williams* v. *Zbarraz,* 99 S. Ct. 2095 and *Quern* v. *Zbarraz* 99 S. Ct. 2095 (1979).
42. 42 U.S.C. sec. 602 (15), 1968 as amended in 1972 to include minors who can be considered sexually active.
43. 42 U.S.C. sec. 300-300 a-6 (1970) as amended.
44. 42 U.S.C. sec. 1397 et. seq. (1975) as amended.
45. P1. 95-626 (S.2910) passed September 29, 1978.
46. McRae, V.: Secretary of Health, Education, and Welfare *et al.* 76-C-1804 E.D.N.Y., 1980.

11 Ethical Issues of Adolescent Pregnancy

Konstantin Kolenda, Ph.D.

When one sees human sexuality from the point of view of ethics one recognizes its vast complexity. Sexuality is a powerful yet problematic, exciting yet often bothersome, aspect of human life. The measures we take to deal with it on personal and social levels may lead at least to partial successes or to destructive failures. It is a fact of our culture that the word sex simultaneously stands out as a tantalizing and a threatening three-letter word. A visitor from Mars inquisitively surveying our scene might conclude that the word denotes either a divinity or a curse or paradoxically both at once.

This confused ambivalence, fostered by some components of our religious traditions and by some patterns of social life, explains the suspicion with which sexuality is approached. On the one hand the libidinal potential of anything and everything is blatantly exploited by advertising. On the other hand concerned parents are anxious for their children not to learn too much about all the ramifications of sex because the very exposure to the subject appears contaminating or threatening. Hence one often senses a slow uphill battle on the part of those who try to see the consequences of this inner cultural conflict without blinders.

Sex and Procreation

In dealing with sexuality one might begin by exploring its interrelationship with all important aspects of life. The most obvious connection is that with human procreation. Concern about the sexuality of teenagers would lose much of its seriousness if teenagers did not get pregnant. But they do—and this is where the obvious hardships and problems are discernible.

These hardships and problems are profoundly ethical in nature from more than just a particular religious or abstractly moral point of view. Pregnancy affects people's lives in the most direct, palpable ways. It is a mistake to think that moral well-being can be attained independent of daily routine. Life is made up largely of simple fundamental tasks. If these daily tasks are too overwhelming or too frustrating, if they prevent

198

our responding to all our normal human potentialities, life becomes a burden.

It is difficult enough to introduce a new human being into the world when it is in the charge of two loving people, who are relatively mature, relatively secure economically and psychologically, mutually supportive, and motivated by the desire to create for themselves and their children a happy family life. Contrast this with the situation of a young and/or unmarried teenager conceiving a baby. What does this condition do to her, to her partner, their baby, and their society? Let us consider each of them in turn.

THE TEENAGER'S ETHICAL RESPONSIBILITY

What is a teenager's main ethical responsibility? Primarily, to grow into a mature, competent, balanced, responsible adult. This task is difficult enough even without special problems, as all of us can testify by looking back to those trying transitional years. But add to the absorbing, often agonizing, issues the teenager has to sort out, the demanding task of bringing another human being into the world. Hardly grown herself, the teenage mother must raise another human being. Is this fair to either? If one considers the abrupt and disruptive changes introduced into a pregnant teenager's life, it is difficult not to perceive a major human failure.

It is a double failure. On the one hand, these changes disturb the normal processes which are required for a teenager to achieve mature stability and independence—physical, economic, intellectual, emotional. On the other hand, she will deliver the baby, the person to be, into most inauspicious circumstances. The teenager not only lacks experience, she is in most respects unprepared to fulfill the tasks of childrearing. Hence, the baby is usually nurtured by someone else. The teenager's family or a foster home usually provides this support and in most cases these settings are likely to involve serious handicaps for the child's optimal development.

THE FATHERING ROLE

Consider the father of the child. Since the conception usually occurs unplanned, without any sense of real belonging and commitment of the two partners to each other or to a potential offspring, the father is likely to experience its coming into the world as an unfortunate nuisance. There were no plans for that human being in their sexual activity, no thought given to what the being might have to face. Instead, there is a sense of detachment, reinforced by an attitude, eloquently confirmed by a shrug of shoulders, that boys will be boys. They believe it is all right for them to have their fun if they can get away with it. Someone else will take care of problems if they arise. Not suprisingly, the male partner often disappears into the background, with the girl carrying the burden, both in the literal and the methaphorical sense.[1]

Even in an exceptional case, when the father is known and acknowledges his own crucial role, what goes for the girl, goes for the boy as well—both are inexperienced and unprepared for the additional time- and energy-consuming task of child rearing. Neither the economic means nor psychologic maturity is present to make them qualified parents. Someone else must pick up the responsibility.

THE ROLE OF THE TEENAGE MOTHER'S FAMILY

The first in line to come to the rescue is, of course, the girl's family, since the boy, if present, is likely to turn into a not-so-innocent bystander. Even presupposing a degree of affluence and goodwill on the part of the grandparents, is it fair to force into their own independent plan of life this additional task, no matter how pleasant and welcome it may turn out to be in the end? Here is an instance of imposing on someone a duty without any antecedent right to do so. No matter how generous and good-hearted the mother of the unexpectedly pregnant teenager may be, she has a legitimate complaint against her daughter, unless, implausibly, one takes the position that teenagers have no responsibilities at all to further the well-being and happiness of their parents.

THE ROLE OF THE COMMUNITY

In the absence of suitable, good-hearted, and self-sacrificing family members who are willing to step in—mothers, aunts, older sisters, grandmothers, cousins—the community, through whatever social services are available, is expected to come to the rescue. Our humanitarian society has some institutions besides the natural family to care for infants—nursery homes or foster homes. Nevertheless, one should not forget that the task of child rearing is difficult and fraught with risks and dangers. We often forget that the task reaches beyond shaping a child in early years. He or she must be schooled and prepared for life on a long-range basis. No society has provisions extensive enough for this, except perhaps a country that is intensively socialized throughout its entire spectrum or one that is regimented on totalitarian political principles.

How much attention is given to the considerations just described, affecting as we have seen, not just the teenage unmarried parent and her baby, but also other individuals and groups? For some reason this explicitly ethical dimension of teenage sexuality, delineating radical displacements that occur in normal developments of persons, families, and whole social groups, does not figure prominently in current discussions of the topic. This is a serious omission, especially since there seems to be a general, diffused alarm about the growing number of teenage out-of-wedlock pregnancies. It is as if the problem were viewed as uncontrollable and irreversible. With this perspective we must resign ourselves to deal with consequences alone and abandon any serious exploration of possible preventive measures.

There is the question, of course, of who can or should do what. As always, it is easier to fall back on the comfortable expectation that someone else will do what is necessary. So the parents expect the schools or churches to do a better job, and those institutions return the compliment. When programs are initiated by schools, or churches, or social agencies and these institutions seem to address themselves openly and vigorously to this complex set of issues, nervous parents often object or interfere, seeing a threat to their cherished but narrowly conceived ethical or religious views. Under these circumstances, little positive change can be expected. All those affected by the problem of teenage pregnancy—private persons, school officials, school boards, and agency personnel on all levels—must bring into the open some obvious and ethically crucial dimensions of human sexuality. Examination of the consequences and ramifications of children being brought into the world by teenagers leads one to the conclusion that they are the most unsuitable group to do so (pace those apologists who find some biologic justification for early motherhood.[2])

Discouragement or Contraception?

If there are weighty ethical grounds for discouraging pregnancies among teenagers, what attitudes toward sexual activity on their part are to be recommended? Two obvious alternatives come to mind: discouragement and contraception. Each of the alternatives presents a wide spectrum of possible policies. Discouragement may consist in restricting or strictly supervising activities of adolescents, or it may take the form of strong indoctrination in homes, schools, and churches against sexual activities for this age group. The accessibility of contraception may also be wide or narrow. Contraception is sometimes available only with difficulty, with special precautionary and supervisory measures, or it may be made easy to obtain, not only on request but also through counseling encouragement.

Both policies have inherent dangers. The policy of discouragement presupposes the possibility of a high degree of control over teenage activities. However, that requirement contradicts the growing degree of freedom and self-responsibility young persons need to develop. Moreover, there appears to be a consensus that intergenerational ties in our culture are not very strong. All too often, they tend to be tenuous and fragile. Perhaps unwittingly we tend to encourage a gap between adolescents and adults by overemphasizing the special, almost wholly autonomous, status of their "subculture."[3] In such a context, restrictions and limitations on behavior appear to adolescents to be repressive and are psychologically and practically resisted. On the other hand the myth of adolescent autonomy and "differentness" makes it easier for adults, parents and teachers, to disclaim responsibility for the adolescent's behavior and development. As a result, more and more teenagers feel emotionally isolated, and often do not even consider the possibility of gaining from resolute and informed guidance by the adult world. That this is likely to impair their already fragile emotional stability should not be surprising.

According to some authorities the advent of the "sexual revolution" has made available to most teenagers sufficient information for them to be in a position to make their own decisions with a high degree of discretion. Moreover, these authorities believe that sexual activity is not only normal but also desirable for satisfactory psychologic and emotional growth, and its suppression is damaging in the long run. Furthermore, they state that with a sufficient degree of care and proper circumstances, teenagers for the most part can manage this admittedly difficult aspect of their growth. Perhaps there is a good deal of unwarranted optimism in this view. Nevertheless it is defended with all seriousness.

For example, at a conference for teachers and youth workers in London, England, in July 1978, Dr. James Hemming, an educational psychologist, used the following argument:

> If adolescents are not allowed to develop responsible love rela-
> tionships with one another during the later teenage years, the al-
> ternative will not be chastity and assiduous application to school
> work but fantasy plus masturbation and an obsession about sex.
> . . . Old-style sexual inhibition has a very bad track record. We
> have around us today not only high figures for divorce but also
> hosts of frustrated marriages and emotionally cold marriages,
> which need never have happened if the partners had had a chance
> to attain sexual maturity by the natural process of growth and
> development.[4]

The opposite approach, to acknowledge the existence of teenage sexuality while encouraging contraception, has its problematic aspects as
well. Although Dr. Hemming claims that his recommendation is "not
a call to permissiveness," to many people promoting contraception is
inviting promiscuity. This belief is based on the assumption that the
possibility of indulging in sexual intercourse without undesirable consequences will obliterate all self-restraint necessary for moral growth.
This view seems to ascribe an irresistible disruptive power to human
sexuality and does not credit young people with discriminating capacities
of their own. Accordingly, the young are judged as incapable of determining to what extent, if any, with whom and for what reasons they
should enter into intimate sexual relations.

Many adults seem to reject the possibility of granting teenagers the
ability to use good sense, believing that the sanction of contraception is
bound to uncontrollably increase the adolescents' impulse to indulge in
sex. This refusal has important ethical and educational consequences: it
postpones self-determination and prolongs parental dominance over children. No doubt, this is a question in which individual discretion is important. To settle the question simply by saying that teenagers are in
principle incapable of controlling their own emotions and behavior is
dogmatic and unfair.

Another argument against contraception is that, since it is not 100%
safe, there will be instances of unwanted pregnancy which without contraception would not have occurred. The implicit assumption of this
indictment is that without the availability of contraceptives sexual intercourse would have been avoided. Thus, some claim, that encouraging
the use of contraceptives actually causes some additional pregnancies.
This argument turns mainly on factual and statistical considerations. To
the extent that contraception on the whole is effective the argument has

little force, especially if one allows for the possibility of abortion in those few cases in which contraceptive measures have failed.

A False Dichotomy?

A moment of reflection may lead us to suspect the dichotomy: discouragement or contraception. We have noted some reasons for questioning the wisdom of absolute discouragement, and we have acknowledged some dangers and limitations of contraception. These two lines of thought need expansion which, if undertaken, may enable us to discern some points at which the two views do not necessarily conflict.

First we should take seriously the supposition that, although inexperienced and rash, teenagers are still full human beings with a potentially effective dose of good sense. It seems unfair and condescending to think of them as hellbent on self-destruction. No one consciously wants his ruin, observed Socrates, and this applies to adolescents as well. Why not assume that when teenagers are given an accurate picture of factors at work, of goals at stake, of dangers to consider, and of alternatives available, adolescents will in most cases arrange their lives in ways beneficial to them and to society?[5] Anyone who dismisses this possibility as ''unrealistic'' may be flirting with cynicism. But cynicism is a dead-end path, while ''unrealism'' often shades into creativity.

What I am suggesting is that we ought to look for a more creative, flexible reappraisal of the whole complex so misleadingly and narrowly covered by probably our most unfortunate short word, sex. That term, by parading its conventional nakedness before us, immediately forces us onto the physical organic plane, quickly bringing to mind sex organs and orgasms. What a Procrustean bed, if there was one! Nor do we help matters much if we talk of people as *essentially* sexual beings. Of course they are that, but also many other things. If our self-concept is mainly in terms of sexual functions and activities, we ignore the rest of ourselves. This is a terrible loss, depriving us of countless other sources of self-esteem and fulfillment.

The best way to discourage undue excessive interest in the purely physical aspects of our sexuality is to reinforce *other* aspects of life. Sexual interests are also *interpersonal,* and therefore a part of sex education should consist in looking *beyond* sex to other activities and relations that enhance people's satisfaction with themselves and with one another.

Since sexual intercourse involves doing some specific things to and with one another, the very specificity of those things is conducive to exploitative attitudes. You do something for (or to) me, and I'll do some things for (or to) you. In concentrating on bare doings, the rest of the personal relationship is submerged, ignored, shunted aside, resulting in what in other contexts goes under the name of prostitution.

But suppose we encourage young people to look at one another as partners in *multiple* sorts of relationships, in which the ability to please and to be pleased is as wide as possible. Suppose we try to defuse the highly charged biologic elements by placing them in the context of attention to activities not primarily sexual in nature but exhibiting characteristically personal features. We should reinforce consideration, kindness, delight in each other, not just for looks and sex appeal, but also for the ability to amuse, to entertain, to help, to support, to cooperate, to be interesting. In the context of this generalized interest and delight in each other adolescents are likely to include physical tokens of tenderness and affection, sometimes even including sexual favors. Since the relationship to start with is built around consideration, mutual respect, and the desire to avoid inflicting hardship and hurt, it is most likely that the sexual activity, if it takes place, will include concern for avoiding harm to one another—physically, psychologically, emotionally, economically. If a relationship is not impulsive and one-sided and if sexual activity develops, the people involved would take precautions against pregnancy.

Contraception would not be a hurried stopgap measure, resented rather than appreciated. It would be seen as a sensible means of safeguarding physical and esthetic satisfaction while involving a minimum risk of undesirable consequences. The characteristics associated with contraception—it is secretive, naughty, adventurous, and strictly mechanical—would be viewed critically. Contraception would be seen as a rationally controlled component, designed to express the presence of concern and goodwill toward one another on the part of the partners.

What contraception is *contra* to is not just conception. If we keep in mind the consequences of conception, discussed in the first section of this chapter, we may see it as also aiming at preventing ethically undesirable hardships for all concerned—the parents, the potential baby, the family, the society. Contraception should be seen as not just a mechanical act of preventing a process by which two members of the opposite sex conceive another human being. It is an ethical policy designed to avoid the starting of this process under conditions that are detrimental to the well-being of all concerned, including the potential human being conceived under those conditions. With such an understanding of contraception, it will cease to be seen as "antilife," but as "prolife," as designed to promote conditions under which human beings are likely to prosper not suffer.

When both discouragement and contraception are perceived in this broader light, we will not be saddled with a simple-minded either/or. Adolescents will understand what is being discouraged and why. Should they nevertheless decide to be sexually active in the light of their total attachment to someone they deeply care about, they will also be more intelligent, careful, circumspect in their use of contraception. They will understand it to be not a shady, semicriminal act, but an intelligent policy to plan their lives according to their long-range objectives and designed not to impose unnecessary hardships on anyone—each other, members of their families, and society as a whole.

Normative Considerations

We have brought to attention the complexity of the problems connected with sexuality as it affects teenagers. We are now in a position to turn to some general normative considerations underlying our discussion and the distinctions made within it. What is our basic ethical concern? It certainly includes the desire to do all we can to make human lives fulfilling, meaningful, and happy. This concern has as its corollary objective the avoidance of situations that produce opposite results. We tend to look at the whole issue of human procreation in the light of this basic concern; procreation should be managed in ways that minimize human frustrations at all stages and on all levels. In our culture, the pregnancy of unmarried teenagers is ethically undesirable precisely for this reason. It sets in motion a chain of frustrations and hardships, beginning with teenagers themselves, extending through their families and communities, and including a difficult, uncertain future for the offspring.

It is appropriate at this stage of the discussion to formulate in a positive way the normative ideal underlying our conclusion. Among the recent statements of this ideal Professor David L. Norton's (1976) provides an excellent philosophic foundation for our analysis. Professor Norton argues that the ethical cornerstone of our policies should be the creation of conditions under which people can grow into mature, responsible, autonomous human beings. Traditionally our entire political and economic system is based on respect for the individual. Leaning on the ancient Greek notion of *daimon,* a personal self-concept of having one's own individual set of propensities, bents, talents, and abilities which are discovered in the process of growing up, Norton suggests that we should deliberately and consciously promote all policies on individual and social levels in such a way that they encourage persons to move toward the optimal attainment of a personally conceived and pursued life plan. The underlying proviso is, of course, that pursuits and activities that prevent others from seeking the fulfillment of their personal destinies are ethically wrong.

Norton's name for this ethical ideal is *eudaimonism,* with the word "eudaimonia" standing not for happiness as it has been commonly translated, but as a state of affairs in which human beings are allowed to fulfill themselves in optimal ways. Happiness is relevant, but not as something directly aimed at. It is more likely to come when people are able to live and to act in the light of their *daimon,* of their own rationally and creatively perceived set of potentialities. These potentialities are, of course, not arbitrary, brought into being by persons *ex nihilo,* but are discerned in the wide experience of mankind. Sound education includes making available through study of history and of literature an open-ended set of models on which we may draw, in every case adding to the educational process our own experience, imagination, and opportunities. To lose sight of this objective is to run the danger of diminishing human well-being by failing to develop one's own autonomous life plan. That life plan certainly should include the management of our sexuality and of procreative activities.

I have placed this philosophic normative interlude at this stage of our discussion for a purpose. Rather than using it as a starting point, it seems to be better to lean on it as providing an ethical foundation for delineating desirable practices in dealing with the problems of teenage pregnancies. Having noted the undesirable ways of managing our sexuality, and especially its procreative aspects, and having connected them with the question of the alternative policies of discouragement of sexual activity or contraception, we were led to question the resulting dichotomy. Our normative logic allows us now to see why it is a false dichotomy. It is false because it is avoidable, not inevitable. When and by whom can it be avoided? It can be avoided by those who desire to fulfill the long-range ethical objectives for all persons involved: the teenagers, their families, their societies, and the potential offspring. Having stated this goal, let us now turn to some specific policies that may be conducive to its realization.

Practical Suggestions

We need sex education programs that will put sex back into its proper significant role in life. The very idea of sex education as confinable to a narrow range of human behavior is grossly misconceived. To have a proper perspective of human sexuality is to see it belonging to a wide spectrum of activities, needs, and goals. The same kind of disjunction occurs when we talk of sexual encounters as exclusively revolving around the production of physical pleasure for the partners. We have seen that the psychologic separation of sex from procreation leads to irresponsible ways of bringing into the world and raising human beings at a terrible cost to everyone concerned. One often has the suspicion that when physicians, psychologists, or social workers refer to people as "sexually active," the entire focus is on physical intercourse. But are not people "sexually active" in a variety of ways? The relation between the sexes is replete with a variety of sexual responses.

We need to remind ourselves and our teenagers that sexual interaction takes place on many levels—speech, looks, conversation, exchange of ideas and emotions, forming friendships, giving encouragement, cooperation, taking part in short-range and long-range plans and activities.

One area in which this rootedness of sexuality in life appears to be incomprehensibly forgotten is the discussion of explicit sexual activity itself. Most books about sex for adults or adolescents are written from physiologic and/or purely technical points of view with occasional concessions in prosaic, pseudoscientific and unimaginative terms to the need for mutual respect, tenderness, and other emotionally stimulating intangibles. It may be that in this age when we rely on "experts" on anything and everything, we feel that we must turn to "experts" in sex as well. But if the connection of sexuality with life is as broad as I have been trying to suggest, then sexuality cannot have experts. One cannot do justice to it when one ignores all its crucial ramifications.

Human sexuality, broadly conceived, has been a subject of close and intense study by another large class of people throughout human history, and yet that class of careful students is completely ignored by modern

See the mountains kiss high Heaven
    And the waves clasp one another;
No sister-flower would be forgiven
    If it disdained its brother;
And the sunlight clasps the earth
    And the moonbeams kiss the sea:
What is all this sweet work worth
    If thou kiss not me?

209

While turning to other sources we need not turn our backs on physiologic, clinical, or psychologic information derived from narrowly conceived "expert" books as long as we do not see them as presenting the *only* relevant material on the subject of sex. One practical suggestion would be to design a text resulting from a collaboration of teachers of poetry and literature with physicians or clinical students of sex behavior. If there is one area in which the "two cultures"—the sciences and the humanities—can meet, that area is sexuality. For the topic of sexuality cuts across all human experience. If sex education is exclusively in the hands of physicians, clinicians, and psychologists, that education is in the wrong hands, for they address themselves only to a part of what is relevant. In this area of human knowledge the hands, the head, and the heart must collaborate to produce healthy results. In sex education the health professionals cannot be successful if their own orientation is narrow. We are dealing with an area in which the whole person must be taken into account and no partial practitioner can deal successfully with the whole. This is the reason why reports about human sexuality derived exclusively from purportedly scientific and objective research are likely to be at best fragmentary and at worst distorting.

As it is a mistake to lift sexuality out of the entire fabric of life, so it is also a distortion to see in sexuality the primary and dominant mode of activity. The Freudian representation of life forces as essentially libidinal, confines all forms of human activity to the same preconceived mold, thus inviting us to look for sexual meanings where there are none. When all art is seen as a sublimating repression of sexual impulses, the conclusion is derived from a reductionist theory. Freud and his followers such as Herbert Marcuse or Norman O. Brown may be right in calling attention to many instances in which healthy erotic impulses are denied or frustrated by ideologic considerations or political and economic forces. But they are victims of overgeneralized theory if they attempt to see *all* life in sexual or erotic terms. Life includes sexuality but is not reducible to it.

One helpful way to recognize a special role of sexuality is to draw a distinction between it and eroticism as Professor Paul Kurtz has done in his book *Exuberance* (1978). Without claiming that the erotic mode of existence is dominant, he suggests that many erotic pleasures are not to be directly connected with sexual impulse. Even if we regard eroticism as diffuse sexuality, its objectives are separable from sexual objectives and should be seen as continuous with other humanly rewarding pursuits.

Putting an arm around a friend's shoulder has in it the satisfaction of physical closeness, but are we justified in always reading it as a sexual overture? In many, probably most instances, it is just a concrete, but symbolic, gesture of friendship, companionship, good will. To refuse it this status on the basis of a universal reductive theory is to fly in the face of obvious facts. Professor Kurtz's approach seems to strike the proper balance when he says that "the erotic per se cannot be identified solely with either sex or love." He continues:

> The erotic, no doubt, has its roots in sex and its highest fulfill-
> ment is in romantic love; but it is limited or thwarted, in my
> judgment, unless it can be intimately diffused with a whole vari-
> ety of human experiences. The erotic is related to sensory stimu-
> lation in a most fundamental way. There is a good deal of psy-
> cho-biological evidence that humans and other primates need
> sensory or tactile sensations, if they are to develop normally.

The appreciation of diffuse eroticism should not prevent us from ac-knowledging the *power* of the sexual urge. Here again we can learn from poets. Rainer Maria Rilke in his *Duino Elegies* (1939) gives a poetic account of the evolutionary biologic stream of life which can be presumed to be present in every individual encounter between two lovers. Our sexuality, according to Rilke, discloses to us a disturbing fact: we *can* become playthings of the overwhelmingly large and powerful cosmos. Sex can be seen to have a terrifying aspect. The overpowering ancestral urge asserts itself early, even in the dreams of the adolescent who feels "the floods of origin flowing within him." Rilke's Third Elegy is a phenomenological commentary on what Freud called "the libido." Its concrete physical dominance is explained by Rilke in evolutionary terms. Sexuality is a fact not about individuals but about the entire hu-man race. Every person is a carrier of the procreative instinct of nature, and we must acknowledge the physiologic underpinnings of our roman-tic love. In singing the beloved we are also in the service of "that hid-den guilty river-god of the blood." Mixed with our romantic attraction to a specific person there is also the procreative urge which reaches through an unbroken chain to all our ancestors who bestowed life on us by paying homage to that river-god within our blood. Rilke points to this connection as accounting for the power, intensity, and irresistible attraction of the sexual impulse.

> Look, we don't love like flowers, with only a single
> season behind us; immemorial sap
> mounts in our arms when we love.

To see oneself as a carrier of this immemorial biologic energy is potentially destructive to our fragile psyche. For the essence of romantic love is concentrated on the individuality of the beloved. The lover believes that it is she, her looks, her beauty, that mobilizes in him the sexual desire. But the presence of the ancient urge is always there to create a sense of doubt: do I really want her or just her body? This unpoetic vulgar way of putting the question does not diminish its relevance, and Rilke perceives that it may lead to a sense of guilt. The lover wants to single out, to sing, to celebrate his beloved, and yet he also knows that he is at the service of this "Neptune within our blood with his horrible trident." The guilt may follow from the uncertainty as to which force is the dominant one in the encounter of two lovers. The deflation and disillusionment is reinforced when the romantic attraction passes. Alternatively, when the attraction to another person is explicitly and exclusively physical, the guilt takes on another form; it is the guilt of *using* the person, of not appreciating personal qualities of the individual. (The guilt about prostitution, affecting both the prostitute and her client, stems from this realization.)

Human sexuality, since it calls for a *personalized* expression, separates individuals from the overwhelming ancestral biologic stream. But the personalization is only tentative and temporary. A sense of guilt is generated by a suppressed anxiety that we do not manage to reconcile the claims of the race with the expression of devotion to particular individuals we profess to love. Here we have a potent source of disillusionment with the human condition.

It is because Rilke sees the presence of this strong biologic urge of the human race in individual encounters that he sees the need to *counteract* its power by consideration, tenderness, and kindness of the lovers to one another. His perception of the situation supports the view defended in this essay that human beings have the capacity to acknowledge and appreciate the strength of the sexual impulse, but that they can also understand its complexity and relate it to a wider context of important human activities and goals. As in all other areas of life, our aim should be to bring about a greater understanding of self and autonomous self-control, enabling us to achieve the many and varied objectives of our personal and social existence.

Conclusion

To translate into practice the objective outlined in this essay—to broaden considerably our concept of sex education—is not an easy matter because the relegation of sex to its special, narrowly defined realm is too pervasive in our culture to be modified quickly. But we must begin. One obvious place is the area of the health professionals themselves. If they begin to see sexuality as connected with other areas of life, they will communicate this perception—in their speech, writings, and behavior—not only to their immediate clients, the teenagers, but also to the rest of the concerned public—parents, school officials, and social agencies, thus creating a ripple effect of the whole society. On such a pervasive issue only a gradual change can be expected. But even a slow change, if it is in the right direction, is preferable to *ad hoc* measures that do not address themselves at all to the inherent complexity of the issue. To effect a change in entrenched habits of thinking we should avoid a head-on approach, but we should try to reach as many as possible of the persons capable of shifting their vision. The only lasting effect can be brought about by educating the educators, and that takes time. Because of that, any further waste of time is to be avoided. The place to begin is with ourselves.

Notes

1. In this regard, there seem to be some subcultural differences. I have heard from a competent source (a teacher who taught for a number of years in a predominantly black high school) that black males tend to accept with pride the responsibility for having fathered a child—a cultural phenomenon, a deeper analysis of which may reach into our darker historical past, that of the slavery period.
2. "There is considerable evidence that youth and strength are on the side of the teenage mother and that, where she is not under an income handicap, her experience of motherhood has a high probability of success " (Kasun 1978).
3. Some undesirable effects of *creating* gaps where none exist by an unsuitable use of language I have discussed in "The pathology of Gap-ology" (Kolenda 1977).
4. Christine Farrell argues that the British law, setting 16 as the age of consent for heterosexual acts, may actually be doing more harm than good to the young

girls it is supposed to protect. "If the law is to maintain its protective function, there would seem to be a strong case for encouraging (these) girls to come earlier for advice by lowering the age of consent. One of the (teenagers') most common complaints about sex education is that they were told too little, too late." (Farrell 1978).

5. "If we accept the premise that an adolescent is a responsible, valuable human being in his own right, then we must agree that, as such, he is entitled to the basic facts about the heritage of the past that have been preserved and have stood the test of time." (Juhasz 1976). John Wilson also claims that we are "not entitled to indoctrinate children about sex, but only obligated to educate them" (Wilson 1965).

References

Farrell, C. *My mother said*. London: Routledge & Kegan Paul, 1978.

Juhasz, A. M. A cognitive approach to sex education. In *Understanding adolescence*, ed. J. F. Adams. Boston: Allyn and Bacon, 1976.

Kasun, J. Teenage pregnancy: epidemic or statistical hoax. *USA today,* July 1978.

Kolenda, K. The pathology of gapology, *Intellect* 105:437–438, 1977.

Kurtz, P. *Exuberance*. Buffalo, New York: Prometheus Books, 1977.

Norton, D. L. *Personal destinies: a philosophy of ethical individualism*. Princeton: Princeton University Press, 1976.

Rilke, R. M. *Duino Elegies,* Translated by J. B. Leishman and S. Spender. New York: W. W. Norton, 1939.

Stallworthy, J. *A book of love poetry*. New York: Oxford University Press, 1974.

Wilson, J. *Logic and sexual morality*. Harmondsworth: Penguin, 1965.

12 Sex Education

Peggy B. Smith, Ph.D.

Background

Historically, sex education as an educational concern can be traced back to the late 1880s when a variety of groups sponsored meetings and panels dealing with sex-related topics. In 1892 the National Education Association at its annual meeting discussed the role of sex education in the curriculum. In 1905 the initial impetus for sex education in the schools was instigated by Dr. Prince Morrow when he organized the American Society for Sanitary and Moral Prophylaxis. The primary focus of this organization was to irradicate diseases that threatened the social order, specifically, venereal disease. The recognition that this end could be accomplished through public education created the thrust for the development of broader sex education programs (Carrera 1972). In 1912 the National Education Association passed the first resolution recommending special training for sex educators.

Some recognition of the need for sex education occurred on the federal level in 1932 when the White House Conference on Child Health and Protection produced a pamphlet entitled "Social Hygiene in the Schools." This document suggested that the primary goal of social hygiene is to preserve the family and to improve and enrich family life. Such goals would later be broken down into specific objectives.

While the need for the introduction of sex education in the schools was accepted even in the thirties, the approach was still quite conservative in comparison with present day methods. Fear of possible side effects from the consequences of human sexuality education were quite prevalent in the earlier works of writers such as Kirsch and Bigelow (1934). However, during the 1940s sex education appeared to be making a broader impact in the United States. Gallup polls taken in 1934 and again in 1948 revealed substantial general support for the inclusion of sex education of public schools. This was a reflection of the popularity of sex education throughout all geographic regions, although the feeling was not as strong in the South (Carrera 1972). Moreover, Kinsey's (1949) work initiated during this period reflected the prevalence of interest in human sexuality.

During the 1950s national leadership in family life education was assumed primarily by the American Social Health Association (ASHA).

Aided by private philanthropic support, ASHA orchestrated five regional projects involving 23 states and the District of Columbia. The objectives of ASHA were organized by means of a strategy which as Somerfield (1971) points out

> . . . did not start with assumptions of the superiority of one discipline over another in family life education responsibility. Perhaps more important than its consequent ability to gain greater cooperation among various disciplines was ASHA awareness of the focality of teacher preparation and its attempts to involve teacher education institution in regional projects.

As a result of its activities, quality regional curricular materials, workshops, resource guides, and television series were developed and made available for secondary school and college use.

A significant effort to promote sex education in the 1960s was the establishment of the Sex Information and Education Council of the United States (SIECUS). This voluntary health organization's purpose was to create in-depth knowledge, to stimulate community concern, and to mobilize community action in the area of sex education. With the leadership of Dr. Mary Calderone, strides were made in the development of community awareness and in a general acknowledgement of the need for human sexuality education. In her organizational statement concerning sex education (1965), Dr. Calderone states:

> SIECUS is definitely health centered, with purposes that are clearly positive rather than negative. These purposes aim not to eradicate something so much as to create something new in the world: Knowledge in depth and attitudes in breadth, about the part of the human individual that is so central to his total being, his sexuality.

While Calderone's approach met with some community resistance (Allen 1969), SIECUS nevertheless successfully provided some professional stature and recognition for the development and dissemination of materials related to human sexuality.

In 1967 The American Association of Sex Education Counselors and Therapists (AASECT) was created. A national interdisciplinary interest group, AASECT stated as its central purpose for the provision of training, education, and research. One of the important activities of this group is to develop competency standards for sex educators, counselors and therapists. Other professional groups also encouraged greater involvement in the teaching of human sexuality. Three such organizations, The American Institute of Family Relations, The Institute for Sex Research and The Institute for Family Research and Education are some of the professional entities which have sponsored supplemental training in the area of human sexuality.

Professionals from the international health milieu also underscored the importance of sex education. The World Health Organization (WHO) in its technical report series also endorsed the development of expertise in the area of human sexuality through the provision of training for professionals. Couched in the terminology, sexual health, WHO believed that health workers in the area of human sexuality must have accurate scientific knowledge, know the common sexual problems, and must recognize when the solution to problems is beyond their ability and qualifications. WHO also endorsed a change in professional attitudes toward human sexuality. The need for a more accepting approach was particularly important. Reflecting its medical background, this organization strongly encouraged that human sexuality be integrated into all aspects of education and become a required course in the medical school curriculum.

Source of Sex Education

As a result of the growing endorsement by a variety of professionals concerning the need for sex education, several traditional institutions have been identified as important community resources. The parent, the school, and the church are usually the predominant sex educators, either by default or design. Moreover, a variety of specialized groups have also become involved in sex education. The source of sex education has taken on increasing importance. The providing agent, by virtue of its position in the community, determines the content, philosophy, target audience, objectives, teaching techniques, and, to some extent, the ultimate community acceptance. For ease in interpretation, several sources of sex education will be discussed separately.

PARENTS

With renewed national emphasis on the role of the family in American life as reported in the popular press (*Newsweek* 1978), parents have once again been designated as the primary educators of their children. Although

217

federal endorsement of the importance of the family unit has been recently reaffirmed, as evidenced by the proposed White House Conference on the Family, some professionals (Gordon 1974, 1977) have been longtime advocates of this parental responsibility, especially in regards to sex education. As the first teachers of the child, parents are in a unique position to convey factual information to their progeny about sex. Parents are also able to convey to the child, at a very early age, the individual familial attitudes toward human sexuality. Special religious and moral codes which affect individual human sexual behavior are most effectively cultivated if training is woven into the fabric of daily family living.

Educational activities should optimally begin at birth. Aside from overt instruction, several factors facilitate the child's learning process. Accidental learning, which usually peaks out by age five, may provide a crucial orientation to such concepts as gender identity (Broderick 1974), sex roles (Athanasiou 1973), and interpersonal relationships. The occurrence of the basic developmental stages may also provide fertile ground for positive learning experiences concerning human sexuality. For example, all children must develop bowel and bladder control. The experiences surrounding this developmental step have direct relationships to the child's orientation to his body, his sexuality, and the way he can communicate with his parents concerning sex.

The organized scheme of human development not only provides specific and replicable examples, but also presents overall structure which can enhance cumulative learning. Information concerning human sexuality can therefore be presented in a sequence sensitive to the emotional and intellectual capacity of the child. By using this gradual approach parents can eliminate the fragmented or shotgun efforts in which "too little too late" is presented to adolescents.

In the first ten years of life, parents have the major responsibility of educating their child about sex. Elias and Gebherd (1969) surveyed children, four to fourteen years of age, concerning their source of sex education, and noted that the school teacher as a formal teaching entity was not mentioned by any of the children as the main source. In fact, the authors note

> throughout the study the contribution of the teacher and the
> school system to the child's information about sex was too low to
> be statistically significant.

However, while parents are encouraged to bring sex education back into the home—where it belongs (Gordon 1976)—parental leadership has not been forthcoming. Libby (1976) found that most parents expressed a desire to talk to their children, but just did not know how. Such a problem probably reflects a combination of factors. Some parents may lack the basic technical vocabulary to discuss sexual concepts. This verbal deficiency may be the result of conflicting attitudes towards sex which are manifested in a rejection of sexual terms and language (Johnson and Belzer 1973). Parents who are uncomfortable using the correct terminology for physical anatomy resort to juvenile or slang expressions, reflective of infantile patterns of communication. Such words lack emotional and cognitive sophistication and become effective stumbling blocks when more sophisticated concepts of human sexuality are presented. Some parents are unable to adequately communicate sexual concepts to their children primarily because their own childhood training lacked such instruction. Libby and Nass (1971) found most of the parents surveyed felt that their own sex education was unsatisfactory. Others have difficulty communicating sexual information and material to their children because of their own sexual orientation. Some adults are unable to discuss human sexuality without emotionally replaying their own sexual conflicts.

Sol Gordon (1974) has stated that the heart of the matter arises from the inability of such adults to deal with their own sexuality. Parents may be out of touch with their own feelings or may have possibly forgotten that before they were parents, many were lovers. Some parents may not provide any sex education because of personal feelings of anxiety concerning the content often reflected in defense mechanisms of rationalization or denial. In Furstenberg's (1976) study of unplanned parenthood, three-fourths of the parents questioned stated that most of the teens in their neighborhoods were sexually active. However, 77% of the mothers reported that they were very surprised when they learned that their daughters were pregnant. Moreover, fewer than one in four admitted any prior knowledge of their daughters' sexual activity. Such a false confidence that their own daughters are not sexually active not only diminishes possible parental anxiety concerning such acts, but also absolves the mothers of the responsibility for deliberate actions to prevent a conception from occurring.

Once parents overcome initial inhibitions concerning sex education, however, significant communication problems may still exist. While the majority of teens (Libby 1974) like and respect their parents, communication seems to break down when sex is discussed. Such psychological barriers are indicative of the developmental stage and are in keeping with the adolescent's attempts to master his environment. Substantive sexual dialogue does not occur. This communication problem may also reflect adolescent reaction to general parental conservatism. In addition, the messages that parents try to communicate may not be the messages teens want to hear. Moreover, communication problems may also reflect prudish orientations to sexual matters. Sex education which transpires under such circumstances is usually vague and unclear with advice focusing on nonsubstantive issues. An example of such verbal admonitions would be "keep your knees together."

Ironically, adolescent groups that spring from parents with rather rigid orientations towards human sexuality are often sexually active at very young ages. Elias and Gebherd (1969) found that three times more blue collar prepubescent boys have had or have attempted coitus as have their white collar counterparts. It should be mentioned that cognitively the white collar boys had higher levels of sexual knowledge. This phenomenon may result from the milder parental orientation toward sexuality of the middle class.

The content of parental communication may not be what the adolescent needs or wants to know. While initially well intentioned, some parents indirectly control their children's behavior by selective presentation of content matter. Libby (1970) in a survey of parental and student attitudes towards the content of high school sex education programs found a polarization of content. Parents preferred content which stressed the dangers of premarital sex and venereal disease. Teens on the other hand preferred information which stressed openness and which helped them to explore themselves and the value system most suited to their self-concept, including discussion of actual behavior. It appeared that some parents presumed that presentation of the negative consequences of coitus would discourage adolescent sexual activity. However, as Gordon (1974) has indicated, young people have sex whether parents like it or not.

Despite the aforementioned problems of parental involvement in sex education, a broad-based effort has commenced to enhance and develop the skills of parents in the area of human sexuality. The Institute for Family Research and Education (1977), working from the premise that parents want to educate their children but often feel inadequate or afraid, conducted a three year pilot community sex education program for parents. While looking towards the school in a supportive way, the program appeared to demonstrate that the most effective ways to provide sex education for children was to educate parents and to take creative advantage of the media young people most common consult. Caution, however, was urged in the following way. Gordon (1977) urges program implementers to be aware that sex education programs primarily attract parents who are already involved with their children. This audience's need is to improve already open channels of communication and levels of factual information. Groups which do not have an already established positive rapport may need substantially different types of experiences.

THE SCHOOL

Even when parents have fulfilled their responsibility to educate their children concerning human sexuality, their exclusive domain over this subject matter is short-lived. Lieberman (1969) points out that usually other children, television, domestic animals, and other pregnancies and births contribute substantial information and confusion. Reinforcement and support from professionals and institutions can facilitate and complement this parental task. This viewpoint is reinforced by Libby (1974) who found that while parents viewed the home as the most significant sources of sex education, parents requested that strong links with the school be forged, so long as the home was not supplanted. Moreover, in some cases children do not always reside with their parents, relegating total responsibility for sex education to other community institutions. Thus, the school is logically seen as assisting with (Anastasiow and co-workers 1975) or being the primary teacher (Osofsky and Osofsky 1971) of sex education.

Support for school leadership comes from a variety of professions. The medical and allied health professions have endorsed the supplementary role of the school in assisting the parents with sex education. From surveys conducted among pregnant teenagers, various researchers (Zelnick and Kantner 1973; Furstenberg 1976) reveal the lack of basic knowledge concerning human reproduction. Furthermore, many teenagers who have found themselves pregnant indicated that they were operating under misinformation (Presser 1974; Reichelt and Worley 1975). While the availability alone of basic knowledge and information does not preclude the possibility of conception, many medical professionals feel that access to this information through the schools will minimize the risk of an unplanned pregnancy.

Such sponsorship by the school has met initially with community approval (Lipson 1972) and has received positive expectations from parents, students, and professionals in the field (Dearth 1974). A recent Gallup poll (Gallup 1978) has reinforced this general public support of the school

entering into sex education curriculum. Seventy-seven % of those interviewed in 1977 stated that sex education should be taught in the schools.
Even the controversial topic of contraception received more than plurality
support. Sixty-nine percent supported the teaching of birth control information in such courses in the schools. However, such warm endorsements may lose their strength when specific human sexuality issues are
subject to closer scrutiny (Blake 1973).

The Language of Sex Education Curricula

One of the difficulties encountered by school officials in the area of human
sexuality and specifically in the development of sex education curriculum
is the lack of consensus over the terminology used for the subject area.
Broderick and Bernard (1969) point out that there appears to be a strong
taboo surrounding the semantics of sex education which in the past has
excited fears and stimulated a narrow and limited approach. The problem
is exacerbated by the fact that professional support sprang initially from
prophylactic attempts to prevent negative consequences of human sexuality, such as unplanned pregnancies and venereal disease. Recently,
phrases such as family life and development, personal and social guidance, population education, and even education for parenthood reflect the
variety of terms being applied to the same content area. While this broad
range of titles may reflect growing social acceptance, Force (1970) has
pointed out that in the past the selected definition and terminology for
the course carried subtle social and political overtones which diffused the
course definition so as to make communication among school professionals difficult. This sensitivity to the selected labels in the area of human
sexuality is not only predominant among professionals, but is also a
strong concern among parent groups. In an article by Dearth (1974)
surveying parental and student expectations for course design, it was
found that the more explicit titles of Human Sexuality or Sex Education
were unacceptable. Moreover, this conservative approach was also reflected in the discomfort stimulated among parents over possible usage
of common four letter words in the course of instruction. Force (1970)
in her regional survey evaluating the formats of family life education,
also found that the broad concepts included in family life education were
difficult to interpret and that basic philosophical differences among professional educators accounted for a wide diversity in terminology and
approach.

The inability to agree on a singular title for the subject matter also reflects the difficulty of defining the objectives of sex education courses. The goals and objectives of available sex education courses span a wide range of approaches, philosophies, and needs. As previously noted, in the initial developmental phases of sex education curricula, the emphasis was primarily on the consequences of sexual intercourse. The original recommendations were usually health oriented. As a result, the goals and objectives of sex education efforts demonstrated a limited scope. The need for parents to keep their sexual lives private and to supervise their children "less they fall into evil ways" were predominant issues in the earlier works on human sexuality. Broderick and Bernard (1969) pointed out that some of the most inflammatory issues were masturbation and nudity in the home.

A more positive approach to human sexuality, however, has gradually evolved. The negative aspects of human sexuality and the limited content have been augmented with information concerning human relationships, values clarification, and decision-making processes. The goals of present day sex education are broader with objectives defined in a continuum of terms. Exemplary objectives today include character education (Gendel 1960), preventive medicine (Calderone 1968), learning satisfying relationships and value systems (Force 1970), preparation for social puberty through the development of moral responsibility (Thornburg 1974), and the provision of information that teenagers need to know (Gordon 1974). Schiller (1977) states that sex education "identifies our gender, our anatomy and physiology"—all essential attributes of our personal identity. Implicit in such objectives and/or definitions is the concept that sex education is just one component of preparation for effective living in every phase of the life cycle.

Specific Curricular Goals and Objectives

The curricular objectives of sex education programs are greatly shaped by the underlying motivations of their planners. As previously mentioned, the most popular objectives are prevention or reduction of adolescent pregnancy and reduction of venereal disease. While some curricula are prohibited from explaining just how one contracts the disease or gets pregnant, the widespread incidence of gonorrhea and syphilis among adolescents (Mumford, Smith and Goldfarb 1977) and its recent appearance in pediatric cohorts (Litt, Edberg and Finberg 1974) provide some rationale for group discussion.

Broader based objectives, such as the understanding of population

223

growth, are more widespread and, predictably, carry less notoriety and controversy. Almost by definition, discussion of reproduction and family planning can be avoided. The focus of these objectives switches from pregnancy to epidemiology. Moreover, such objectives can be inserted into a broader spectrum of established curricula. Diverse subjects such as geographical social studies and math can all legitimately address these objectives.

A small group of programs has selected a values-oriented paradigm for the objectives of sex education. Self-fulfillment, augmentation of self-esteem, and the development of an awareness of one's own sexuality are some of the objectives. These focus on the development of self and its relationship to sexual behavior. These objectives are quite ubiquitous, finding relevancy for a diverse grouping of material, and may not even focus on sex. The emphasis is concentrated on the decision making process not on the action or behavior itself. Such programs discuss how one makes decisions and assumes responsibility for one's actions. Sexual intercourse is just one of many behaviors in which one must accept the consequences of one's actions. The technique of values clarification is a method used in such an approach (Morrison and Price 1974).

This discussion is by no means all inclusive. In many programs various combinations of objectives are arranged with great variety, each program reflecting its community's unique needs. Furthermore, similar titles and phraseology may only describe the general content of individual programs while the specific courses may treat quite different subject matter.

Implementation of Sex Education in the School

The actual implementation of any information concerning human sexuality in the school setting requires important preparatory tasks. Experts in the field (Institute for Family Research and Education 1977) indicate that the planning stage prior to the actual development of sex education curriculum is a crucial part of the educational experience. This planning includes needs assessment, community education and involvement, format selection, educational institutional endorsement, teacher selection and training, and ongoing evaluation. Deliberate and well-thought out strategies will contribute to the successful acceptance of the program and its maintenance.

Needs assessment is the usual point of departure for program initiation.

Concern is usually raised over precipitating problems such as the rise of adolescent pregnancy or venereal disease in adolescents. Individuals who have been successful in initiating sex education classes in the schools (Thoms and Tatum 1977) recommend that planners listen to what people in groups have to say. Implicit in this listening exercise is the identification of the feelings of parent groups and individuals who support traditional programs. Personal dialogue with parents who work in the schools is also of importance. The securement of their support can take a variety of forms. In Maryland (Terry and Woodward 1976), professionals initiated community support for the introduction of a five year sex education project in the school system by sponsoring two ten day work-shops to examine curriculum designs, to identify health problems unique to the state, and to attempt to formulate a design of curriculum for grades K through 12. Leadership in this endeavor combined the expertise and efforts of the State Department of Education, State Health Department, and the medical field.

Besides sponsoring workshops to obtain needs assessment, other alternatives have been suggested and developed. Schiller (1977) suggested that a committee of key people be formed to investigate and determine the receptiveness of parents whose children will have classes in sex education. If any negative reactions are discovered among parents then professionals will meet with this group to answer their questions and to help them overcome anxiety. From past experience, most questions pertain to the content of program, the values to be taught, and/or to the qualifications of the teachers. One ancillary problem concerning implementation of sex education in the school (Libby 1974) is the difficulty for some parents to distinguish between learning about sex and learning how to be sexual. Professional sensitivity should respond to this issue early in the program development.

Some professionals (Dearth 1974) have used needs assessment techniques to determine the public's expectations for sex education in the schools. In general, such studies reveal that parents, experts, and students expect positive results from human sexuality courses in the school curriculum. Once the needs have been identified, a subtle educational campaign should begin. Without broad-based community support, any effort in the area of human sexuality, however well intentioned, will reach less than positive resolution. Middlewood (1969), in her comparison of two community education projects, points out that in the final analysis gradual activity with minimal publicity may have more positive benefits than a task force approach with media blitz. Middlewood points out that the key factors of successful programs were: (1) it was initiated in the school; (2) the community was involved but not allowed to impose its views; (3) the consistent goal was to educate all ages from kindergarten to adults with the school assuming responsibility for preschool and adult education; (4) the energy was generated within the planning group itself rather than from outside authorities; and (5) there were no unnecessary public meetings.

After the development of broad-based support and endorsement by the community, the project can then be initiated. The actual implementation of curriculum must include the choice of format. This decision should be predicated on the specific objectives identified for each community where projects are implemented. The alternatives for format are varied. Gordon (1974) suggests five basic prototypes, each appropriate for a variety of teaching situations. The reproductive system model is the first suggested prototype; it emphasizes physiological development, particularly menstruation and changes at puberty. The content is biologically oriented. The second format is the consequences model. In this curriculum attention is paid to the physical, psychic, and economic cost of premature sexual experiences and unwanted births. Emphasis is placed on issues such as venereal disease, illegitimacy, economic strain, and medical complications. The economic cost of child rearing, early marriage, and the advantages of population limitations are also usually covered. The morality model is the third format where emphasis is placed on decision making and exploration of the variety of value systems in a pluralistic society. The fourth format suggested by Gordon is labeled the integrated model. Teaching areas such as biology, economics, history, health, language, and physical education address the issues from the standpoint of the individual disciplines. In the student centered curriculum model, the final format suggested by Gordon, the students themselves structure the content by identifying their own concerns and interests. The entire program is student planned and organized with school-wide participation and heavy use of outside professional resources.

A variety of approaches exist in addition to the ones delineated, but any selection should reflect the individual needs of the community and the needs of the schools themselves. Gordon indicates that the successful approach to sex education can only be determined after assessing the situation in the individual school. If the school has a low morale with great student distrust, apathy, or animosity then an objective presentation of essential facts is the most realistic approach. However, if the students enjoy the school, a great deal can be accomplished. In an environment that is emotionally positively reinforcing, schools may be able to help adolescents develop a better awareness of their sexuality with greater sensitivity to others.

Once the approach has been selected, the next step is to establish the mechanics of incorporating the information concerning human sexuality into the school setting. Schools, procedurally, must decide in what curricular structure the content can be logically placed. One organizational option categorizes human sexuality material as a separate curricular option and/or elective. This approach can minimize the problems of compatibility that result from combining curricula from diverse disciplines. The separate curriculum approach was indirectly endorsed by SIECUS.

Experiences of other educators, however, have indicated that the curriculum of sex education lends itself to an integrated approach. Some believe that if sex is pulled out of context, the material will be spotlighted in an undesirable way. Thoms and Tatum (1977) in their approach to human sexuality recommend that curriculum should be more geared to grade levels at which instruction is planned and not primarily focused on separate curriculum:

> We should back sex education not, as ''now we will have a class in sex education,'' but in terms of these larger ideas of human personality and sexual identity. Just as we would not discuss with a five year old the complicated interaction between human beings on a personal and/or conversational level, we would not discuss with the same five year old complex ideas about sexual behavior. We have to gear what we teach, when we teach it to the particular developmental level of the students we are teaching.

Gordon (1974) also endorses the integrated approach citing excellent examples concerning human sexuality that are naturally present in other educational fields:

> A separate course for sex education is not only artificial but unnecessary. It is important to consider in English classes why George Eliot had to publish under a man's name or what D. H. Lawrence's concepts of women and sex had to do with his writing. History classes must understand sex roles in the nineteenth century to understand British politics or reactions of women's suffrage movement. And surely, no study of Freud's work would be complete without discussing sexuality.

Implicit in the integrated approach, however, is the premise that teachers from a variety of disciplines are or can be qualified to teach human sexuality. This issue of qualifications, discussed in the next section, is of crucial importance.

Teacher Training

While planning community education and curriculum development are priorities in the implementation of sex education in the schools, probably the most important component is the training of the professionals who will present the curriculum. Schultz and Williams (1968), Ready (1973), Gordon (1974) and Schiller (1976) have given this issue top priority in the field of human sexuality. In spite of the consensus concerning the importance of this factor, widespread availability of such training is not present (Force 1970). Broderick and Bernard (1969) and later Schiller (1977) indicate that this lack of preparation opportunity for teachers is the greatest problem in the field.

Some professionals (Forman 1969) have even asserted that if sex education staggers and falls, the fault will probably rest with an ill-equipped or inept teacher. The National Commission on Family Life Education also asserts that "confidently prepared family life educators are crucial to the successful realization of goals." Without the basic foundation of qualified teachers even the best curriculum material will remain on the shelf or will be implemented in such a way to stimulate community anger and student indifference. Some professionals (Graves 1974) feel that the professional level of the field will be better accepted and enhanced when adequate teacher training programs are established.

With a few exceptions, available training experiences are minimal. In a review of the history of sex education (Schiller 1977) reported in a work by Malfetti, of the two hundred and fifty institutions which responded to a questionnaire concerning course offerings on human sexuality for potential teachers, only 21% offered a specific course in the curriculum area. These findings are especially disheartening when one examines the activity in other countries. While a cross-cultural comparison is beyond the scope of this work, the efforts in the United Kingdom, because of the mutual cultural heritage, merits reporting. Burke (1974) reports on a study conducted in 1964 which surveyed the amount of training and sex education given to student teachers in the United Kingdom. Of those replying to the questionnaire, 38% of the preparatory institutions offered formal courses in sex education. Moreover, the majority of respondents appeared to include sex education in a wider content of other courses. Thirty-two % of the institutions actually provided teaching techniques in the area of sex education. Although the quality of such curriculum material is not externally documented, 90% of the institutions concerned with teacher training reported that they felt the offered courses were adequate. Some difficulty was indicated, however, in finding a suitable person to undertake the training aspect.

Several factors have been cited which have contributed to the dearth of training opportunity. Calderone (1968) cites vocal and well-orchestrated protest from minority groups as a key factor in the limited offerings in human sexuality. Carrera (1972) cites the lack of agreement of what actually should be taught as a significant factor, resulting in the lack of quality control, curriculum, and standards. Gordon (1974) indicates that the lack of systematic training also complicates the issue. As a result, the majority of sex education teacher training opportunities that are offered are usually short weekend workshops or limited inservice experiences. The optimal format of semester experiences (Munson 1976) are the exception rather than the rule. Kirkendall and Libby (1969) indicate that while some teacher training programs provide basic information on psychology, human growth, personality development, and social awareness, few preparatory curricula deal directly with sexuality itself or recognize the importance of sex education as an aspect of providing information in the public schools.

IMPORTANT COMPONENTS OF TEACHER TRAINING

Up to this point, we have focused on the gaps that exist in teacher training. However, some information is available on significant components in the training experiences for teachers in the area of human sexuality. The National Council on Family Relations recommends that those who teach in family life and sex education programs need to have certain academic and field experiences along with opportunities for self-awareness and practicum experience. This issue of certification is not without its problems because as Somerfield (1968) points out, there is still disagreement in institutions of higher learning as to which disciplines should be involved in the offering of core experiences. Reed and Munson (1976) indicate that the primary prerequisite for teachers in the area of human sexuality is the possession of a positive attitude toward ones own sexual identity. Such an orientation is crucial before any teacher can enter the class. Johnson (1974) and Mundy (1976) distinctly indicate that one must come to grips with ones own sexuality with special attention to the affective level. In order to be comfortable with one's own sexuality, certain issues must be reconciled. Reed and Munson (1976) underline the necessity of accepting and allowing alternate sex lifestyles, especially when they differ from one's own value system. The importance of non-exploitation of other individuals and the joy of being humanly sexual are also components which are posed as prerequisites in the teacher training curricula. Munson (1976) recommends that teachers also need to have a working knowledge of adolescents as well as a facility with the language of human sexuality and a sensitivity to one's own identity and experience level. Schiller (1973) indicates that the training experiences of the sex educator should consist of three primary parts—content, attitude, professional behavior, and skills. Moreover, sex education requires a high level of responsibility and calls for perception and sensitivity. Thus, as Mundy (1967) points out, training opportunities must present more than factual information. Teacher training programs should provide a number of opportunities for self-examination and the resolution of personal conflict. Role play and values clarification will provide some of the vehicles for staff attitude assessment.

Problems with Sex Education in the School

During the last forty years tremendous professional interest has been directed towards establishing and implementing quality sex education. In addition to the recommendations of physicians (Mecklenburg 1973), educators (Carrera 1972), sociologists (Presser 1974; Furstenberg 1976), and epidemologists (Jekel 1977), the Sixth White House Conference on Children and Youth recommended that

> . . . school curriculum includes education for family life, including sex education, family life courses, including preparation for marriage and parenthood, be instituted as an integral and major part of public school education from elementary school through high school . . .

However, when the fruits of such efforts are assessed, very few accomplishments are identifiable on a local level. Several inherent issues associated with sex education may be responsible in some part for this low level of long term productivity. One of the first issues is the lack of local and regional political leadership. In spite of federal encouragement and recommendations for the initiation of courses in human sexuality in the public school sector, territorial prerogatives still rest with local and state political forces. The foundation for such control is almost simplistically clear. Elementary and Secondary Education, with few exceptions, is financed entirely through state and local bodies (Ambrose 1976). It should be pointed out that such regional politics may not completely be anti-sex education. However, individuals in these systems may be more vulnerable to minority group pressure. Moreover, accessibility to such policy makers is enhanced by close geographical proximity. Protesters who may not make themselves heard in Washington, D.C. can usually be quite vociferous on the steps of the state capitol or city hall.

One reason for local leadership reluctance may arise from the psychological deterrents. The implementation of sex education programs even under optimal circumstances is a very difficult task. The responsibility for such programs, however, is all too frequently dumped in the lap of school administrators who lack trained staff, instructional material readily acceptable to the community, and, in some cases, minimal interest. Even when rudimentary support systems are available, many teachers have been unable to adequately challenge the students' already existing attitudes. The "tabula rasa" that may provide fertile ground for some disciplines has already been imprinted with emotional bias in sex education.

The lack of scientific information in sex education curricula may also impede acceptance by some groups. One of the milestones in the establishment of a discipline or area of academic endeavor is to statistically document that exposure to the particular educational tenets will actually affect outcome or behavior. In the domain of sex education, results would demonstrate that groups who participate in sex education classes experience a lower prevalence of venereal disease, unplanned pregnancy, or induced abortion. However, very few programs in elementary and/or secondary schools have been able to approach such an empirical design. Moreover, in the majority of cases no evaluation is attempted to ascertain the real effects of exposure to such curricula. Because of the dubious status of sex education, Chilman (1969) stated that it was impossible to substantiate her ideas concerning sex education because

> . . . no research has been done concerning how information
> about sex is best imparted, what its content should be, or what
> the effects of sex education are.

However, in spite of the identification of such a substantive gap, assertive efforts in the area of program assessment have not materialized. Somerfield (1971) indicates that the present state of the art prevents or impedes them. Diversity of course goals, time, quality of facility, and school atmosphere often make such comparisons unfeasible.

Such assessment difficulties still appear to exist. Sol Gordon (1974) attributes this lingering conceptual deficiency to the lack of specific objectives and terminology in sex education courses. As a result "except for studies of isolated courses, there is no research on how well sex education is carried out today."

The Church

Religious institutions have historically influenced thought and custom concerning human sexual behavior. Some historians (Cole 1966) have indicated that even from early times, sex and religion have been fundamentally intertwined. Johnson and Belzer (1973) indicate that in pagan cultures the worship of sex organs was basic to organized religion. The phallic sign became an overt symbol in many phases of pre-Christian worship. This significance is also demonstrated in the Hindu religion where the phallus, in this case referred to as Lingam, has protecting and saving powers.

The significance of sexual influence is not limited to the pagan tradition; the sacred writings of the Judeo-Christian ethic are also heavily influenced by human sexuality. In examining the Old Testament, human sexuality, sexual behaviors, and reproduction were assigned positive or negative values. In the Jewish tradition, a woman's reproductive capacity (Genesis 16 and 30) as well as her sensual ability to please (Exodus 21: 8–11) could determine her fertile future.

The relationship between sex and religion was maintained and reinforced in the Christian ethic as well. While Jesus did not spend significant time defining behaviors concerning human sexuality, some of his followers became quite involved in the definition of sexual morality. Cole (1966) points out that the gospels are quite silent with respect to

Jesus's interpretation of sex. However, there is some consistency with his teaching in that he emphasized relationships and attitudes rather than independent or isolated actions. In the fourth gospel, Jesus accepted and forgave a harlot. He was not shocked by her sexual sin; moreover, she received the same treatment from him that he accorded the publicans. In his eyes sensuality was a minor vice beside the enormous spiritual pride of the Pharisees.

This emphasis was not carried out by Paul, however. Throughout his epistles, repeated reference is made to the merits of celibacy and to the inferior status of women. Cole (1966) softens this authoritarian position by stating "the truth of the matter, however, is simply that he (Paul) suffered from a malady which most members of his sex reflected, mainly male arrogance. He believed that men are superior to women, that God intended from the very beginning that men should exercise authority over their wives."

Probably one of the most far reaching theological positions in the Christian world in the area of human sexuality is the work of St. Augustine. Augustine, in an attempt to justify the fall of man and his subsequent punishment linked sin and sexual intercourse. Johnson and Belzer (1973) state:

> St. Augustine had to wrestle with a very difficult theological problem. This was his problem: God who is good and just not only punished Adam and Eve, but their blameless offspring throughout the ages without end for the original sin of disobedience. How could a good God be perpetually cruel? . . . St. Augustine found the solution to both problems in sexual intercourse. Adam's sin of disobedience led to God requiring people to propogate sexually, in lust, self interest and in pleasure—that is in sin.

With the establishment of the relationship between sex and sin by the early theologians, all forms of sexual behavior became evaluated in an increasingly negative way. Morality and sexuality were placed in antithetical positions, with legal institutions often enforcing control over human sexuality. Reflections on the Inquisition of the Middle Ages reinforce the powerful system of control. In more recent times, the Puritan mentality also maintained social and sexual mores. The Puritan mindset very clearly saw that sex and the flesh were significant threats to society and therefore should be rigorously persecuted.

233

American religious heritage possesses complex and, in some cases, contradictory messages concerning human sexuality. This same heritage, however, also contains positive forces for leadership roles in the area of human sexuality. The teaching role of the clergy for most religious sects is a legitimate activity. Church services, sermons, and scripture interpretations have common educational components. In fact, in the Jewish tradition, the term Rabbi has, as its semantic origin, the word teacher.

In recent times the involvement of church groups in their area of sex education seems to be a promising endeavor. Some professionals (Gordon 1974 and Schiller 1976) feel that the churches more than any other entity are able to move with more freedom in the area of sex education. Smith (1975) seems to collaborate this activity potential by stating that a definite trend has recently occurred in the churches and that they are actually providing more sex education.

Church endeavors in the area of human sexuality are both passive and active. Passive activities may take the form of endorsements by individual religious groups concerning the merits of sex education and the appropriateness of school participation. The Methodist Church has sanctioned involvement in the following way:

> We support the development of school systems and innovative methods of education designed to assist each child towards full humanity. All children have a right to full sexual education, appropriate to their stage of development that utilizes the best educational techniques and insights.

Such statements may also reflect collaborative endorsements as in the interfaith statement on sex education released by the National Council of Churches, the Synagogue Council of America, and the United States Catholic Conference, Family Life Bureau which states:

> Human sexuality is a gift of God to be accepted with thanksgiving and to be used with reverence and joy. It is more than a mechanical instinct. Its main dimensions are intertwined with the total personality and characteristic of the individual. Sex is a dynamic urge or power arising from one's basic maleness or femaleness, and having complex physical psychological and social dimension. These dimensions, we affirm, must be shaped and guided by spiritual and moral considerations which we derive from our Judeo-Christian heritage.

234

Statements of endorsement occasionally become more than an affirmation of the need for education in human sexuality; some religious groups actually take sides in specific conflicts. During the 1968–69 public controversies concerning SIECUS, several church groups supported this organization's activity when it was under strong attack (Smith 1975).

Some church groups have been able to move out of the arena of global endorsements into the actual development and implementation of curriculum and teaching materials. Some outstanding materials have been developed by church groups. Curriculum has been developed by the Presbyterian Church of the United States, the Unitarian Universal Association, and the Roman Catholic Church. The Jewish Faith has also developed curricular modules through their national organization and has provided educational opportunities to their congregations as well. Educational activities of church groups include more than curriculum development. Middlewood (1969) points out that church groups play an important role in community education, as both the Methodist and Catholic churches have conducted community workshops for their congregations. In addition, the United Church of Christ has implemented youth programs in the area of sex education.

PROBLEMS OF CHURCH LEADERSHIP IN SEX EDUCATION

The problems and dilemmas which have plagued the school and parents have also confronted the church in its role as sex educator. The crucial problems stem from the limitations of a specific religious philosophical orientation and the acceptance of this view by the target audience. In a pluralistic society churches must often reconcile their specific morality with lifestyle alternatives that exist in the present-day culture. Some congregations, by definition, are unable to compromise or even accept deviation from the norm. As a result, issues such as abortion and homosexuality are approached in a moralistic rather than objective way. The democratic humanism advocated by Gordon (1974) in the area of human sexuality is, for some religious groups, categorically impossible.

Even when less controversial philosophical issues are addressed, some religious groups do not feel adequately represented by the majority position. Kushner (1975) has indicated that the Jewish culture has a significantly different approach to sex education. This unique approach is based on the historical fact that in the Judeo ethic the model for marriage was a covenant, not the idealized love presented in the Christian tradition. Thus, any teachings of sex education which deviate from the contractual aspect of matrimony cannot adequately or validly represent the Jewish concept.

Even when basic philosophical problems are reconciled, educators in the area of human sexuality still must evaluate the potential of the church as an attractive source of sex education to the target audience, in this case adolescents. Some studies have indicated that the credibility of this institution as a sex educator is quite low. In Sorenson's (1973) study most of the adolescents surveyed felt that the church's sexual attitudes were negative or ineffectual and that nearly half of the adolescents believed that the church taught that sex is sinful. This conclusion is not difficult to draw. Greeley (1972) in his essay concerning Catholic sexual teaching points out that the official Catholic position concerning birth control is still punitive, with 42% of Bishops refusing to give absolution to a penitent who would not promise to give up contraception.

Even if one neutralizes the negative image of church teaching concerning sex education, leadership in this area still encounters difficulty. In a study by Libby, Acock, and Payne (1974) the church was identified as an insignificant source of information for either sex. The fact that teens do not evaluate the church as a primary source of sex education may indicate several things. Some sects by Canon Law require that ordained ministers be celibate and chaste. Therefore, such clergy may lack the ''credentials'' to speak with authority concerning human sexuality. Moreover, teens may perceive that his lack of first hand experience establishes an orientation that is less understanding and flexible on the subject of teenage sexuality. Thus, if teens know in advance that their behavior will be evaluated negatively, there is little incentive to seek counsel from religious sources.

References

Allen, G. Sex education problems. *American Opinion,* March 1964, pp. 1–34.

Ambrose, L. Sex education in the public schools: the need for official leadership. *Family Planning/Population Reporter* 5:78–80, 1976.

Anastasiow, N.; Grimmett, S.; Eggleston, P.; and O'Shaughnessy, T. Educational implications of earlier sexual maturation. *Phi Delta Kappan,* 1975, pp. 198–200.

Athanasiou, R. A review of public attitudes on sexual issues. In *Contemporary sexual behavior: critical issues in the 1970's,* ed. J. Zubin and J. Money. Baltimore: Johns Hopkins University Press, 1973.

Bigelow, M. A. Sex education and sex ethics. *Encyclopedia of the social sciences.* New York: Macmillan Inc., 1934.

Blake, J. Teenage birth control dilemma and public opinion. *Science* 180:708–712, 1973.

Broderick, C. B., and Bernard, J. ed. *The individual, sex and society.* Baltimore: The Johns Hopkins Press, 1969.

Burke, S. Sex education in the United Kingdom. In *Sex education: rationale and reaction,* ed. R. Rogers. Cambridge: Cambridge University Press, 1974.

Calderone, M. The sex information and education council of the U.S. *J. Marriage and Fam.,* 1965, pp. 533–534.

Calderone, M. S. Sex and the adolescent. *Clin. Pediatr.* 5:171–174, 1966.

Carrera, M. A. Training the sex educator: guidelines for teacher trainer institutions. *Am. J. Public Health* 62:233–243, 1972.

Chilman, C. S. Some social and psychological aspects of sex education. In *The individual, sex, and society,* ed. C. B. Broderick and J. Bernard. Baltimore: Johns Hopkins Press, 1969.

Cole, W. G. *Sex in christianity and psychoanalysis.* New York: A Galaxy Book, 1966.

Dearth, P. B. Viable sex education in school—expectations of students, parents and experts. *J. Sch. Health* 44:190–193, 1974.

Elias, J., and Gebhard, P. Sexuality and sexual learning in childhood. *Phi Delta Kappan* 50:401–405, 1969.

Force, E. Sex education: a regional survey. *The Family Coordinator,* October 1970, pp. 295–298.

Forman, I. Sex and family living. *American Education* 5:11–13, 1969.

Furstenberg, F. F. The social consequences of teenage parenthood. *Fam. Plann. Perspect.* 8:148–164, 1976.

Gallup, G. Epidemic of teen pregnancies: growing number of americans favor discussion of sex in the classroom. *The Gallup Poll,* News release, Princeton, New Jersey, January 23, 1978.

Gordon, S. Freedom for sex education and sexual expression. In *Sexuality today and tomorrow,* ed. S. Gordon and R. W. Libby. North Scituate: Duxbury Press, 1976.

Gordon, S. *The sexual adolescent: communicating with teenagers about sex.* North Scituate: Wadsworth Publishing Company, 1973.

Gordon, S. Why sex education belongs in the home. *The PTA Magazine,* February 1974, pp. 15–17.

Greeley, A. W. *Priests in the United States.* New York: Doubleday and Company, 1972.

Institute for Family Research and Education. *Community sex education programs for parents.* Syracuse, New York, 1977.

Jekel, J. F. Primary or secondary prevention of adolescent pregnancies. *J. School Health* 47:457–461, 1977.

Johnson, W. R., and Belzer, E. G. *Human sexual behavior and sex education.* Philadelphia: Lea and Febiger, 1973.

Kantner J., and Zelnick, M. Contraception and pregnancy: experience of young unmarried women in the U.S. *Fam. Plann. Perspect.* 5:21–35, 1973.

Kirkendall, L. A., and Libby, R. W. Trends in sex education. In *The individual, sex, and society,* ed. C. Broderick and J. Bernard. Baltimore: The Johns Hopkins Press, 1969.

Kirsch, F. *Sex education and training in chastity.* New York: Bezinger, 1930.

Kushner, L. C. Sex and judaism. In *Sexuality today and tomorrow,* ed. S. Gordon and R. W. Libby. North Scituate: Duxbury Press, 1976.

Libby, R. W. Adolescent sexual attitudes and behavior. *J. Clin. Child Psychology* 3:36–42, 1974.

Libby, R. W. Parental attitudes toward high school sex education programs. *Family Coordinator,* 1970, pp. 234–247.

Libby, R. W.; Acock, A.; and Payne, D. Configurations of parental preferences concerning sex education for adolescents. *Adolescence,* 1974, pp. 73–80.

Libby, W. R., and Nass, G. D. Parental views on teenage sexual behavior. *J. Sex Res.,* August 1971, pp. 226–237.

Lieberman, E. J. Leveling with young people about sex. *JAMA* 210:711–712, 1969.

Lipson, G., and Wolmon, D. Polling Americans on birth control and population. *Fam. Plann. Perspect.* 4:39–42, 1972.

Litt, I. F.; Edberg, S. C.; and Finberg, L. Gonorrhea in children and adolescents: a current review. *J. Pediatr.* 85:595–607, 1974.

Mecklenburg, F. E. Pregnancy: An adolescent crisis. *Minnesota Medicine,* Feburary 1973, pp. 101–104.

Middlewood, E. Sex education in the community. In *The individual, sex, and society,* ed. C. B. Broderick and J. Bernard. Baltimore: Johns Hopkins Press, 1969.

Morrison, E. S., and Price, U. M. *Values in sexuality: a new approach to sex education.* New York: Hart Publishing Company, Inc., 1974.

Mumford, D. M.; Smith, P. B.; and Goldfarb, J. L. Prevalence of venereal disease in indigent pregnant adolescents. *J. Reprod. Med.* 19:83–85, 1977.

Munson, H. E. What teachers think they need to be sexuality educators. *Health Education* 7:31–40, 1976.

Special report: saving the family. *Newsweek,* May 15, 1978, pp. 63–90.

Osofsky, H. J., and Osofsky, J. D. Let's be sensible about sex education. *Am. J. Nursing* 71:532–535, 1971.

Presser, H. Early motherhood: ignorance or bliss? *Fam. Plann. Perspect.* 6:8–14, 1974.

Ready, J. L. The current status of family life and sex education in the public schools of Illinois. *J. Sch. Health* 43:49–51, 1973.

Reed, D. A., and Munson, H. E. Resolution of one's sexual self: an important first step for sexuality educators. *J. Sch. Health* 46:31–34, 1976.

Reichelt, P. A., and Werley, H. H. Contraception, abortion and venereal disease: teenagers' knowledge and the effect of education. *Fam. Plann. Perspect.* 7:83–88, 1975.

Schiller, P. *Creative approach to sex education and counseling.* New York: Association Press, 1977.

Schulz, E. D., and Williams, S. R. *Family life and sex education: curriculum & instruction.* New York: Harcourt Brace Jovanovich, Inc., 1968.

Smith, L. Religion's response to the new sexuality. In *Sexuality today and tomorrow,* ed. S. Gordon and R. W. Libby. North Scituate: Duxbury Press, 1976.

Somerfield, R. M. Family life and sex education in the turbulent sixties. *J. Marriage and Fam.,* February 1971, pp. 11–35.

Sorenson, R. C. *Adolescent sexuality in contemporary America.* New York: World Publishing Company, 1973.

Terry, D. E., and Woodward, L. H. A five-year plan for designing and implementing a statewide health education curriculum in Maryland. *J. Sch. Health* 46:282–285, 1976.

Thornburg, H. D. Educating the pre-adolescent about sex. *The Family Coordinator,* 1974, pp. 35–38.

Thoms, G. H., and Tatum, M. L. *Developing family life and sex education programs in the schools.* Falls Church, Virginia: Mason Junior/Senior High School, 1977.

13

Sexual
Counseling
for
Adolescents

Patricia Schiller,
M. A., J. D.

Puberty is occurring at an earlier age than in past generations. At the same time, there has been a major revolution in sexual mores among many youth resulting in more frequent and earlier sexual intercourse, a rise in teenage and out-of-wedlock pregnancy, an increase in venereal disease in youth and young adults, and an increased need for contraception and abortion services. The situation has been further complicated by the fact that some youths are disenchanted with American society today—they have difficulty with school, drop out, become disillusioned with society as a whole, are unwilling to repeat the lifestyle and patterns of their parents, come into conflict with the law, or show other symptoms of alienation and escape, such as using drugs and alcohol. Underlying these problems have been factors such as the weakening of the family and family life in the structure of our society, and the effects of the cycle of deprivation.

It is well known that the period of adolescence is a critical period in the physical and emotional growth and development of the young. It is clear that certain identifiable groups of teenagers are of high risk and need special assistance, including social, emotional, educational, vocational, and health counseling. In spite of this fact, much less emphasis has been placed upon organized efforts to deliver quality health care to youth.

Any plan for training adolescent sex counselors must be based upon the current problems and needs of adolescents, the current resources available, and the resources that need to be developed. People are becoming increasingly aware of the need for sex counseling for their children. Episodes running the gamut from premarital pregnancy to adolescent homosexual play strike terror in the hearts of parents and accelerate the pressure on the schools to establish a sex counseling program.

What often results from this crisis climate is one or two lectures about menstruation and reproduction. Usually the school nurse or a doctor is brought in to help the counselor in this "sensitive" area of counseling. The counselor or the expert proceeds to give the children all the correct terms, using slides and anatomical charts. Sometimes a movie depicting the development from girl to woman and boy to man is shown. The students are permitted to ask questions, but the answers they get are often limited to the anatomical and functional aspects of growth, development, and reproduction.

What is wrong with this kind of sex counseling? Are the youngsters being taught the "facts of life" in an objective, unemotional way, with the correct use of terms, and are they receiving vital information about their bodies? Let me answer on the basis of fourteen years of professional experience in dealing with sexual and family living problems of children, adolescents, and married couples. The short answer is that the information they are learning is necessary to the development of healthy sex attitudes, but is only one aspect of such development. It is sexuality, not the physical act of sex, that is crucial. Human sexuality is what is personally important to the growing child, the adolescent, and the adult. Sexual identity is an important part of the self-image and affects every aspect of life. For example, sexuality determines the names we are given at birth, the toys we play with as children, the clothes we wear, the friends we have, the things we like to do, the courses we take in high school and college, the careers we choose, the way we see our roles and responsibilities in our homes, and last but not least, the ways we satisfy and cope with our sexual needs and urges as responsible and committed human beings.

Asking a few other questions may reinforce the point: Is it enough to teach a ninth grade boy how one becomes a father without teaching him what it means to be a respected man? Don't we also need to teach him the attitudes and behavior that will help him, on reaching manhood, to be a sympathetic, kind, and understanding husband and father? Upset and panicky as we get at the thought of our youngsters' having premarital relations, how much more critical and upsetting is the crisis that will be caused later on if they marry and have children only to end up with divorce and family disintegration.

During adolescence, when youngsters need to discuss their conflicts and concerns with adults other than their parents, it is particularly important for them to have counselors who understand their emotional and social problems. During the transitional ages, particularly in early adolescence, children may have trouble accepting their sexual identity. Some girls feel no pride in their sex and actually fear being a woman. Many boys, especially when they are smaller than their contemporaries, fear that they may not be able to be a real man because they associate masculinity with physical size and development.

Questions that youngsters frequently ask reflect the real worries of

241

youth and indicate that it is mainly their attitudes about sex that constitute a problem for them, for their parents, and for counselors. How can we help them with their bewilderment as to whether the sex urges they feel mean they are in love? How can young boys or girls sort out the various emotions that accompany sexual desires to hug, to kiss, to pet? Are their tumultuous feelings the real thing or just puppy love? Is there a way to work out sex needs, other than in sex play? What are young adolescents to do about the fantasies, fears, and dreams that they experience along with their sex urges?

Human sexuality includes the social roles that men and women play. Many adolescents have difficulty understanding and learning these roles. Those most enmeshed in the dragnet of uncertainty are usually being brought up in disorganized homes (especially where they have little contact with adults of the opposite sex or where parents are passive, resentful, or unable to accept the responsibilities of parenthood).

In recent years, many leading sociologists have stressed the need for boys to develop a strong male image early in life in order that they can later take on their role as fathers. Psychologists and sociologists emphasize the importance of providing male substitutes for absent or rejecting fathers. Whenever possible, male teachers, coaches, relatives, older brothers, recreation leaders, and Scoutmasters should be encouraged to act as models and substitute fathers.

Since over 75% of our population marries at one time or another, the counselor should give young people an opportunity to discuss dating, going steady, engagement, marriage, and family life. A trained sex counselor can help students explore the pros and cons of going steady and the sexual behavior appropriate in pairing.

Sex counseling should encompass human sexuality rather than merely the reproductive aspects of sex. It should deal with the psychological, sociological, economic, and social factors that affect personality and behavior as well as with the biological facts of human reproduction.

Senior High School

During the high-school years, students are interested in interpersonal relationships. Many are dating on a steady basis, a few are planning to marry, and some are parents and living together as married couples or just partners. A significant number are already sexually active. Key concepts to be explored are love, human sexuality, equality, and responsibility. Important areas for study include consideration of marriage, family planning, infant care, vocational choices and opportunities, divorce, unwed motherhood and fatherhood, masturbation, homosexuality, and conflicts confronting young men and women in their social and personal relationships.

Family planning is essential at these grade levels. It should be counseled in the frame of reference that quality of life is the inherent right of each individual and that the potential for reaching this goal is best exemplified by planning parenthood and rearing wanted children. The social and personal need for family planning knowledge is great. It can decrease illegitimacy and venereal disease and help young people and children to avoid miserable lives. Early marriages can often be postponed. Early divorce, broken homes, and homes fraught with emotional tension can frequently be avoided.

If we agree that family planning is an essential part of family life and sex education, who should counsel and in what manner should the subject matter and attitudes be counseled? A counselor who is sensitive and comfortable with the subject ought to be chosen. There are several possibilities—a health counselor, nurse, counselor, psychologist, or practically any competent professional who has a solid interdisciplinary background, is familiar with the subject matter, and is sensitive to the feelings, understandings, and social, religious, and cultural background of those who are being counseled. It is important to avoid a judgmental authoritarian approach. Explaining and clarifying in a supportive, comfortable way the questions of students is most helpful in the process of family planning counseling.

Counseling in family planning, where possible, should include the parents of the young people. The classes for each age group should be held separately, but both might include the same materials. This parallel developmental approach is helpful for improving communication between parents and their children. Many successful programs have included resource people from the community in medicine, nursing, law, and religion.

In group counseling, a student-centered approach where the group can explore and survey differences of opinion and the basis for decision-making can lend reinforcement and strength. Case studies and role playing help the students to explore attitudes and feelings.

From experiences with individual and group counseling, the dominant problems which concern adolescents seem to be: sex education, family planning, parental guidance, parental discord, economic problems, teenage pregnancies, neglect, alcoholism and narcotics, teacher-parent-child problems, lack of motivation, nutrition and health, communication problems, early dating in the elementary schools, sexual promiscuity, inadequate male image, lack of privacy, overprotective parents, boys and girls in the same family sleeping in the same bed after puberty, sexual assaults and incest, one-parent family problems, exposure to adult sex activities and homosexuality.

Training of the Sex Counselor

Sex counselors need to be well informed in the following general areas: (1) social and psychological factors of teenage pregnancy; (2) impact of teenage pregnancy on family dynamics; (3) needs and sensitivities of adolescents; (4) birth control and family planning; and (5) sex and family law. To use this knowledge effectively, counselors must become adept at facilitating individual and group counseling. Therapy will be provided for pregnant teenagers, other teenagers, and parents. Learning how to set specific goals for individual or group therapy and to establish and maintain groups are important skills. An awareness and an appreciation of sensitive issues for adolescents—such as masturbation, homosexuality, obscenity, and premarital sex—also contribute to the sex counselor's ability to communicate well with teenagers.

Adolescent Pregnancy and Parenthood

The Department of Health, Education and Welfare considers the various problems associated with adolescent pregnancy and parenthood to be of major concern. Programs geared toward alleviating these problems are given a high priority in our government's national domestic programs. This is certainly as it should be, considering the appalling statistics and the problem of the neglected young people involved in unwed parenthood. During 1971, one out of every four babies was born to a mother under twenty. One out of every eight thirteen-year-old girls will become pregnant out of wedlock before she reaches the age of twenty, and one out of every four eighteen-year-old girls is currently married. Out-of-wedlock babies mothered by adolescent girls were estimated at 600,000 in the United States in 1977.

PROBLEMS OF ADOLESCENT PREGNANCY

Massive data has been collected on the outcome of early pregnancies. Analysis of this material confirms the assumptions counselors and educators have made about the resulting life style. The findings support the following assumptions:

(1) Adolescent family life is linked to unwanted children who were "accidentally born;"
(2) Family life is fraught with financial, social, and interpersonal problems;
(3) Unfinished secondary (or sometimes elementary) education is common;
(4) Poor health is present or anticipated for mother and infants;
(5) There is a high incidence of separated families and divorce;
(6) Welfare dependency is widespread;
(7) Work potential is reduced because of lack of skills due to the failure to complete educational and/or technical training; and
(8) General frustration results from inability to achieve long-held aspirations and desired life goals.

It is apparent from these findings that the adolescent boy and his family need guidance as much as the unwed mother and her family. Aside from attending to the manifold frustrations and anxieties of the young people, parent counseling is also essential. The parent in the home is the most consistent and long-term counselor for better or worse, and most young parents need guidance and training.

Recommendations for Current School Counseling Programs

These recommendations, drawn from several studies of pregnant adolescents, are designed to improve sex counseling in the schools.

(1) A follow-up process should be established to ensure that girls re-enter school as scheduled and that contact is maintained with them during the first crucial year to provide the needed support.

(2) Greater effort should be given to helping school officials, teachers, and counselors to understand the problems and needs of returning school-age mothers. Encouraging school continuance by these girls should be seen as a total school responsibility.

(3) Adequate and accurate birth control information should be included in health instruction and in discussions of developing quality family life; and

(4) Young men who become fathers should partake in school-sponsored programs that are designed to help them and their partners achieve maturity and thereby become more able to cope with the problems of parenthood. Where schools are not ready to carry on the work, community programs will be needed to fill the gap.

Other types of programs need to be developed for the parents and guardians of young adolescent parents. Group-counseling and education sessions could be held during lunch hours while others could be conducted during evening hours. The following subjects should be discussed:

(1) social-sexual needs of adolescents; (2) opening up communication between adolescents and parents; (3) building a sense of maleness and femaleness in children and youth; (4) teaching human sexuality before children reach puberty; (5) parents as sex counselors who from the time children are born communicate attitudes and values in verbal and non-verbal ways; (6) available community, social, and health resources to adolescent parents and their families; (7) moral issues in family planning and birth control; (8) nutritional needs of adolescent pregnant girls; and (9) infant care and development.

At the present time, community health centers, maternal and infant care centers, family-planning centers and planned parenthood organizations are deeply involved in educating and counseling the adolescent parent. However, there is a lack of jobs, manpower training, continuing counseling programs, and decent child-care centers which will care for infants under one year of age. These deficiencies are seriously hampering the ability of the young people to make the fullest use of their opportunities.

On the positive side, as more competent educators and counselors work with these young people in a supportive way, these adolescents develop values toward themselves and each other that hold out the promise of a cohesive family life filled with loving and caring people.

Abortion Counseling in Adolescent Pregnancy

Despite the legalization of abortion in all states and the emergence of medically effective abortion clinics, abortion for counselor and counselee and for sex educators remains a difficult and, in the words of David R. Mace, ''agonizing decision.'' Sex educators and counselors need to comprehend the social, legal, religious, and personal attitudes, values, laws, and conflicts involved in the issues of problem pregnancies and abortion.

The client seeking counseling is unable to reach a firm decision on her own. She is looking for clarification, interpretation, more facts, and a warm, accepting person who can help her reach a decision that will help her and her partner, and that will give her comfort. The sex educator and counselor, in addition to being a knowledgeable and patient listener, should be prepared to help the client move toward exercising the most realistic option available in making a prudent decision. The necessary knowledge for the client would include: (1) abortion as a medical operation; (2) attitudes of the family, close friends, and the community; (3) moral issues; and (4) practical personal concerns.

Sex counselors should specifically provide patients an opportunity to freely discuss the various emotions that torture them. A major one is the fear of being rejected if they have an abortion or conversely if they have the baby. The counselor also needs to be prepared to deal with the patient's anger, withdrawal, and fear. David R. Mace in his book *Abortion—The Agonizing Decision* (1972) lists the five following requirements that need to be explained to the patient before she is ready for an abortion:

(1) She understands what abortion means and is sure that this is what she wants;
(2) Her own judgment is not being unduly subverted either for or against abortion by coercion from her husband, her parents, or friends;
(3) In making her decision she has considered how it will be likely to affect her conscience and her value system;
(4) She has thought through the possibility of accepting the pregnancy as an alternative to abortion; and
(5) She is knowledgeable about effective methods of contraception and their availability.

The process of problem-pregnancy counseling is a difficult aspect of sex counseling. The counselor must be as prepared and experienced as all other types of sex and pregnancy counselors.

Sex Education and Counseling of the Handicapped

Unfortunately, our children, youth, and adults who are categorized as "handicapped" have all too frequently been deprived of the generally available sex counseling offered to normal young people in the same school district, county, social, or health agency. Many teachers and counselors have reported that the "handicapped" children under their care resort to masturbation and other auto-erotic activities as a source of release of tension. They also report there is a great need among the children to cling to and touch each other and adults for emotional security, perhaps more so than children who are not handicapped.

Mrs. Medora S. Bass, a sex educator and counselor, deserves much credit for researching and pulling together the bits and pieces of research and curriculum materials that are currently available (1964). She notes that parents of retarded children are "extremely afraid of any kind of sexual expression on the part of their adolescent children. There seemed to be an underlying fear that their children will become involved sexually, or that they will take advantage of someone else. There also exists the fear that more retarded children will be born as a result of the sexual encounters of their children."

These fears have a basis in fact, but keeping both child and parent ignorant about human sexuality only aggravates the problem. Sex education for handicapped children which accepts that they are sexual human beings with sexual needs will help promote realistic programs geared to the limitations imposed by the form of the handicap, and so help the children and their parents to cope effectively with sexual pressures and urges.

As people considered severely retarded are not permitted to marry in some states, the sex educator and counselor should check on these laws in the state where sex counseling occurs in order to plan and develop a realistic curriculum with realistic objectives. It is important to note that the wisdom of such laws has been questioned by some specialists (Bass 1964). Many of these experts feel that severely retarded couples should be sterilized and then permitted to marry. In this way they could partake in the satisfactions of married life without the great responsibilities of childrearing. However, the National Association for Retarded Children considers marriage for those with IQs between 25 and 50 to be inadvisable.

Most experts in sex counseling believe that courses for the retarded ought to include decision-making problems around the issue of having children. This exercise would be constructive in many ways. Retarded students would learn about the process of reproduction. They would accept their limitations as they relate to the responsibilities of parenthood and would begin to form a realistic self-concept.

Special-education counselors recommend social-drama techniques with puppets, painted paper bags, pictures, and simple drawings as visual aids in counseling the retarded about boy and girl social-sexual attitudes and behavior. The special-education teachers feel that formal sex education for the handicapped should begin at the preschool level as with normal children. The physical sexual development of the retarded children follows the same pattern as with normal children and the need for sex counseling appears to be just as great or even greater than with normal children.

Our rapidly growing experience has made it clear that adolescent pregnancies, abortion counseling, and problems of the handicapped call for special training skills and knowledge. Teachers or counselors can carry their fair share of the responsibility when they are particularly aware of the unique methods suitable for counseling the handicapped. When the counselor is sensitive to the many delicate dilemmas which confront the man and woman involved in a problem pregnancy, he or she can move with patience and rational thought in a manner which is suitable to the patient's needs and readiness. Counseling in these areas is a science and an art.

References

Bass, M. S. Sex education for the handicapped. *Family Life Coordinator* 13(3):59–68, 1964.

Mace, D. R. *Abortion—the agonizing decision*. Nashville, Tennes- see: Abdingdon Press, 1972.

Schiller, P. *Creative approach to sex education and counseling* (2nd ed.). New York: Association Press, 1977.

INDEX

Perihepatitis, 105
Peritonitis, 105
Permissiveness
    attitudes toward, 203
Personality traits
    of adolescent mothers, 24
    Erikson's theory of, 26
Pharyngitis, 103
Physicial examination, 35. *See also*
    Patient care
Physicians
    contraceptives prescribed by, 179
    role of, 213
    in teenage pregnancy programs,
        79, 80, 81
Piaget, Jean, 4
Pill. *See* Oral contraceptives
Placental assessment, for diabetics,
    44
Planned Parenthood, 246
    clientele of, 147
    report of, 9–10
    sex education of, 152
    on teen services, 89
*Planned Parenthood of Central Mis-
    souri v. Danforth*, 182
Podophylin, 128
Poe School (Baltimore, Md.), 82
Poetry, 209
Poe v. Gerstein, 181
Population control, national impor-
    tance of, 20. *See also* Family
    planning
Postpartum classes, in hospital-based
    programs, 80
Postpartum complications, in adoles-
    cent pregnancy, 46–47
Poverty. *See also* Socioeconomic sta-
    tus and early childbearing, 66
    and premature parenthood, 71
    and teenage pregnancy, 27
Preeclampsia
    among diabetics, 43

follow-up for, 42
incidence of, 41, 42
treatment of, 41–42
Pregnancy, adolescent
    abortion counseling for, 247. *See
        also* Counseling
    adolescent development and, 5
    adverse effects of, 32–33
    approaches to, xv
    chronic medical problems associ-
        ated with, 42–44
    common medical problems associ-
        ated with, 37–41
    counseling for, 244
    early works on, 25–26
    emotional support during, 42
    financing medical costs of,
        185–191
    health benefits for, 186
    historical perspective on, 17–18
    hypertension in, 41
    medical complications of, 33–34
    national concerns about, 18
    nutrition during, 36
    paternal involvement in, 92. *See
        also* Fathers
    postpartum complications of,
        46–47
    prevention of, 143. *See also*
        Contraception
    problems of, 245
    psychiatric aspects of, 23–29
    rate of, 12
    research on, 52–54
    and socioeconomic status, 16–17,
        19
    spontaneous abortion during, 46
    statistics on, xiii–xix, 1
    and syphilis, 115–116
    termination of. *See* Abortion
    treatment for syphilis in, 118
Pregnancy, premarital
    incidence of, 73

tradition of, 50
Pregnancy Disability Bill, 186
Pregnancy prevention, as service delivery goal, 86–89, 93
Pregnancy testing, in school setting, 83
Premarital sex
counseling for, 244
Prematurity. *See also* Neonate
and herpesvirus, 39, 121, 123, 124
rate of, 34
Prenatal care, 195. *See also* Patient care
of adolescent, 34–37
gonococcal culture during, 109
Presbyterian Church, 235
Pre-School Inventory, 70
Princeton Center for Infancy, 155
Privacy
right of, 176, 178, 180
Supreme Court on, 183
Probabilistic thinking, 10–11
Procreation
ethical issues involved in, 198, 201
Programs. *See* Educational programs; Social programs
Project TALENT data, 65
Promiscuity
attitudes toward, 203
definitions for, 6
Protein, during pregnancy, 36
Psychopathology, and illegitimacy, 24–26
Puberty
onset of, 2, 240
Public assistance, 59. *See also* Welfare assistance
Public Health Service, U.S.
recommendations of, 109–110
Public Health Service Act
Title X of, 191

Public school systems
pregnant teenagers in, 35
sex education in, 215, 229. *See also* Sex education
Puritan mindset, 233

Race
and coital experience, 51
and concerns about teenage pregnancy, 2
and incidence of sexual intercourse, 52–53
and parenting education, 164
and presentation for abortion, 142–143
Rape, and state funding of abortions, 189–190
Rap sessions, 91, 150, 152. *See also* Counseling
"Reality training," xvi
Religion, and sex education, 232–235. *See also* Sex education
Renal disease, 44
Reproductive system model, of sex education, 226
Retarded
sex counseling for, 248–249
Rhythm method, 149. *See also* Contraception
Richmond, Julius, 18
Rights. *See* Legal aspects
Rilke, Rainer Maria, 211, 212
Risk-taking behavior, 3, 6, 11
Roberts, Francis J., 169
Robertson, M., 16
Roe v. Wade, 180, 182, 190
Roman Catholic Church, 235
Romantic love, 211
Rorschach Test, 24
Rothstein v. Lutheran Social Services decision, 90
Rubella, 39